Praise for *A More Perfect Union*

"America stands on a knife's edge. If we are to survive this moment, with its pitfalls and perils, we have to figure out how to be together differently. Rev. Adam Russell Taylor offers a path forward to making real the Beloved Community—a new consensus—for our time. Together, let us get about the hard work of building a new America."

—Eddie S. Glaude Jr., author of *Begin Again: James Baldwin's America and Its Urgent Lessons for Our Own*

"When we relaunched the Poor People's Campaign in 2018, we stood on the National Mall and said this movement must be a national call for moral revival. This book explores the rich moral vision of Beloved Community. Read it and join the long struggle for a more perfect union in this land."

—Rev. Dr. William J. Barber II, president of Repairers of the Breach and author of *We Are Called to Be a Movement*

"In a toxic world filled with bold dreamers, Adam Russell Taylor offers affirmation of dreams past and present, and accompaniment into what can be a world that sustains us in Beloved Community."

—Rev. Traci Blackmon, Associate General Minister, United Church of Christ

"An old and deep vision that needs to be rediscovered to make our union more perfect. Adam Russell Taylor is one of the leaders who will help us restore and rekindle it. This essential book reframes and renews the vision."

—Jim Wallis, founder and ambassador of Sojourners, and *New York Times* bestselling author

"There are books that are worth reading, and then there are books like this one that desperately need to be read, and by as many people as possible."
—Rev. Michael B. Curry, presiding bishop of The Episcopal Church and author of *Love Is the Way* and *The Power of Love*

"This book is a powerful and desperately needed message for our nation. At a time when the United States is anything but united, Adam Russell Taylor offers a sober diagnosis and a compelling prescription for a way forward by envisioning the Beloved Community in which all people can flourish."
—Richard Stearns, president emeritus of World Vision US and author of *The Hole in Our Gospel* and *Lead Like It Matters to God*

"An urgent and eloquent volume. Adam Russell Taylor invokes history, theology, and organizing experience to make clear that the idea guiding the witness of Martin Luther King Jr. and John Lewis should be our North Star in leading toward redemption, renewal, and social reconstruction."
—E. J. Dionne Jr., author of *Our Divided Political Heart* and *Code Red*

"With a deep commitment to reimagining an America where all can breathe free, Adam Russell Taylor brings light to powerful traditions often made invisible by a nation at times afraid of the music and stories birthed by people who sing the blues and simultaneously preach the gospel. *A More Perfect Union* is a call to fight for a nation that is not yet but will be if we listen to this prophet in our midst."
—Otis Moss III, senior pastor at Trinity United Church of Christ in Chicago, Illinois

"Adam Russell Taylor offers a relevant, practical, and contemporary strategy for realizing the dream and vision that counter the polarizing politics of our day. Moving from a truthful diagnosis of our nation's mis-truths and polarizing toxicity into the building blocks of a reenvisioned Beloved Community, Taylor leaves no stone unturned and no lie unad-dressed. A must-read for all who are fatigued by the divisions and injus-tices that bombard us daily and are losing hope of a way forward into a more just and inclusive nation."

—Howard-John Wesley, senior pastor at Alfred
St. Baptist Church in Alexandria, Virginia

"Adam Russell Taylor paints a clear and compelling vision for a way beyond the fragmentations we experience. For those who have long been on this justice journey, and for those just joining, Taylor provides excel-lent analysis and tangible actions. He helps us to dream bigger and usher the Beloved Community into our neighborhoods."

—Nikki Toyama-Szeto, president of Christians for Social Action

"Adam Russell Taylor is an American treasure, and this book shows why. Beautifully weaving spiritual principles with American possibilities, Tay-lor provides a new narrative of interfaith Beloved Community worthy of Dr. King's legacy."

—Eboo Patel, founder and president of Interfaith
Youth Core and author of *Out of Many Faiths:
Religious Diversity and the American Promise*

"As a Jew and a rabbi, I couldn't be more inspired by Adam Russell Tay-lor's remarkable call for a renewal of the Beloved Community, which our nation–and our world–needs now more than ever. *A More Perfect Union* echoes the enduring Jewish commitment to *tikun olam*: repairing the world. May this book bring us together across all kinds of lines to become the community of justice and love for which we yearn."

—Rabbi Jonah Pesner, director of the Religious
Action Center of Reform Judaism

"In this book, Adam Russell Taylor invites you not to settle for the past, or even for the present. He urges us all to raise the bar for the future and to usher in God's dream for our country and for our world—which is nothing less than Beloved Community."

—Shane Claiborne, author, activist, and
co-founder of Red Letter Christians

"In a timely tome, Adam Russell Taylor has masterfully called us back to those unassailable principles necessary for building the Beloved Community in the midst of persistent racial and economic inequity. For those of us committed to the work of justice, *A More Perfect Union*, with its insight, honesty, and hopefulness, is a clarion call to not relent until this work is done."

—Rev. Gabriel Salguero, president of the National
Latino Evangelical Network (NALEC)

"Adam Russell Taylor expresses a depth of theology drawn from the breadth of the church and calls us to a life together in community that is thoughtfully explained with clarity. Taylor's call to a common narrative rooted in what can and should be the expression of the common good in the Beloved Community is the fresh word we need in our church and in our nation."

—Soong-Chan Rah, professor at Fuller Theological Seminary
and author of *The Next Evangelicalism* and *Prophetic Lament*

"In this book, Adam Russell Taylor has beautifully woven the rich tapestry of his own diverse background and identity into a moral vision of an America that values and celebrates the image of God in all people. This must-read book offers healing springs to the parched souls of people of color and allies deeply wounded by the all-consuming nightmare of a nation teetering dangerously between apartheid and a restored democracy. *A More Perfect Union* invites us all on a refreshing, hope-filled journey toward a reimagined America, where all systems impacting human life and flourishing truly reflect the Beloved Community."

—Dr. Barbara Williams-Skinner, co-convener of the National African American Clergy Network, president of the Skinner Leadership Institute, and author of *I Prayed, Now What?: From No Faith to Deep Faith*

"As a Muslim, immigrant, North African woman who chose to make the United States home and witnessed the unbelievable savagery—and heroism—of America over the last twenty years, I find Rev. Adam Russell Taylor's book healing. It is a roadmap of how the sacred can respond to the profane to build the America of love, resilience, and the triumph of the collective human spirit—the Beloved Community."

—Azza Karam, secretary general at Religions for Peace

"At this historic moment, we need a book that seeks to both bring us together and stand up for our deepest spiritual values and their implications for our life together as a society. Rev. Adam Russell Taylor brings both his own life experiences and a variety of inspiring stories of a cloud of witnesses to the task. This is an important book, particularly for those of us who care about holistic mission to read and to discuss."

—Rev. Dr. Alexia Salvatierra, Assistant Professor of Integral Mission and Global Transformation at Fuller Theological Seminary

"In *A More Perfect Union*, Adam Russell Taylor tells the story that America needs to hear about itself, including its repressed transgressions and inviting ideals. This book is a civic gift for our future, demonstrating the galvanizing vision of the Beloved Community. Taylor masterfully weaves his own powerful story into this narrative for the nation, revealing his insightful and incisive prophetic voice. If you want to choose one new book offering a spiritually grounded pathway forward for America at this time, here it is."

—Wesley Granberg-Michaelson, author of *Without Oars: Casting Off into a Life of Pilgrimage* and former general secretary of the Reformed Church in America

"At this time of growing crisis for our democracy and our culture, Adam Russell Taylor makes a compelling case that love is the only impulse of the human heart strong enough to overcome the powerful forces that are pulling us apart and pulling us down, and that the spiritually grounded vision of the Beloved Community is the only social vision that can give us the solidarity and the passion to build a society in which all can flourish. This must-read book marks Taylor as a young leader who deserves our attention, respect, and support."

—Robert A. Boisture, president and CEO of Fetzer Institute

"Drawing on reasons for hope from communities all across the nation, Adam Russell Taylor has issued a clarion call for us to embrace the moral vision of the Beloved Community—a story drawn from the deepest wells of America's civic and religious values. This book reflects Taylor's dual sense of calling as bridge-builder and truth-teller. There are tensions between those roles. But as the great novelist F. Scott Fitzgerald observed many years ago, the ability to hold two opposed ideas in the mind at the same time, and retain the ability to function, is the mark of a first-rate mind."

—Tim Dixon, co-founder of More in Common and former prime ministers' speechwriter

A MORE PERFECT UNION

A NEW VISION FOR BUILDING THE BELOVED COMMUNITY

ADAM RUSSELL TAYLOR

BROADLEAF BOOKS
MINNEAPOLIS

A MORE PERFECT UNION
A New Vision for Building the Beloved Community

Cover design: Juicebox Design

Print ISBN: 978-1-5064-6453-4
eBook ISBN: 978-1-5064-6454-1

Printed in Canada

CONTENTS

FOREWORD

Ten years ago, I shared these words about Adam Russell Taylor for his first book, *Mobilizing Hope*: "Adam Taylor has made conscious decisions to get in the way of injustice—whether it's the AIDS pandemic, the pervasive scandal of poverty, or in ending the genocide in Darfur. . . . I'm proud to see the struggle to build God's Beloved Community continue through the creative maladjustment of a committed minority of transformed nonconformists highlighted in these pages."[1] Now Adam brings forward his latest book, which feels both timely and necessary, wherein he reimagines and recasts the moral vision that animated and fueled the civil rights movement, the vision of the Beloved Community.

Our nation desperately needs this vision in this crossroads moment of deep reckoning and renewal. In this continued season of national awakening around police violence, systemic racism, and coming through a devastating COVID-19 pandemic that has further laid bare deep-seated racism, Adam offers a bold and transformational vision for what can and must replace a politics of fear, division, and contempt.

In *A More Perfect Union: A New Vision for Building the Beloved Community*, Adam builds the clear case for America's need to come to terms with and repent for the ways it has woefully fallen short of extending the full meaning of its creed to *all*. Without that change, Adam insists, we will never realize our full potential, and we will remain hopelessly divided. Looking back is not enough, he argues; we must also lean forward in embracing and communicating a radically more unifying and compelling moral vision of the America that we sustain and that sustains us. This vision builds upon the solid foundation of our shared and most deeply held civic aspirations and spiritual values.

I have spent a lifetime getting into good trouble, all for the sake of building the Beloved Community. In the course of my lifetime as a freedom rider, young activist, and chair of the Student Nonviolent

Coordinating Committee, and most recently, representing Georgia's Fifth Congressional District, I have been a part of seeing the Beloved Community being built—and have glimpsed how that community might grow. I've also experienced the pain and bitter disappointment of our nation's backtracking from the premise that all people are created equal and deserve equal justice under the law. In the height of the protests that helped change our nation in the early summer of 2020, I cheered on with pride and joy a new generation of Black Lives Matter activists rising up and getting into good and necessary trouble to end police violence and dismantle systemic racism.

After decades of protests, forty-five arrests, and thirty-three years in Congress, I still believe in the power of the Beloved Community vision to ultimately transform our nation into a more perfect union. I still believe that we will create the Beloved Community, we will redeem the soul of America. I still believe we shall overcome. With great urgency, clarity, and hope, this book provides a moral road map showing us how.

United States Representative John Lewis (1940–2020)
July 2020

PROLOGUE

As we headed into the 2020 election season, I recalled the night after Election Day 2016. At three a.m. our bedroom door swung open, interrupting my very restless sleep. Half-delirious, I could see the silhouette of my then five-year-old son Joshua standing over me and my wife. Joshua had a distraught look on his face. He told us that he "needed to know who won the election."

As much as my wife and I had tried to shield our two sons from the toxic rhetoric that characterized so much of the 2016 presidential race—a seemingly impossible task when living in the Washington, DC, area—our sons had internalized far more than we had realized. My wife and I exchanged a pained look and then stumbled through a barely coherent explanation of Mr. Trump's likely victory. Joshua responded, "I don't understand how someone who has said and done such mean things can win."

His poignant comment triggered deep anguish within me—not just because of the electoral results, but due to the troubled state of our nation's soul spotlighted by the outcome. At a profound level, my son had articulated why I felt such heartbreak and trepidation that night. His young mind had intuited something more substantial than simple political disappointment: I felt a deep sense of betrayal by the electoral outcome—but not because our nation had elected a president whose ideology and policy priorities diverged from my own. Rather, it was because so many Americans, particularly white Christians, voted for a candidate despite (and in some cases because of) the fact that he falsely represented himself as an economic populist and ran a campaign based on fear and hate, exploiting and manipulating some of our nation's worst impulses.

After seeing our tortured reaction, my son—in what felt like a reversal of roles—said reassuringly, "It will be OK because you and Mommy will make it OK." At that moment, I felt the weight of the world on my shoulders.

That night, my wife and I had a serious argument. She is a Canadian and Jamaican citizen, and we argued vociferously about whether we should consider moving our family to Canada. She didn't make this impassioned argument because she doesn't appreciate America. We both love America, but the dystopian version of the nation around which Trump campaigned was barely recognizable to us, and it made us worry even more for the welfare of our two young Black sons. I tried to reassure her that the election outcome was the byproduct of long-gestating causes and that we needed to stay to fight for the America we believe in. I told her I still had faith in the potential of the American project and in the promise of American ideals, even as compromised as they have been and then appeared.

I'm sure many can empathize with how we felt that night. We were faced with a choice to either withdraw into cynicism and disillusionment or redouble our efforts to stand up for the very ideals that make the American project worth redeeming and defending. Meanwhile, another part of America was celebrating Trump's improbable victory, believing that he was either the best of two bad choices or that he would restore America's greatness and fight for them.

As I tried to answer my son's continuing questions, I was responding not just as a father but in particular as the father of two Black boys who will grow up in the midst of a racially polarized America. I was responding as the son of a Black mother and white father who made the controversial decision to marry soon after interracial marriage was made legal across the country by the 1967 *Loving v. Virginia* Supreme Court decision. I was also responding as a Christian and an ordained minister of a gospel that mandates that I love my neighbors *and* my enemies and teaches me that ultimately, I must put my hope and trust in God, not in politics or political leaders.

The magnitude of the emotion I felt in that moment came from all these converging parts of my background and identity. I couldn't simply write off every person who voted for Donald Trump as being motivated by racism, misogyny, or xenophobia; I also couldn't ignore how many voters either ignored Trump's appeals to these vices or were actually motivated by them. Like many, I knew that the election outcome had some deep, painful, and sometimes illuminating lessons to teach me and that the degree of alienation, grievance, and anger felt in much of the country—expressed in support for Trump—was something I barely understood, let alone had enough direct contact with.

At the time, I was leading the Faith Initiative at the World Bank Group. But that morning after the election in 2016, I knew in my spirit that it was time to leave my comfortable position there. My work at the World Bank was meaningful, but I knew I would be unable in that role to engage in the kind of advocacy and transformation that would be necessary in light of the new political context in this country. It took a year to make the transition, but I then rejoined the Christian social justice organization Sojourners, where I had served as senior political director and board chair and where I am now president.

The voice of my son—his trust that I would be part of "making it OK"—had ignited a restlessness in me and made it clear that it was time to more fully engage in the struggle for "a more perfect union," the struggle for the soul of our nation and a radically more just society. If my family were to stay, I needed to be all-in. I needed to join forces with others who were determined to mobilize around a different story of America, one that embodies our deepest civic and religious values.

The many troubling and traumatic events of the Trump years—from the Muslim ban to the brutal policy of family separation at the border, from the incessant attacks on truth to the misuse and abuse of power, from the resurgence of white supremacy to the insurrectionist storming of our Capitol—have stirred in me a fresh insistence that change needs to happen, that a radically different moral vision is needed. And the COVID-19 pandemic has turned everything upside down as well. The virus exposed and was exacerbated by long-standing disparities and fissures in our society and politics. The public health crisis coincided with a racial justice awakening that followed the brutal killing of Ahmaud Arbery, Breonna Taylor, George Floyd, and so many others.

During the height of the pandemic, in my daily morning ritual I watched part of the *Today Show* and *Morning Joe*. Inevitably, this led to uncontrollable tears of lament and moral indignation for the dehumanization of Black lives and the fact that so much political delay, denial, and incompetence had sabotaged our nation's window of opportunity to contain the virus. More tears followed for the staggering suffering the coronavirus and the long-standing virus of racism were inflicting upon families and communities—with Black and brown and Indigenous communities hit hardest. I also shed tears of hope as I watched the selfless heroism of nurses, doctors, and first responders, as well as so many workers who were suddenly understood as essential—from farmworkers to grocery store clerks to delivery drivers.

Our better angels were often on display. Many of us showed a great commitment to be our brothers' and sisters' keepers and to protect the most vulnerable, acting in awareness that our lives are truly interdependent, and enhancing our sense of community. People took to the streets in a declaration of our common humanity, as Black Lives Matter protests occurred in almost every city square. It is these better angels—tied to our most sacred civic and religious ideals—that must prevail in the recovery of the nation. And living into these ideals is more urgent than ever in the project of making our unfinished democracy a more perfect union.

After the 2016 election, many looked for ways to create transformational change. Rev. William Barber II, founder of the Moral Mondays movement, said, "I believe the turmoil we are witnessing around us today is in fact the birth pangs of a Third Reconstruction."[1] And in his 2020 book *Begin Again*, Princeton professor Dr. Eddie S. Glaude Jr. echoes this call: "A moral reckoning is upon us, and we have to decide, once and for all, whether or not we will truly be a multiracial democracy. We have faced two such moments before in our history: (1) the Civil War and Reconstruction, and (2) the Black freedom struggle of the mid-twentieth century. One has been described by historians as our second founding; the other as a second Reconstruction. Both grappled with the central contradiction at the heart of the Union."[2]

Glaude describes the need for what he calls a "third American founding," arguing, "Our task is to work, with every ounce of passion and every drop of love we have, to make the kingdom new."[3] Shawn Barney, who leads a racial equity initiative in New Orleans, describes the COVID-19 pandemic as "a moment for a #hard-reset,"[4] similar to other historical times, such as the Great Depression, which led to the introduction of the New Deal, a series of efforts to redesign society in fundamentally more equitable ways.

Each of these calls—for a Third Reconstruction, a third founding, a hard reset—is ultimately a choice about what kind of country we will be and a commitment to build a radically more just and inclusive society.

Despite our deep divides and the sense of growing losses, we must continue to ask: How can America be remade, even reborn, in ways that repair our democracy and move us forward in building the Beloved Community? How can we root out a politics of division and replace it with a politics that prioritizes truth, justice, and the common good?

With its seeds planted in the anguish of the 2016 election *and* my son's words of hope, and through the uncertainty and trauma of the pandemic and the 2020 election, this book has been a labor of love. It has also been a challenging exercise to honor my dual calling to be a prophetic truth-teller *and* a builder of bridges. Both approaches are needed right now. Sometimes they can be—and should be—in conflict with each other. Our nation's reckoning in the past few years around issues of police violence and systemic racism inspired me to rewrite much of this book, as did the 2020 presidential campaign and its aftermath: a president embracing the big lie of a stolen election and refusing to condemn white supremacists in ways that threatened the very institutions of our democracy and led to the violent assault on the US Capitol as the seat of that very democracy. The silence, sometimes ardent support, and even taking up of arms by so many white Christians in response to Trump's appeals to white supremacy and nationalism shook my faith in the moral vision of the Beloved Community. I questioned whether this ideal could really bridge our deep divisions and unite Americans around a redemptive new story.

Inauguration Day 2021, however, restored some of my hope in these ideals and the potential for a new national story. Seeing our nation swear in Kamala Harris, the first woman and first person of African and South-Asian descent to serve as vice president; hearing President Joe Biden offer a sermon-like inauguration speech that carried a message designed to start healing and unifying a deeply divided nation—these were profoundly meaningful parts of the celebration. But the most hopeful moment for me came in the brilliant and edifying words of Amanda Gorman, the young African American poet who captured in spoken word so much of the vision that this book seeks to cast. As she recited her poem to and for the nation, her words spoke about a deep commitment to reckon with our nation's history while embracing the strength of the nation's diversity across all of its cultures, colors, and personhood, poignantly declaring at the end that,

> *. . . being American is . . .*
> *the past we step into*
> *and how we repair it*[5]

In the midst of this trying and tumultuous period, Gorman's words, above all else, helped me tap into a deeper well of hope as I become ever more convinced that building the Beloved Community is a vision that can—and must—transform our nation.

INTRODUCTION

AMERICA IS A NATION, BUT IT IS ALSO AN IDEA. IT'S AN IDEA CONSTANTLY BEING contested and perfected, built on the profound premise of "we the people."[1] Initially, the aspirational creed that all people are created equal was considered the right of only white men, "endowed by their Creator with certain unalienable Rights, that among these are Life, Liberty and the pursuit of Happiness."[2] But these noble ideals have been compromised and imperiled by sharply conflicting conceptions of exactly whom America includes and whether these ideals truly extend to everyone.

America entered the COVID-19 crisis deeply and dangerously divided. It entered the protests after the killing of George Floyd, and then the 2020 elections, also divided. What has often felt like a cold civil war has long been at the threshold of erupting into outright enmity and violence—a threshold broken by the insurrectionist attack of the US Capitol on January 6, 2021. This is not a new revelation, nor is it hyperbole. There are many reasons for these divisions, from the long-standing fault lines of race, economic insecurity, and growing inequality to the ways in which the media, including social media, have exacerbated polarization, instigating a politics of fear and contempt that has coarsened our political culture. These divisions have also been exacerbated by the us-vs.-them and zero sum form of politics pursued by many politicians and mastered by former president Donald Trump. This politics has weaponized obstruction, stoked racial animus, and exploited wedge issues.

But all these forces are symptoms of an even deeper malady, and we must wrestle with these important questions:

- Do we hold enough shared values and aspirations to keep us together as a nation, or has that well run dry?
- Are we able to see each other's full humanity, or are we too blinded by prejudice and fear of the other?

- How do we solidify the civic and spiritual glue that can bind us together?

We can't afford superficial or shallow answers to these questions. We must delve into symptoms and systems to provide appropriate treatments, which will involve addressing the deepest roots of these and other problems.

How can Americans hold such conflicting stories of what America is, where we have been, and where we should be going? Until we have a better common understanding of our nation's history, including the myths and contradictions that have shaped it, and unless we can unite around a shared moral vision for our future, we will continue to retreat into partisan and cultural camps; we will fail to forge common ground that bridges our differences and advances the common good.

We must craft a new common story for our nation. As Harvard historian Jill Lepore puts it in her book *This America*,

> Nations, to make sense of themselves, need some kind of agreed-upon past. They can get it from scholars or they can get it from demagogues, but get it they will. The endurance of nationalism proves that there's never any shortage of fiends and frauds willing to prop up people's sense of themselves and their destiny with a tissue of myths and prophecies, prejudices and hatreds, or to pour out the contents of old rubbish bags full of festering incitements, resentments, and calls to violence. When serious historians abandon the study of the nation, when scholars stop trying to write a common history for a people, nationalism doesn't die. Instead it eats liberalism.[3]

Historians haven't been the only ones who have failed to communicate a common story for America. Too few civic and religious leaders have done so in the public square, enabling others with a more populist but corrosive agenda to highlight their own distorted version. To make matters worse, too many only told their story in the echo chamber of their own political party or cadre of like-minded people, thus failing to reach the many Americans motivated by the Make America Great Again fallacy. And far too many simply withdrew or gave up in cynicism due to the nation's broken and self-serving politics.

Only a more compelling, inspiring, and persuasive story can replace a distorted and dystopian one.

Since the 2016 election, I have found myself in a seemingly endless stream of conversations about the troubled state of our nation's democracy and its far-less-than-perfect union. Inevitably, these various discussions reached a similar conclusion: Our nation lacks a desperately needed common moral vision capable of uniting the country around a shared purpose, ideals, and values.

Gouverneur Morris is credited with coining the phrase "a more perfect union." Morris, now largely forgotten, was one of our nation's founders. "The wealthy 35-year-old New Yorker was, in effect, the first communications consultant to the not-yet-fully-formed U.S. government," according to journalist and marketer Kirk Cheyfitz.[4] In 1787, at the Constitutional Convention in Philadelphia, leaders tasked Morris and other members of the "Committee of Style" with polishing the draft of the country's founding document. Morris added an introductory paragraph—the Preamble to the Constitution. The founders ultimately embraced the aspirational language of "a more perfect union" in its reference to the project of uniting thirteen disparate colonies into one nation. While Morris's preamble has no legal validity, it remains the most timeless, best-known, and most quoted part of the Constitution. The preamble confers the document's moral authority and communicates its bold vision for the creation of a new nation.

Princeton's Eddie S. Glaude Jr. provides an invaluable counterweight to any blind or unconditional embrace of a more perfect union. "Ours should be a story that begins with those who sought to make real the promise of this democracy," Glaude writes in *Begin Again*. "Put aside the fairy tale of America as 'the shining city on the hill' or 'the redeemer nation,' and recast the idea of perfecting the Union not as a guarantee of our goodness but a declaration of the ongoing work to address injustice in our midst."[5] Glaude argues that we must contextualize the concept: "'A more perfect union' can also operate," he told me, "as one of America's myths, enabling us to cover up and evade our past sins. It can be misused to reinforce a perfectionist impulse that has been one of the mechanisms to maintain our innocence and lend a blind eye to the lie of white supremacy, which has disfigured American democracy from our nation's inception."[6]

What we hold as a promise and an ideal, the pursuit of a more perfect union, can't be used to excuse or ignore our past, particularly because our past continues to show up in our present. If we do ignore it, we will remain captive to our history, and the umbilical cord of white supremacy will continue to choke off our potential and promise.

Confronting the past can be uncomfortable and inconvenient. But our past makes up the very DNA of this nation: as William Faulkner put it, "The past is never dead. It's not even past."[7] There is no easy path to a more perfect union. If the path is too easy and doesn't require sacrifice or change within us and our policies and systems, then clearly we are on the wrong path, since so many mistruths and inequities are deeply entrenched in the core of our being as individuals and as a nation. The challenge is made more complicated by the fact that many of our states function as if they are disparate countries, with their own distinct cultures and worldviews, as well as by the divide between rural and urban communities and the deep racial and ideological divisions that separate us.

Unions of any sort require a shared sense of purpose and vision. They need a basic set of shared values, as well as a willingness to compromise in ways that don't violate those fundamental values. While marriage is an imperfect metaphor for political unions, we can glean a great deal from the most ubiquitous and, arguably, the most important union in our social and religious life. I remember going through premarital counseling with my wife, Sharee, and learning about the importance of building and maintaining trust, identifying shared values and priorities, cultivating open and honest communication, developing an understanding of our past and how it has shaped us, and recognizing the importance of forgiveness and reconciliation—all of which form the lifeblood of a healthy marriage. What is true for couples is often true for communities and nations.

The escalating cold civil war that has crippled our politics and divided our nation over the past few decades is a warning sign, portending America's continuing disunity and decline. This understanding is not based on partisanship; no president or Congress, as important as they are, will deliver our country to the promised land. True and lasting transformation will require considerable pressure from outside of elected office, as well as transformational leadership at every level and from every sector.

We need a moral vision that draws from our most sacred civic and religious values and transcends our partisan loyalties, cultural and racial fissures, and ideological blinders. That moral vision, I believe, is a reimagined vision of the Beloved Community.

The groundbreaking report *Hidden Tribes*, produced several years ago by the organization More in Common, revealed that most Americans yearn for a more inclusive and unifying story of us, one that communicates a sense of common purpose as well as shared goals and aspirations.[8] While no single narrative or moral vision will resonate with all Americans, the continued absence of one will leave our nation like a castle made of sand—blown apart by competing winds of tribalized identity, hyperpartisanship, and ideology.

A shared moral vision wouldn't be a panacea—it wouldn't solve all our nation's ills. But how will we come together to confront the very real challenges facing us without at least attempting to construct and unite around a common vision? Our very real challenges include the dire need for a full and more equitable economic recovery, the increasingly devastating impacts of climate change, continued transformations in our economy due to automation and technology, extreme and often racialized inequality, and persistent poverty, among others. While a new moral vision and story won't immediately heal polarization and transform our nation, they could offer a desperately needed starting point.

The vision of the Beloved Community animated the civil rights movement, but since then it often has been overshadowed and derailed. Bridging the deep divides among us will not come purely through an electoral outcome or a change in political leadership, as important as these shifts may appear. Due to distorted incentives in our politics that favor extremism, blame, and zero-sum thinking, it is increasingly unlikely that a unifying moral vision will come primarily out of the political realm.

My Black mother and white father were married in 1968, the same year Dr. Martin Luther King Jr. was assassinated and not long after interracial marriage was legalized across the country. My parents instilled in me a deep and abiding conviction that my biracial background was a source of strength and not a weakness. In a similar light, they helped me see that our nation's rich diversity was an incredible asset and gift, not a liability. Through the convictions they built into our family and those I grew to embrace through the lens of my faith, I have seen that politics isn't the only realm through which to seek the Beloved Community. And politics alone isn't strong enough to hold a moral, unifying vision. The deeper foundation is the divine imprint instilled by God in each person, which means that everyone deserves and possesses equal dignity and worth.

I first heard the term *the Beloved Community* when I learned about the Montgomery bus boycott in my high school American history class. I was mesmerized by Dr. King's statement at the end of the boycott campaign, in which he saw beyond that finite but seminal victory and tapped into the broader vision of the civil rights struggle, which he saw as the realization of the Beloved Community. When I read those words, I recognized in them my own convictions about the moral vision that was needed to animate change. I recognized in them the questions my parents raised as they wondered what kind of world would embrace their biracial children.

I became infatuated with the civil rights movement, reading every book I could find, including Taylor Branch's series, *America in the King Years*. I repeatedly watched the groundbreaking documentary series *Eyes on the Prize*. I became convinced that my generation had inherited the unfinished business of the civil rights movement—and that we must make this moral vision our own. This infatuation from high school through college was probably a little much for some of my friends and family, but I believed then as I do now that a commitment to a broader moral vision helps prevent moral indignation against injustice from devolving into shrill self-righteousness.

The vision of the Beloved Community is an old story, but it's also a new narrative with the potential to inspire and unite Americans across generational, geographic, racial, and religious divides. The Martin Luther King Jr. Center summarizes the basic idea of the Beloved Community as one in which people of different backgrounds recognize that our individual well-being is inextricably linked to the well-being of others—including those we consider "the other." It is a society based on justice, equal opportunity, empathy, and love.[9] Building on this foundation, I believe the Beloved Community requires constructing a society in which neither punishment nor privilege is tied to race, ethnicity, gender, gender identity, or sexual orientation and where our diversity as a community and nation is celebrated and embraced as a source of strength rather than weakness. The Beloved Community taps into and is based upon religious values and mandates, such as the Golden Rule and the biblical concept of shalom, as well as civic values tied to the founding ideals of our nation and to documents such as the UN Declaration of Human Rights.

This moral vision is broad enough to include disaffected white, working-class Americans who feel left behind and have been swayed by a politics of fear and grievance instead of by a politics of justice and inclusion. The Beloved Community has arms wide and strong enough for all of America, including those known as Dreamers and others in immigrant communities, those from religious traditions considered outside the mainstream, and those who have been left out and left behind—from Midwestern towns and rural farms to Indigenous reservations and blighted cities or suburbs—red, blue, and everything in between.

Building the Beloved Community requires truth-telling and repentance about our past. Instead of inciting guilt and casting blame, the Beloved Community is built on a foundation that generates empathy and galvanizes a greater commitment to justice. It will involve communicating a compelling moral vision and a persuasive practical case for why the multiracial democracy that we are increasingly becoming can generate greater belonging, shared thriving, and common purpose for all Americans.

Building the Beloved Community is never a simple task. If it were, we would not be in the national conflict and crisis we are in now. But I have the audacity to believe that despite the founders' flaws and prejudices, they understood something deeply profound when they fashioned America's ideals and set us on a path of constant striving to achieve a more perfect union. Yes, the American project is worth redeeming and fighting for. And the imperative to build the Beloved Community requires the involvement of all of us.

Numerous books have been written in recent years about how America's democracy and "soul" are in jeopardy. Many of them offer prescriptions about how to restore our values and heal our broken democracy. Saving America's soul became a theme of Joe Biden's 2020 presidential campaign, and the phrase was echoed in different ways by many others. I too am deeply worried about the soul of our nation and the state of our democracy, so my hope is that this book will play a part in repairing and strengthening both, by offering something foundational, beginning with how we define America and what it will take to realize the full promise of the nation.

This book looks at the meta-story that we tell ourselves and hold as true about our nation's history, character, and ideals. It is about replacing distorted and sometimes destructive myths and stories with a larger narrative based on a more honest and holistic understanding of our nation's history and our most cherished ideals. It is about embracing a moral vision for our future that is aligned with our deepest religious values and civic ideals. It is about telling a bigger story of us, which I believe can be best told through the story of building the Beloved Community.

And it is about applying that moral vision to many of the most intractable and pressing issues facing our nation and world—from gun violence to immigration, from protecting life at every stage to transforming our policing and criminal justice system, from ending extreme poverty to combating climate change. This book is about seizing this opportunity to form a more perfect union by building a radically more just nation and in the process experiencing the Beloved Community together.

The book is divided into three parts:

Part I makes the case for why the nation needs a new unifying vision of the Beloved Community. This new vision requires examining and replacing spiritual lies and distorted narratives with redemptive truths that help move the nation from our current state of hyper-polarization toward justice and community.

Part II addresses the building blocks of the Beloved Community. Each building block requires overcoming forces and trends such as toxic polarization, a nationalistic form of patriotism, and mistruths and misunderstandings of our nation's history.

Finally, Part III explores the practical questions, as well as core attitudes and commitments, around realizing that vision.

Each chapter in Part III details a "beatitude" (literally, blessing) consisting of a fundamental value that is a component of building the Beloved Community. These beatitudes include a renewed investment in equality, interdependence, radical welcome, environmental stewardship, nonviolence, and dignity for all. Living out these vital "beatitudes" can help us address the most vexing and pressing social and political issues we face.

While the concept of the Beloved Community and my own approach are rooted primarily in the Christian faith, the Beloved Community intentionally incorporates and walks alongside other faith traditions. In that spirit, I hope this book will be a companion for many readers from different faith expressions, including the growing number of those who identify as spiritual but not religious, as well as for other people of conscience. The vision of a Beloved Community finds expression in many images and traditions, and within a variety of racial and ethnic communities—as we'll see, for example, in the value systems of *familia justicia* in the Latino/a community, *jeong* in the Korean community, and shalom in the Jewish tradition.

The dangers of extreme polarization, the rise of hate groups and white nationalism, and the ascendance of populist strongman leaders are not solely American challenges. These have become global contagions, infecting countries across the world. While many lessons can be learned from other countries, ultimately the project of building the Beloved Community in the United States will require solutions specific to American politics and culture—though I hope some of the antidotes and commitments I identify can inspire transformation in other countries as well. Our increasingly interdependent world, in which our prosperity, security, and livelihoods are inextricably tied to our neighbors and the rest of the world, demands a global worldview. America's rebirth will also enable the nation to better serve as a vehicle for hope and dignity on a global scale.

In his final book, Martin Luther King Jr. asked the still salient and provocative question "Where do we go from here: chaos or community?"[10]

Just before his assassination, King sensed that the nation was at a danger-ous crossroads as he witnessed the stall of the civil rights movement and the rise of rampant violence. The country was embroiled in the Vietnam War and was coming apart at the seams due to culture clashes. We are again at a crossroads moment, which has been exposed by the COVID-19 crisis, the virus of systemic racism, and the January 6, 2021, insurrection at the US Capitol. We can choose the path of resignation and accept continued, crippling polarization and entrenched inequality, or we can choose the path of transforming our culture, politics, and economy according to the beatitudes of the Beloved Community.

Our choice is between the vicious cycle of a fear-based politics fueled by distrust of and contempt for the "other" and another, more virtuous politics grounded in deeper listening, truth-telling, bridge-building, and common problem-solving. It is time to choose a path that acknowledges and repents for the ways we have failed to live up to America's ideals. It is time that we boldly pursue a shared vision of a future rooted in our most deeply held religious and civic values. It is time to embark with even greater urgency on the task of building the Beloved Community, which will enable us to achieve a more perfect union and a radically more just nation.

Part One

THE VISION OF THE
BELOVED COMMUNITY

Chapter One

EMBRACING A BIGGER STORY OF US

If we are to have peace on earth our loyalties must become ecumenical rather than sectional. Our loyalties must transcend our race, our tribe, our class, and our nation, and this means we must develop a world perspective. —Martin Luther King Jr.

A new Americanism would require a clear-eyed reckoning with American history, its sorrows no less than its glories. A lie stands on one foot, as Benjamin Franklin liked to say, but a truth stands upon two. A new Americanism would reset on a history that tells the truth, as best it can, about what W. E. B. Du Bois called the hideous mistakes, the frightful wrongs, and the great and beautiful things that nations do. —Jill Lepore

I HAVE LONG BEEN A BELIEVER IN THE POWER OF STORIES, OR WHAT MY FORMER professor Marshall Ganz refers to as "public narrative," to capture people's moral imagination and to fuel social and political change. Stories help us make sense of the world. Stories transmit and shape our most fundamental values. Stories have the power to change hearts and minds.

The United States needs a new story, a bigger story of us. We need a story that is steeped in a more honest account of our founding story but that is also forward-looking, enabling us to see beyond our deep divisions and the myriad of social, economic, and political challenges we face.

Research by the group More in Common concludes that "a bigger story of us" is what is needed to anchor us in shared values and a more inclusive and hopeful American story. That bigger story will help us counter entrenched polarization. According to the *Hidden Tribes* report, "The forces that are driving polarization and social fracturing are profoundly powerful: from rising inequality and economic insecurity to the media echo chambers and the bewildering pace of social and demographic change. All this is happening against a backdrop of fears of crime and terrorism, which further heighten people's perception of threat and accelerate their retreat into their tribal identities."[1]

This groundbreaking research also found that most Americans yearn for a bigger story of us. According to the study, while 87 percent of Americans believe that "the country was more divided than at any point in their lifetimes,"[2] 77 percent say that "our differences are not so great that we cannot come together."[3] We may be perilously divided, but most Americans haven't fallen off the cliff of fatalism and hopelessness; rather, they still hold to the belief that our differences are not irreconcilable. To bridge this divide, the report's authors suggest, we need to find a bigger story of us.

The challenge is that stories also have the power to deceive, to mislead, and to mutate into false narratives and mistruths. It is far too easy to exploit the long-standing fissures in American society to paint false narratives, such as that our nation's growing diversity represents a threat rather than a strength or that liberals and conservatives don't share a love for the nation and its future. At its best, a common aspirational story of us represents a bridge for crossing into a more perfect union and a catalyst for building the Beloved Community.

While a great deal binds us together, there are powerful forces tearing us apart as a nation. It's difficult to change or influence people's minds simply with a barrage of facts or purely through reason. Instead, we must tap into the emotive power of inspiring narratives to change people, to move beyond purely self-interest to also appeal to their conscience and capture their moral imagination. We need to replace narrow and fear-based sources of belonging with a shared understanding and belief in the growing reality that we are all in this together. But to convince Americans that we are all in this together, we need more persuasive and inspiring stories.

Dr. Ganz's course on "People, Power, and Change," which I took while a student at Harvard's Kennedy School of Government in 2000, transformed my thinking about the primary importance of public narrative to bring about change. Public narrative, he says, is how we learn to make choices and construct our identities—as individuals, as communities, as nations. Ganz builds on a famous quote by Rabbi Hillel—"If I am not for myself, who will be for me? If I am only for myself, what am I? And if not now, when?"[4]—and points out that public narrative is the art through which we combine the story of self, the story of us, and the story of now. According to Ganz, "we are all part of multiple 'us's'"—families, faiths, cultures, communities, organizations, and nations in which we participate with others.[5]

Ganz's course included the following questions that help open up these stories:

- What community, organization, movement, culture, nation, or other constituency do you consider yourself to be part of and connected with?
- With whom do you share a common past? With whom do you share a common future?
- Do you participate in this community as a result of "fate," "choice," or both?
- How like or unlike the experience of others do you believe your own experience to be?[6]

"One way we establish an 'us'—a shared identity—is through telling of shared stories," Ganz explains. These are stories "through which we can articulate the values we share, as well as the particularities that make us an 'us.'"[7] But the way we define that "us" is also something we must constantly interrogate. Every day we see distorted and parochial versions of "us" stories in America—the "us" of red states vs. blue states, rural vs. urban, liberal vs. conservative, Republican vs. Democrat. While these and other examples of "us" have meaning, do they overly or falsely define us? I believe we can and must expand them with a more inclusive and justice-centered us. This will require telling the story of how a bigger us is more in line with our shared religious values and civic ideals. This bigger story will give oxygen to the building of the Beloved Community.

Unfortunately, our ability to receive and embrace a bigger story of us is often blocked by the powerful mental frames already at work in our heads. These barriers are also compounded by confirmation bias in the wiring of our brains, where we push away information and facts that we disagree with or that conflict with our worldview. *Confirmation bias* means we tend to embrace information that confirms our preconceived views, while rejecting information that casts doubt on them.[8] As we own our responsibility to understand our biases and recognize our often unconscious blind spots, we can work to overcome those internal factors that create ill-formed narratives. When we do, we are better able to ground our ideas in clear, factually reliable, and foundational values around an issue. By doing so, we create greater opportunities to unite around shared moral values and civic purpose, opening space for narratives that build the Beloved Community.

When I was leading Global Justice, an organization I cofounded after graduate school to mobilize college students to become champions of global human rights, I served on an advisory group where I helped the Rockefeller Brothers Fund develop a communications guide. This guide, *U.S. in the World*, aided policymakers and nonprofit leaders in communicating persuasively and effectively as they built greater public support for US leadership in the world.[9] The guide leaned heavily on cognitive science and the research of the FrameWorks Institute, which left an indelible mark on my thinking. According to the institute, new information that doesn't fit our mental models, or "frames," often gets rejected outright. And in a rare collaboration between communications scholars and practitioners, FrameWorks has been developing a new approach to explaining social issues to the public, called Strategic Frame Analysis. Recognizing that there is more than one way to tell a story, Strategic Frame Analysis emphasizes the importance of communicating through values, metaphors, and narrative, among other things.[10]

Everywhere and every day, we encounter framing—our own and others'—whether we are conscious of it or not. Framing creates a narrative. That narrative may be shaped by you, by another person, by the media, or by all of the above—as can be seen in phrases such as "welfare queens," "death panels," and "clean coal."

These examples hint at how ubiquitous framing is. "Through 'reframing'—the process of changing the thoughts and actions triggered by messaging cues—we can shift how we and others understand and respond to issues, which can help build and grow movements for change," explain Nat Kendall-Taylor and Sean Gibbons. "To illustrate this, in one study, researchers asked people if, given the importance of *free speech*, they supported allowing a hate group to hold a political rally. Eighty-five percent said yes. When the same question was framed around the *risk of violence* posed by this activity, fewer than half (40 percent) said the same. Changing the frame changed the response."[11]

This research suggests that a bigger story of us will require that we reframe, through metaphor and narrative, who America is, what America stands for, and where America is going. This new narrative can't reinforce biases, simply tout facts, or just pose arguments and policy prescriptions. Instead, it must tell a bigger story of us, tied to where we are now and what we can become in the future.

The wildly divergent public reactions to the slogan "Make America Great Again," which defined so much of Donald Trump's campaigns and presidency, provide an illustration of the power of a distorted but highly effective frame. For many who supported Trump, the slogan served as an effective rallying call to restore America's supposed lost glory and greatness. The slogan carried a narrative within it. For example, for the "values voters"—who dominated the news after the 2004 election and who morphed into what researcher Robert P. Jones refers to as "nostalgia voters"[12]—this slogan symbolized a reminder that the era of white Christians dominating the church and the larger American culture was beginning to diminish. The slogan also appealed to the anti-establishment and grievance-centered politics of the Tea Party movement. This frame tapped into a yearning for the security and control that the past supposedly afforded. Meanwhile, for many others, particularly African Americans and other people of color, the "Make America Great Again" slogan served as a painful reminder of America's history of racism and was coded language for making America white again—a narrative that promised to protect the privileges of whiteness and the penalties that come with Blackness.

Gifted politicians can sometimes use the power of their own story and their vision for our country to inspire swaths of the nation around shared ideals. Former president Barack Obama accomplished this through a hopeful campaign message of "Yes We Can." Unfortunately, this vision soon became absorbed into Organizing for America, a political apparatus that advanced Obama's policy agenda and reelection rather than catalyzing and strengthening independent movements to transform the values and political priorities of the nation. In the increasingly partisan and polarized state of our politics, it's difficult to imagine the political realm producing the kind of unifying and transcendent vision required for transformational change. Instead, the narrative will need to come from sources that lie outside of our overly partisan, and often broken, politics.

During the civil rights era, that narrative came, in particular, from the Black church and our religious leaders. And while institutional religion has taken some hits in terms of its moral suasion and credibility, particularly with younger generations, there's incredible potential for deep spiritual renewal and revival to undergird building the Beloved Community. In *A Stone of Hope*, David Chappell makes a compelling case that the prophetic tradition of the Old Testament, sometimes translated into secular language, fueled the civil rights movement and drove African American activists to unprecedented solidarity and self-sacrifice. Chappell writes,

> The most significant struggle against oppression in modern America—the civil rights movement—defies sustained comparison with any nonreligious movement. It is hard to imagine masses of people lining up for years of excruciating risk against southern sheriffs, fire hoses, and attack dogs without some transcendent or millennial faith to sustain them. It is hard to imagine such faith being sustained without emotional mass rituals—without something extreme and extraordinary to link the masses' spirits. It is impossible to ignore how often the participants carried their movement out in prophetic, ecstatic biblical tones. In this age of declining faith in revolution, the tradition of revivalist religion—commonly understood as the opposite of revolution, indeed the most potent form of the opiate of the masses—might supply the raw materials of successful social change in the future.[13]

As Chappell and many other scholars point out, the civil rights movement was grounded in moral revival that inspired sacrifice, courage, and a prophetic imagination. A deep moral vision, often rooted in an understanding of the Beloved Community, enabled people to see beyond the seemingly immutable status quo and defy often impossible odds to bring about change. The movement's resilient commitment to an ethic of nonviolence and steadfast love was also an informing ethic, providing a potent antidote to narratives inciting hatred and violence.

Even though the country has become more secular, a purely secular or ideological vision will be insufficient to transform America today. In addition to appealing to civic and humanist values, we must tap into the power of faith and spirituality, which are critical for inspiring and sustaining the moral vision of the Beloved Community. As Chappell explains, "The civil rights struggle did not consist entirely of politics and grassroots organizing, as books and documentaries on the subject have so far implied. It also involved a change in American culture, a change in the way Americans thought and felt when they talked about things like freedom, equality, race, and rights. It involved a change in Americans' expectations about these things, what they considered realistic as opposed to idealistic."[14]

Sadly, in recent years, the church's moral authority has been compromised by a series of scandals and challenges, including the sexual abuse scandal within the Catholic Church; the misguided allegiance and seemingly Faustian bargain between the Religious Right and the Republican Party; and increasing perceptions, particularly among young people, that the church is intolerant, homophobic, and hypocritical.[15] The longstanding slide in membership in mainline churches is now happening in evangelical churches as well, many of which are in decline except for the influx of recent immigrants. Despite these challenges, the church and other religious institutions are still among the most influential and trusted transmitters of shared story and identity. The church still holds incredible influence on American politics and culture and has great potential to be a positive catalyst of the bigger story of us.

America is becoming less religious, but spirituality seems to be deepening and thriving. In October 2020, the Fetzer Institute released groundbreaking research on spirituality in America, finding that "more than eight out of ten Americans consider themselves spiritual to some extent and six in ten aspire to be more spiritual." The study also found that the "more people identify as spiritual the more likely they are to vote, speak out about social and political issues, and participate in politics and social movements." The study suggests that the "more strongly someone identifies as spiritual, the more likely they are to hold prosocial attitudes and take civic and community action."[16] After serving on an advisory committee for the study, I offered the following reflections:

> Throughout the nation's history, spirituality and religion have inspired and fueled many of the social movements that have reformed and transformed America, from women's suffrage to the civil rights movement. It has also played a key role in undergirding the pro-life movement and other traditionally conservative causes. While some of the movements of today may on their face seem less rooted in religious institutions than in the past, many activists and leaders, including within the Black Lives Matter movement, continue to be motivated by deep and resilient spirituality. These findings provide further insight and evidence that spirituality provides both fuel and oxygen for social and political change.[17]

My own life story has been inspired by a bigger story of us. And my story is interwoven into America's story. I am the product of two Americas. My mom and dad sacrificed a great deal in deciding to marry. My mom, who grew up in segregated Louisville, Kentucky, was an inspiring trailblazer, becoming the first Black woman to serve as a vice president at both Western Washington University and the University of Arizona. My dad, who grew up in a white rural suburb just outside Cleveland, Ohio, was often willing to go against the grain, which included marrying my mother. In the process, he lost many of his friends and family and compromised some of his own white privilege. Among those ardently opposed to my parents' marriage was my dad's stepmother. Ironically, her most fervent argument was that my parents would be doing a grave disservice to their children because we would be racially homeless and lost. In one confrontation, my dad responded to her disapproval with his signature biting humor, saying, "If God hadn't meant for the races to mix, then God would not have made them sexually compatible." This pointed retort ended the conversation. For her part, my mom sacrificed having as strong a connection to the Black community as she would have liked by relocating and starting a life with my father in Bellingham, Washington, a small city north of Seattle where at that time there was only a very small Black population.

In my early life I was not particularly attuned to skin color or the racial categories so often constructed around it. While I was the only biracial or Black kid in almost all my early classes, I have only a few vivid memories of experiencing overt discrimination or racism. Most of these occasions were tied to kids cruelly excluding me from games because I was Black, and "only white kids [could] play this game." Fortunately, these experiences were the exception and not the norm.

When I was five years old, for a year my family moved to Boston, one of the country's most racially polarized cities, particularly over the issue of mandated school busing. As an experiment and a compromise amid the turmoil, my first-grade class at the predominantly white Brookline Elementary School traded classrooms on alternate Fridays with the first-grade class at a school in almost-exclusively-Black Roxbury. That experience taught me more about the concept of race.

Then, at the age of thirteen, during a trip to visit my Uncle Danny in Chicago, the scales of blindness to racism fell more definitively from my eyes. My uncle was a consummate entrepreneur who had started a major bus company based in Chicago. We took a drive through some of the starkly contrasting neighborhoods of the city, from the Black South Side to predominantly white, affluent neighborhoods. While I had seen media images of dilapidated housing, blighted neighborhoods, and intergenerational poverty, seeing this firsthand sparked a rude awakening for me, but also an overdue education. I now saw Bellingham as a beautiful but sheltered bubble, and I realized that staying in that bubble—now that I was beginning to sense my calling tied to the unfinished business of the civil rights movement—would leave me restless to be part of the change I wanted to and inspire me to work toward a more inclusive us.

A bigger story of us will embrace the positive contributions and attributes of culture, even as we understand culture as dynamic, malleable, and multifaceted. A bigger story of us needs to be a better story, one that more fully includes the diverse cultures of Latino/a people, Asian Americans, African and Caribbean immigrants, and Native Americans. Before Sharee and I got married, we were in serious premarital counseling. It took those sessions for me to fully understand just how different my wife's blended Caribbean and Canadian culture was from my blended American one. I came to understand just how much we learn from the example of our parents and how much we are unconsciously shaped by our upbringing in terms of what we value and how we think about ourselves and others.

A bigger story of us also requires that we learn to tell stories differently, with greater vulnerability and candor. Instead of telling our story from a defensive or wary posture, we can tell it as many people of faith tell the story of their faith journey: in the words of my Baptist tradition, we can provide our "testimony." In the best of the Christian tradition, we are always in the process of becoming and growing into the redemptive story of what a relationship with Christ looks like, because Christ makes all things new. While we inevitably will fall short of God's best for us, we also learn that the most important thing is not to be perfect but to be faithful. In the context of America, this means acknowledging and repenting for our many faults, contradictions, and sins without getting paralyzed by them. This doesn't mean our past has no bearing on our present and future decisions. It means our past profoundly informs and shapes how we work together to build a more perfect union and strive to live up to the full meaning of the American creed, that all people are created equal, and then to apply it inclusively to everyone.

Part of what makes embracing and pursuing this more inclusive story of us so difficult is that many of us, especially those of us who are African American, have grown tired of being gaslighted and constantly having to explain the ugly truths of our nation's history, let alone its present injustices. What is often referred to as "white fragility" prevents many white Americans from hearing some of the hard truths that have reverberated across American history and that continue to shape and contort our present reality. Many of us are fatigued at having to be patient, fatigued at tolerating offensive or misinformed comments, fatigued by questions that are often used to dismiss or deny these truths. We are tired of so often having to be the ones who must initiate dialogue or go out of our way to build bridges and relationships across the fault lines of race. We are tired of the defensiveness that so often comes with having these hard conversations.

At the same time, many white Americans are also tired of feeling guilty or responsible for the actions and sins that took place in the past. They are tired of being told that they are the problem or of being presumed racist or intolerant. Sadly, the word *racist* has become an overly loaded term, and many white Americans have a hard time seeing their relationship to the word or accepting that they benefit from various forms of white privilege—particularly because so much of this privilege has become institutionalized and therefore made invisible. Where do both forms of being tired leave us, other than with racial fatigue and resignation? This conundrum and our current trajectory can feel like a hot mess.

In *White Fragility*, Robin DiAngelo explains why racial fatigue is so common and why we have such a hard time talking about racism. Writing as a white woman primarily to other white people, DiAngelo doesn't mince words:

> White people in North America live in a society that is deeply separate and unequal by race, and white people are the beneficiaries of that separation and inequality. As a result, we are insulated from racial stress, at the same time that we come to feel entitled to and deserving of our advantage. Given how seldom we experience racial discomfort in a society we dominate, we haven't had to build our racial stamina. Socialized into a deeply internalized sense of superiority that we either are unaware of or can never admit to ourselves, we become highly fragile in conversation about race. We consider a challenge to our racial worldviews as a challenge to our very identities as good, moral people. . . . Though white fragility is triggered by discomfort and anxiety, it is born of superiority and entitlement. White fragility is not weakness per se. In fact, it is a powerful means of white racial control and the protection of white advantage.[18]

Race is not the only story of us in America, but it is fundamental and related to almost every understanding of us. It must be part and parcel of our seeing the us that emerges when the church finds its moral authority and joins people of other faith traditions and of humanist values in telling a new story of us. When we do, the vicious cycle of racism, sexism, class-ism, and homophobia can be disrupted by the transformational power of relationships and a commitment to truth-telling that embraces a bigger story of us—one that includes all Americans. Yes, this bigger story will be fraught with difficulty and will engender backlash, and the process of co-creating that story will require some discomfort and courage. But it is the story to which those building the Beloved Community are dedicated.

A bigger, more inclusive story of us cannot be reduced to a story of left or right, Republican or Democrat, religious or nonreligious. Instead, it must emphasize both personal and communal responsibility, com-passion and justice, service and civic activism. The inclusive story of us is quintessentially a both/and story, which is the only kind of story of us that can transcend the brokenness and limitations of our binary minds and fractured politics.

Chapter Two

WHY AMERICA MUST BE REBORN

A nation that will keep people in slavery for 244 years will "thingify" them—make them things. Therefore they will exploit them, and poor people generally, economically. And a nation that will exploit economically will have to have foreign investments and everything else, and will have to use its military might to protect them. All of these problems are tied together. What I am saying is that we must go from this convention and say, "America, you must be born again!" —Rev. Dr. Martin Luther King Jr.

Jesus replied, "Very truly I tell you, no one can see the kingdom of God unless they are born again." —John 3:3

"HEALING THE BODY" WAS THE TITLE OF MY VERY FIRST SERMON, WHICH I PREACHED in 2001 at Union Baptist Church in Cambridge, Massachusetts. I can still remember the overwhelming nervousness mixed with hopeful anticipation I felt in that moment. My scripture came from the apostle Paul's letter to the church at Corinth, where he offers a poignant metaphor comparing the health of the church to the health and functioning of the human body. The apostle wrote, "If one part [of the body] suffers, every part suffers with it" (1 Corinthians 12:26). I preached about my advocacy efforts in the fight against the HIV/AIDS pandemic, which I believed would define my generation. At the end of the sermon, I said that I believed that God has a second definition for the acronym HIV (Human Immunodeficiency Virus)—that it also presented an urgent opportunity to "Heal the International Village" by addressing the underlying brokenness and injustices that fueled the epidemic. We would need to heal the body.

Years later, amid the COVID-19 crisis, I reflected again on the relevance of Paul's words. The pandemic preyed upon many of the weakest members of society, including the elderly and people living with underlying health conditions. The coronavirus magnified many preexisting inequalities in society, evidenced by the disproportionate infection rate and death toll among African Americans, Native Americans, and other communities of color. It also presented a historic opportunity to address those structural and racialized inequalities, as many people realized that when one part of the body was suffering, we all were suffering.

In a practical sense, the pandemic fundamentally changed our very way of life. But in a moral sense, the virus acted like an MRI, shining a light upon the weaknesses and inequities in our society—and pointing to the opportunity to reorder our priorities and reimagine the way we live our lives together, as parts of a body that jointly constitute a whole. Our nation needs a fresh start. In Christian terms, it is a country in need of a rebirth.

There's a well-known story about Jesus, told in the Gospel of John. In this text Nicodemus, a religious leader, approaches Jesus with a penetrating question that cuts to the heart of who we are and what we believe. As a Pharisee, he was part of an ancient Jewish sect focused on keeping strict observance of the law. In the gospels, Pharisees often test Jesus on aspects of keeping the law, seeking to entrap him in his own words and questioning his authority. It's in this somewhat adversarial context that Nicodemus approaches Jesus at night. Perhaps he is ashamed or afraid of being associated publicly with Jesus. But his question is no trap; it is earnest. Nicodemus asks Jesus, "Rabbi, we know that you are a teacher who has come from God. For no one could perform the signs you are doing if God were not with him" (John 3:2).

Jesus responds with the profound statement, quoted at the head of this chapter, about being "born again." He understands that the question isn't just about proving his identity as one who comes from God; it's about Nicodemus's search for truth and filling a deficit in his soul. Jesus's response to Nicodemus's statement contains a curious challenge:

that flesh gives birth to flesh but the spirit gives birth to the spirit. God's work in the world isn't just about fixing our broken pieces, but about breathing new spirit into us and making us into a new creation. And that new creation, that transformation, is nothing short of a rebirth.

One of the defining tenets of my Baptist tradition is to be "born again." Being born again is not simply about conversion; it's also about rebirth and transformation. These can be reflected in moments when we are faced with a life-altering choice. I have long been infatuated with the *Matrix* trilogy, groundbreaking films that came out during my college years. In the first film Neo, a computer hacker, is presented by Morpheus with a choice: to swallow a "blue pill" and stay under the control of machines in an artificial state of denial and indifference, or to swallow a "red pill" and join the cause of confronting injustice and freeing humanity—as Morpheus puts it, to see "how deep the rabbit hole goes." For me, the choices we make to either accept the broken status quo or commit to transforming America are "Matrix moments."

One of my most memorable and formative rebirths took place at the foot of Victoria Falls, on the border between Zambia and Zimbabwe. Two years after Nelson Mandela was elected president of South Africa, I spent a life-changing semester studying abroad in Cape Town. As part of my internship month in an academic program, I lived in Durban and worked at the African Center for the Constructive Resolution of Disputes (ACCORD). There I was put through a crash course in conflict resolution. Before going to Durban, I had been given some tough-love advice from a man named Sizwe, the assistant director of the program. I had told Sizwe that after graduating from college, I felt called to move to South Africa to contribute to the ongoing freedom struggle there. His response has stayed with me: If I really wanted to help South Africa, Sizwe said, I should return to the US and seek to transform the policies of my own country, which would have a much greater ripple effect on South Africa.

Wrestling with this wise and challenging advice, I set off. The conflict resolution center gave me the daunting assignment of working with a group of rival youth activists in Durban who had been perpetrators and victims of a wave of political violence before and after the watershed 1994 election, in which Mandela was elected. I felt powerless to help them heal from the trauma they had experienced, and I wasn't sure how to support them in overcoming the lack of opportunities they faced in a new South Africa. I was guilty of both hubris and naivete in believing I could impart conflict resolution skills I had barely learned to a group of young adults more mature in life's struggles and realities than I was. I fell into an abyss of depression, though I didn't understand what I was experiencing at the time. I became alienated from God, refusing to face my feelings of inadequacy and powerlessness.

After my program ended, my girlfriend at the time traveled to South Africa to see me and to participate in a service program in Johannesburg. I couldn't find the courage to confide in her what I was experiencing. What's more, I knew I needed to end our relationship. Instead of facing my fears, I jumped on a bus heading to Harare, Zimbabwe, a place I had always wanted to visit. As I traveled across Zimbabwe, I felt alone, isolated, and lost.

Drawn to Victoria Falls, one of the natural wonders of the world, I was overwhelmed by the incredible beauty, grandeur, and majesty of the place. It felt as if the powerful yet refreshing wall of mist generated by the sheer force of the falls washed away my guilt and removed the incredible burden I had been carrying. I felt lighter, freer, and more deeply connected to God's grace than ever before. I also felt more committed to discerning and following God's direction for my life. In that moment of complete surrender, I felt a weight lifted; the fog over my spirit and mind evaporated. It felt like a rebirth.

Being born again is not limited to individual experience. Communities and societies can also be reborn as a result of shared transformational experiences. Our shared struggle through the COVID-19 crisis could be such an experience, creating new possibilities for the rebirth of a more united "we the people" and a renewed social contract. With this comparison, I don't mean to diminish the sacredness of the experience of being born again. But the process of rebirth and transformation that has been so central to my own faith journey offers powerful lessons for building the Beloved Community and realizing a more perfect union. America's national identity and character—despite our nation's contradictions, bruises, and flaws—*can* be reimagined, transformed, and even reborn. I have the audacity to believe this because, from my Christian perspective, God can make all things new.

Our nation's rebirth will require coming to terms with our past and making amends while we embrace a new set of commitments for the future. None of this is inevitable, and there will likely be backsliding into old habits, attitudes, and temptations. But if we remain steadfast in claiming and living out our best religious and civic ideals, we can and shall overcome.

Many factors have contributed to our current crisis and explain why a rebirth is needed. Money increasingly distorts our politics. Trust in our political institutions and politicians has plummeted. Far too many congressional seats are so gerrymandered—enabling politicians to choose their voters rather than the other way around—that the only real contests are in primaries, a situation that often favors the most strident and ideologically extreme candidates. In addition, the normalization of lies, disinformation, and even conspiracy theories in our public life has eroded the moral core of our nation.

The cutthroat and us-vs.-them nature of our politics suffocates our ability to find common ground, let alone seek compromise. Political campaigns and rhetoric have often been characterized by increasing amounts of animus and vitriol, with candidates often not simply treating the opposing side as wrong but impugning them as un-American or as the "enemy." What was once dislike or discomfort for the other side or the opposite party has morphed into distrust and even hatred.

The health of our union isn't measured only through the lens of our broken and polarized politics. Its troubled state manifests in our communities, illuminated through a series of alarming statistics that only rarely break into national headlines and have yet to become political priorities. These include the 47,173 suicides recorded by the Centers for Disease Control and Prevention (CDC) in 2017;[1] the 420,000 Americans who died of overdoses in 2016;[2] the numbing frequency of mass shootings and the loss of life due to gun violence in our inner cities; the one in five children in America who grow up in the quicksand of poverty;[3] the alarming rise of racially motivated violent extremism;[4] the surge of hate crimes directed at Asian Americans in the context of the COVID-19 pandemic;[5] and the fact that the US has the highest incarceration rate in the world, with 716 per 100,000 of the national population behind bars.[6] These and other sobering trends point to a crisis that is not just political but also spiritual and existential. As a nation, we rarely examine the root causes of these trends, yet they represent clear assaults on human dignity and pose grave threats to our lives and livelihood. With a nation so troubled at many levels, it is time we move beyond platitudes and blame.

In the biblical book of Matthew, Jesus calls on his followers to be "the salt of the earth" (5:13). The brokenness of our society is tied in part to many branches of the Christian church losing their "saltiness," becoming complicit in and co-opted by distorted narratives and misguided theology. Clearly there is not, nor has there ever been, only one Christian perspective on American politics. Disagreement over how to best apply biblical values and truths to complex political issues is inevitable and can even be healthy. But since its inception in the early 1970s, the Religious Right has been in lockstep with the Republican Party, a movement co-created as it was by GOP political operatives such as Paul Weyrich and prominent conservative church leaders such as Jerry Falwell. The initial focus of the Religious Right was to resist the federal government's efforts to force Christian colleges and schools to admit Black students after the passage of the 1964 Civil Rights Act. These racist origins continue to have a corrosive impact on the Religious Right today and explain in part why many white evangelical leaders overwhelmingly supported a president who stoked racial animus and fear. It is also why so many leaders within the Religious Right—including Rev. Franklin Graham, Jerry Falwell Jr., Ralph Reed Jr., and Rev. Tony Perkins, to name a few—entered into what I have called a Faustian bargain with President Trump: overlooking his significant moral indiscretions, pathological lying, and appeals to racism and white nationalism as long as he appointed conservative justices, opposed abortion, and protected them from perceived attacks on religious liberty.

Robert P. Jones, CEO and founder of the Public Religion Research Institute (PRRI), has done extensive research and reporting on President Trump's support among white evangelicals. Jones found that Trump addressed several central concerns of white evangelicals, including their declining influence and the realization that the majority-white Christian nation they dreamed of was being eclipsed.[7] Similarly, historian John Fea of Messiah University explained that white evangelical Trump supporters "look away from the moral indiscretion in order to get their political agenda in place . . . they want to reclaim, renew, restore what they believe was a Christian culture, a Christian America that has been lost."[8]

It seems paradoxical that many white Christians, particularly white and conservative evangelicals who voted overwhelmingly for Trump, also claim to be restoring and saving America. One of the major reasons Trump enjoyed such resilient support among white evangelicals and other white Christians is that even as many understood his character flaws and acknowledged his poor ethical choices, they believed he was willing to fight for them, protecting and advancing their values and battling to restore what they felt was under attack and had been lost. The Democratic Party's track record of reticence and at times even hostility toward religious groups, particularly toward evangelical Christians, has only reinforced the victimization mindset of many evangelicals.

The white Christian church is no longer as dominant in American culture and society as it once was, but that doesn't mean all of Christianity is in decline or has lost its way. Rather, the church in America is increasingly becoming much more diverse and less Eurocentric, mirroring the tectonic shifts taking place within global Christianity over the past few decades.

America's rebirth will require the emboldened moral leadership of the church, the synagogue, the mosque, the temple and more. While religion doesn't possess a monopoly on morality, religious institutions and traditions play a significant role in shaping the values, behavior, and worldviews of the majority of Americans. The compromised and corrupted witness of some parts of the church has contributed to the atrophy of America's spiritual and moral grounding. But we have also seen how, at their best, religious leaders have the capacity to inspire and challenge us to live out the full meaning of our creed. Churches and faith leaders have been at the center of most of the major movements that have successfully reformed and transformed our nation's politics—including movements inspired by the call to build the Beloved Community.

This rebirth, this new formation of the Beloved Community, will require the renewal of religious priorities and spiritual practice. For those of us who identify as Christian, this will require a radical realignment with the teachings, values, and priorities of Jesus. Rev. Jim Wallis aptly describes the problem in his book *Christ in Crisis: Why We Need to Reclaim Jesus*: "We have become disconnected from Jesus. We are not standing and acting in his name, with his values, action, and inspiration. We have lost Jesus—lost our connection to him. This explains why our actions and words lack the power evident in the early church."[9] As people of faith and conscience, we cannot build the America we believe in if we still prioritize partisan loyalty and ideological purity, particularly when it comes at the expense of the common good.

Dr. King captured the civic vocation of the church best when he said, "The church must be reminded that it is not the master or the servant of the state, but rather the conscience of the state. It must be the guide and the critic of the state, and never its tool. If the church does not recapture its prophetic zeal, it will become an irrelevant social club without moral or spiritual authority."[10] That vocational call applies also to the synagogues, mosques, and temples of this country, as well as to every nonprofit and civic organization committed to advancing a more just country and world.

By serving as the nation's conscience, we will help sow the seeds of the nation's rebirth and pave the way for that long-sought "more perfect union."

Chapter Three

E PLURIBUS UNUM:
OUT OF MANY, ONE

One Love! One Heart! Let's get together and feel all right.
—*Bob Marley*

There is no separate black path to power and fulfillment that does not intersect white paths, and there is no separate white path to power and fulfillment, short of social disaster, that does not share that power with black aspirations for freedom and human dignity. We are bound together in a single garment of destiny. The language, the cultural patterns, the music, the material prosperity, and even the food of America are an amalgam of black and white. —*Martin Luther King Jr.*

WHILE IT WAS NEVER CODIFIED INTO LAW, E PLURIBUS UNUM, OR "OUT OF MANY, one," was the de facto motto of the United States until 1956, when Congress adopted "In God We Trust" as the official motto. This is a real loss, because at its best, the former served as a reminder that America's strength does not derive from an assimilating uniformity but instead from the richness of authentic expressions of diversity. The older motto was inspired in part by the words of Roman statesman and philosopher Marcus Tullius Cicero, who wrote, "When each person loves the other as much as himself, it makes one out of many" (*unus fiat ex pluribus*).[1] Our oneness is also not found in a single culture, language, or place of origin but rather in our shared ideals, values, and aspirations, as well as in our commitment to love the other as much as ourselves.

Underlying our deep polarization is a growing recognition that within a few decades, white people will constitute a minority of the country's population. This inevitable demographic shift has been a source of great trepidation, anxiety, and fear among many white Americans, even as it serves as a source of hope and pride for many others, particularly people of color. If the nation doesn't embrace this trend, the fault lines of race and color will continue to pull us apart.

As long as America is defined by the normalization of whiteness and the primacy of white culture and people, we will remain stuck in a vicious cycle of crippling division and acrimony. Donald Trump's rise to the highest office in the land felt like a last gasp, a reassertion, of the lie of white supremacy, a lie that has haunted our nation and disfigured our democracy from its beginning. This lie manifests itself in racist and xenophobic rhetoric that asserts that white people are the true or original Americans. It's also evident in the claim that racism is a vestige of the past, or that it's only tied to individual actions—fallacies that rationalize and perpetuate long-standing inequalities and injustices that are so often systemic in nature. Our attempts to build the Beloved Community will be futile as long as these lies and inequities remain unchallenged and deep wounds remain unhealed.

After race riots raged across the country in the late 1960s, President Lyndon Johnson appointed the Kerner Commission to investigate the causes. The commission's report shined a necessary spotlight on deep-seated poverty and institutionalized racism, warning that the United States was poised to fracture into two radically unequal societies— one Black, one white. The report's research and recommendations are still deeply instructive and relevant to the ongoing pandemic of systemic racism, including the report's prescient conclusion that "discrimination and segregation have long permeated much of American life; they now threaten the future of every American. This deepening racial division is not inevitable. The movement apart can be reversed. Choice is still possible. Our principal task is to define that choice and to press for a national resolution. To pursue our present course will involve the continuing polarization of the American community and, ultimately, the destruction of basic democratic values."[2]

During the 2020 presidential campaign, President Trump and Vice President Pence proclaimed that systemic racism was not a real issue in American life, as though racism has been reduced to the isolated attitudes and actions of individuals. Whitney Parnell, founder of Service Never Sleeps, points out: "Racism was constructed to uphold white supremacy. It manifests on individual, interpersonal, and institutional levels to create its systemic nature."[3] Likewise, Jim Wallis argues effectively in *America's Original Sin* that "whiteness is not simply an artificial sociological construct; it is also, in spiritual and religious terms, a form of idolatry, a sin that separates us from God and from each other."[4]

An illuminating look into whether we Americans see our increasing diversity as a strength or a liability is provided by a "Pluralism Survey" conducted in 2018 by the Public Religion Research Institute (PRRI) and the *Atlantic*.[5] The survey found that fewer than half of Americans generally support a racially and ethnically diverse vision of the United States, with the most significant differences in response related to political party affiliation. When asked to put themselves on a scale, where one end is the statement "I would prefer the US to be a nation made up of people from all over the world" and the other end is the statement "I would prefer the US to be a nation primarily made up of people from Western European heritage," 47 percent of Americans "mostly agree" with the first statement, while fewer than one in ten (9 percent) of Americans "mostly agree" with the second statement, and 39 percent place themselves in the middle of the scale.[6] Stark political divisions on this issue remain deeply ingrained. Nearly two-thirds of Democrats, compared to only three in ten Republicans, mostly prefer a country with racial and ethnic diversity.[7] The survey also found the following:

> Overall, a majority (62 percent) of Americans agree that the country's diverse population, with people of many different races, ethnicities, religions, and backgrounds, makes the country stronger. About one-quarter (23 percent) say this diversity makes the country neither stronger nor weaker, and only 13 percent say it makes the country weaker. Among political groups, Democrats are likeliest to say that diversity makes the country stronger. More

than three-quarters (77 percent) of Democrats say that the country's diverse population makes it stronger, while only 55 percent of independents and 51 percent of Republicans agree. Notably, one in five (20 percent) Republicans say that the country's diverse population makes it weaker.[8]

These statistics, while discouraging, also contain seeds of hope, signaling that significant opportunities still exist to engage and move the majority of the country—particularly Republicans and white Americans who place themselves somewhere in the middle on these questions—toward embracing our nation's growing diversity. While those in the middle likely harbor some concerns about the nation's growing demographic diversity, they also may be open to embracing the changing face of America and perhaps can be persuaded to see diversity as a strength rather than a threat. This transformation will not come primarily through marshaling facts and arguments. Deeper transformation is often catalyzed by the power of relationships and people's stories.

When I married my wife, Sharee, who is from Jamaica, I felt as though I became an honorary Jamaican, having joined her gigantic blood family and her even larger family of friends, many of whom she also refers to as "uncle" or "auntie." Through family bonds and the amount of time I've spent on the island, I have developed a deep kinship with Jamaica. Sharee, who was born in Kingston and spent a significant portion of her life in Montego Bay, taught me the importance of the Jamaican national motto, which is "Out of Many, One People." Four months after the 1962 approval of the motto, which points to the country's multiracial roots, Jamaica became independent from Britain. And while Jamaica still faces issues of discrimination and violence, the motto stands as a sign of the country's aspiration to move forward together.[9]

Jamaica's version of e pluribus unum captures the power and promise of diversity. Rather than being viewed as an abstract goal, the Jamaican motto ties the benefits and richness of diversity to real people. Until the US becomes more a people with a *shared* memory, history, and future, we will be stuck in the cycle of "us vs. them" and a limited-good mentality. Such a mentality says that the more you give access and opportunity to others, the less access you will have for yourself. This seductive and dangerous mentality makes you afraid of anyone getting access to the privileges and opportunities that you enjoy, which makes equality for others seem like a threat to your own pie. These mindsets of us vs. them and limited good are antithetical to the emphasis on interdependence and abundant life in our faith traditions. At worst, they are seeds that could lead to our nation's dissolution.

In our political history, including in recent times, we have seen the commitment to being a nation exalted over the commitment to being a shared community of diverse peoples. Being a nation first without also striving to be a people easily leads to destructive forms of nationalism and idolatry—forms that we witness daily in overt and insidious ways and that fueled the January 6, 2021, insurrection, which will remain a stain on our democracy.

The pressing question is this: Is America truly a people in addition to being a nation? Or do our ethnic and racial identities and divisions make it impossible to identify as a common people with shared values, aspirations, and experiences? How do we combine the best of our distinctive racial and ethnic cultures with a shared sense of peoplehood rooted in an embrace of our beautiful diversity? How do we evolve into an even more diverse, multiracial nation in ways that inspire all Americans to desire the benefits of being on the same, larger team?

How can white Americans affirm our growing diversity, rather than overly identifying with being white, which has often meant denying or downplaying other rich cultural connections and traditions tied to ancestry from various European nations? Given our nation's history, it is almost inevitable that having a central identity of whiteness is based on a false sense of superiority or a nihilistic rejection of being something else. An intentional investment in becoming more of a people—those who are part of and engaged in building the Beloved Community—is one of the most important ways to deliver whiteness from the destructive temptation of superiority. James Baldwin understood, as Glaude put it, "that in this so-called democracy, people believed that the color of one's skin determined the relative value of an individual's life and justified the way American society was organized. That belief and justification had dehumanized entire groups of people. White Americans were not excluded from its effects." Baldwin argued, "In this debasement and definition of black people," white people "debased and defined themselves."[10] Developing or restoring pride in a white cultural identity is important, but it must be tied to a commitment to antiracism and cutting the umbilical cord that binds white identity to superiority.

Becoming one people and one nation requires that we make a firm choice in favor of embracing a multiracial, multireligious democracy. This requires letting go of the notion that white and/or Christian America is the true America or that America is only for certain types of people. The Republican Party's recent embrace of Trumpism and its focus on appealing to an increasingly dwindling majority of white voters can no longer win a majority of votes in national elections. This means that unless the GOP is willing to change course, the only way left to win national elections is to continue to rig the rules and suppress voters of color to delay the impact of demographic change. The future of our democracy would be much more promising if, instead, the GOP decided to actively compete for the votes of communities of color, which would require greater outreach and relationship-building as well as a significant revamping of policy priorities and rhetoric.

As a biracial Black man, I often have had the opportunity to serve as a bridge between worlds. I've understood the strength of diversity within my own life story. It's personal. And for me it is tied to Beloved Community–building. The elements of my life story have given me firsthand experience that diversity serves as an asset rather than a liability.

I agree, as some have explained, that race is a social construct created for the purposes of subjugation and oppression. But as Ta-Nehisi Coates writes in *Between the World and Me*, "They made us into a race. We made ourselves into a people."[11] There are many ways in which distinctive and multifaceted cultures, including Black culture and community, have evolved out of particular histories. Black culture, language, art, and music, in all their authenticity, diversity, and beauty, are byproducts of our efforts to survive and thrive despite systemic racism. Racism also transcends simply a black and white paradigm, it encompasses and harms Asian-Americans and Pacific Islanders, Latino/a Americans, Native Americans, and more. One alarming example has been the surge of violence and harassment directed at Asian-Americans and Pacific Islanders during the COVID pandemic, which was fueled in part by the racist rhetoric of former president Trump and others who scapegoated the AAPI community by referring to the virus as the "China virus" and "Kung Flu."[12] Stop AAPI Hate documented 3,795 incidents of self-reported hate crimes toward the AAPI community nationally between March 19, 2020 to February 28, 2021.[13] Asian-Americans and Pacific Islanders are often either stereotyped as the "model minority" or treated as perpetual foreigners, which contributes to both invisibility and exclusion.

Because racism permeates the air we breathe and so profoundly shapes our experiences and daily reality, the idea of a so-called post-racial America—a nation supposedly free from racial divisions, or that doesn't "see" race—became a major topic of debate after Barack Obama's historic election as the nation's first Black president. But a post-racial America is a mirage. Though the construct of race has evolved in some positive ways—such as into unique cultures and communities—the pursuit of a post-racial America is the wrong goal. Instead, our aim should be to build an America that is antiracist, committed to building the Beloved Community.

Throughout my life, I have sought opportunities to advance both reconciliation and justice. Serving as a facilitator of prejudice reduction and diversity trainings through the National Coalition Building Institute (NCBI) was one of the most formative experiences in my four years as an undergraduate student at Emory University. NCBI's diversity, equity, and inclusion emphasis was ahead of its time in enlisting people to interrupt all forms of prejudice and modeling a now popular commitment to allyship. The model emphasizes celebrating our similarities and our differences, recognizing misinformation that people learn about various groups, and identifying and healing from internalized oppression (when oppressed groups who suffer discrimination harbor self-destructive views of themselves and each other). NCBI emphasized that when members of oppressed communities claim pride in their identity and better understand the personal harm of prejudice, they can be better equipped to address and heal from bigoted comments and behavior. While at Emory I facilitated dozens of these workshops, at one point as a leader of a team of trained facilitators who led workshops for the university's entire entering class during freshman orientation. During these sessions I had to develop a thick skin and enduring patience, as I listened to countless students struggle with their own deep-seated prejudice, much of which they weren't even conscious of or were in denial about. I realized just how challenging this work can be. But starting the journey of prejudice reduction is half the battle.

A glaring weakness of the NCBI model, at least at the time I was involved in the 1990s, was its almost exclusive emphasis on challenging and changing personal attitudes, comments, and behaviors rather than on systems and policies that perpetuate and give license to discrimination. Put in more recent terms, the model focused mostly on disrupting and preventing microaggressions, a term coined by Harvard psychiatrist Chester Pierce in 1970. As Ibram X. Kendi explains, "Pierce employed the term [*microaggressions*] to describe the constant verbal and nonverbal abuse racist white people unleash on Black people wherever we go, day after day." Since 1970, the concept of microaggression has expanded to apply to interpersonal abuse against all marginalized groups, not just Black people. In the last decade, the term has become popular in social justice spaces through the defining work of psychologist Derald Wing Sue. He defines *microaggressions* as "brief, everyday exchanges that send denigrating messages to certain individuals, because of their group membership." Kendi provides a provocative response to the concept of microaggressions: "What other people call microaggression I call racist abuse. And I call the zero-tolerance policies preventing and punishing these abusers what they are: antiracist. Only racists shy away from the R-word—racism is steeped in denial."[14]

Robin DiAngelo, in her book *White Fragility*, also warns against an overly interpersonal and individualistic understanding of racism: "Our simplistic definition of racism—as intentional acts of racial discrimination committed by immoral individuals—engenders a confidence that we are not part of the problem and that our learning is thus complete." As DiAngelo puts it, "Racism is a structure, not an event." She adds, "Similarly, racism—like sexism and other forms of oppression—occurs when a racial group's prejudice is backed by legal authority and institutional control. This authority and control transforms individual prejudices into a far-reaching system that no longer depends on the good intentions of individual actors; it becomes the default of the society and is reproduced automatically."[15]

Kendi's bestselling book *How to Be an Antiracist* also roots the work of antiracism in dismantling and challenging systems, not just attitudes and individual behaviors. While the term *antiracist* has been around for quite some time, Kendi's book popularized it and made it more mainstream. Kendi makes the case that *racist* "is not the worst word in the English language; it is not the equivalent of a slur. It is descriptive, and the only way to undo racism is to consistently identify and describe it—and then dismantle it. The attempt to turn this usefully descriptive term into an almost unusable slur is, of course, designed to do the opposite: to freeze us into inaction." He rightfully points out that "there is no neutrality in the racism struggle. The opposite of 'racist' isn't 'not racist.' It is 'antiracist.' What's the difference? One endorses either the idea of a racial hierarchy as a racist, or racial equality as an antiracist. One either believes problems are rooted in groups of people, as a racist, or locates the roots of problems in power and policies, as an antiracist. One either allows racial inequities to persevere, as a racist, or confronts racial inequities, as an antiracist."[16] Determining which laws, policies, and decisions are antiracist versus racist is not always simple or obvious; however, we must be guided by their ultimate impact and not their intent. Kendi offers an important reminder that "the movement from racist to antiracist is always ongoing—it requires understanding and snubbing racism based on biology, ethnicity, body, culture, behavior, color, space, and class. And beyond that, it means standing ready to fight at racism's intersections with other bigotries." It is "the struggle to be fully human and to see that others are fully human."[17]

In her engrossing and provocative book *Caste: The Origins of Our Discontents*, Isabel Wilkerson helps to sharpen our analysis and understanding of our racial dilemma by comparing America to a caste system. First, Wilkerson uses a haunting metaphor to describe our country: "America is an old house. We can never declare the work over. Wind, flood, drought, and human upheavals batter a structure that is already fighting whatever flaws were left unattended in the original foundation. . . . The owner of the house knows that whatever you are ignoring will never go away. Whatever is lurking will fester whether you choose to look or not. . . . And any further deterioration is, in fact, on our hands."[18] I love this metaphor because the flaws and dangers of an old house kept in disrepair impact and harm us all. Wilkerson writes,

Like other old houses, America has an unseen skeleton, a caste system that is as central to its operation as are the studs and joists that we cannot see in the physical buildings we call home. Caste is the infrastructure of our divisions. It is the architecture of human hierarchy, the subconscious code of instructions for maintaining, in our case, a four-hundred-year-old social order. . . . The hierarchy of caste is not about feelings or morality. It is about power— which groups have it and which do not. It is about resources—which caste is seen as worthy of them and which are not, who gets to acquire and control them and who does not. It is about respect, authority, and assumptions of competence—who is accorded these and who is not. . . . In America, race is the primary tool and the visible decoy, the front man, for caste.[19]

Wilkerson powerfully reinforces the reality that racial hierarchy is deeply ingrained in our consciousness, our systems, and our structures and that small upgrades or fixes will not be enough—what is truly needed is a complete rebuild.

I was first exposed to the concept of antiracism by Crossroads, an organization that has been working for decades to train and equip Christians to actively dismantle racism. For Christians, the challenge of moving from personal and interpersonal concepts of racism to the systemic understanding is often made more difficult due to the theological malpractice of an overly privatized and individualistic interpretation of scripture. We often export our cultural and political biases and assumptions into scripture, at worst making God into our own image. It is important to remember Paul's statement in the letter to the Ephesians that "we wrestle not against flesh and blood, but against principalities, against powers" (6:12). The problem is that for far too many churches, their understanding of injustice still focuses on personal behavior rather than on social systems. This phenomenon has also distorted our understanding of reconciliation.

The call to reconciliation is a deeply biblical one. Unfortunately, a pathological individualism has often reduced reconciliation to the interpersonal realm rather than the systemic one. Erna Kim Hackett writes, "Racial reconciliation centers language with which white people and their allies are comfortable. Racial reconciliation moves at the pace that whiteness dictates. It focuses on making sure white people don't feel guilty, but not on the systemic disenfranchisement of [people of color]. It will talk about redeemed white identity without teaching about white supremacy. It will lament but not repent with action." Later in the same article, Hackett uses the metaphor of the canary in a mine to capture the often costly and difficult work of decentering whiteness and advancing justice:

In the olden days, miners would take a canary into coal mines because their delicate lungs would more readily be impacted by deadly gases and alert the miners that they should leave before they died of poisonous gases. In the racial reconciliation model, the death (or departure) of [people of color] is sad and sort of confusing, but is seen as an indicator that the bird was just not a good fit for the mine. They bring down another canary, try to put a tiny mask on it, and get confused when it dies as well. At no point is there a discussion that the mine is toxic. The white supremacy framework says, HEY! That bird died because your well-intentioned mine is toxic. It is on you, it is on the mine, to stop being toxic. It is not on the canary to become immune to deadly fumes. The term white supremacy labels the problem more accurately. It locates the problem on whiteness and its systems. It focuses on outcomes, not intentions. It is collective, not individual. It makes whiteness uncomfortable and responsible. And that is important.[20]

Speaking from my own experience across my professional career, including now leading Sojourners, I've learned the work required to live into a deep commitment to justice, equity, diversity, and inclusion involves transforming culture and more fully embracing antiracism. This work is hard but necessary. It involves all of us and places a particular responsibility on those who benefit the most from various forms of privilege.

My perspective and passion for antiracism and for diversity, equity, and inclusion work were also significantly shaped by a formative set of experiences while I co-led a program in graduate school. When I was a graduate student at the Kennedy School of Government at Harvard, I was invited to join the leadership of the Race, Ethnicity, and American Leadership (REAL) program. The program was initiated by students to create a space for fresh, honest, and productive dialogue about race and to form a community where students with diverse viewpoints could develop the tools, insights, and personal awareness to become more effective citizens and leaders in a multiracial democracy. Many students of color had identified a serious gap in the Kennedy School curriculum, in which issues of race were often invisible or ignored despite the reality that race and ethnicity color the way we perceive and enact public policy. While most students yearned for more conversations about the nexus between race, public policy, and leadership, the space for such conversation was often limited, and many students lacked the tools or comfort level to engage openly in these discussions. While REAL was a voluntary program, we worked hard to recruit many white students who, we knew, came from more conservative and homogenous backgrounds. The program enabled me to deepen relationships with students I would otherwise never have gotten to know. Many participants thanked me and others in the program for creating a space in which they could engage in candid dialogue without fear of judgment or embarrassment. It was clear that the five ninety-minute dialogues we held helped us all, particularly the white participants, build greater stamina for real racial dialogue that has the potential for mutual transformation. I was heartened to learn that after the horrific murder of George Floyd, the dean of the Kennedy School announced the addition of a required course for master's-degree students on racism and public policy, as well as an orientation-week session on antiracism and allyship.[21] I believe our efforts in the REAL program laid the groundwork for this overdue addition to the core curriculum.

The work of antiracism often requires building bridges and trust across our racial divides. A formative and transformational experience from my time in college stands out. I was a sophomore adviser in the dorm where it happened. Two female freshman roommates, one Black and one white, had got into a heated argument that allegedly turned physical. The white female student's white boyfriend intervened and ended up pushing and assaulting the Black female student. When word spread about the incident, four Black male students confronted the white male student in his dorm. Words were exchanged, and the Black male students said that if circumstances were different, the white student would be a dead man. This perceived threat on the white boyfriend's life led to the police taking the four Black male students into custody; under Georgia law, they faced possible felony charges for threatening someone's life. (Ironically, this severe punishment was put in place years before as a result of the civil rights struggle, when Black civil rights leaders' lives were constantly under death threats.) Many students were outraged that the white student continued to walk free while four Black students faced possible criminal charges, jeopardizing their academic careers and lives. To add insult to injury, the campus student newspaper released an article mischaracterizing the entire incident as "an altercation" between two female students rather than acknowledging that the real issue was that a white male allegedly assaulted a Black female student.

In the aftermath, the campus was in an uproar. Black student leaders and Emory University's predominantly white campus administration were at a standoff often speaking past each other. Dr. Theo Harris, a well-respected Black professor, and I, as a dorm advisor and leader in student government, stood in the middle of the meeting as mediators trying to bridge this chasm and open dialogue, recognizing that we had to overcome a great deal of pain, anger, and distrust and that our attempt might fail. Administration officials were upset by the torrent of criticism the university had received after an email that they felt mischaracterized the racially charged incident went viral, bringing bad publicity to the university. They were also perturbed that Black student leaders and organizations had issued a series of demands that the administration viewed as unrealistic and overly militant, including that the white student involved in the assault be expelled, that Residence Life issue a public apology for the lack of responsiveness, and that an investigation be launched into the Emory Police Department's treatment of the whole episode.

As a Black student, I was among many who were tired of empty rhetoric and broken promises from the administration. We were fed up with long-standing patterns of racial injustice and discrimination on campus. The racially charged assault was a match that had ignited an existing tinder box of frustration and grievance. Black students had endured discrimination for years. We were tired of constantly being stopped by the campus police for no apparent reason and being asked to show our student IDs. We were tired of advocating for the hiring of more Black faculty members, with few results. We were tired of the fact that underneath the surface of a progressive and prestigious university were the skeletons of racism. For example, each year one of the fraternities performed a Confederate ceremony celebrating its "Southern pride," in which members placed cannons directly facing the only Black fraternity house on campus, which happened to be my own Mu Alpha chapter of Alpha Phi Alpha Fraternity, Inc.

Dr. Harris and I knew that trust would not be built overnight and that we couldn't solve everything in one meeting. But we had to reopen a line of communication and begin the difficult process. Harris and I were willing to put our relationships and our reputations on the line because our campus community was unraveling, and just like a house, a campus divided against itself cannot stand.

After this long opening meeting with administrators and outraged students, the wall of ice was cracked. It wasn't easy, but the tensions had been reduced and progress had begun. The administration agreed to engage in further dialogue and to set up a commission to investigate patterns of discrimination on campus. The process started with a focus on a particular incident, but it shifted to deal with ongoing patterns, policies, and systems that needed to be transformed. Initial attention on the interpersonal became appropriately focused on underlying root causes and on commitments to seek systemic change, all of which were prerequisites to restoring trust and rebuilding a sense of community on campus.

In the context of e pluribus unum and building the Beloved Community, relationships matter and are in fact indispensable. It is much harder to feel empathy or compassion toward someone who is different from you if you have no real relationship with them. And far too many Americans have intentionally kept themselves within racial enclaves in neighborhoods, schools, and churches—in our social interactions as well as our social media and online interactions. While much progress has been made since the victories of the civil rights movement, America's racial geography continues to be profoundly and stubbornly segregated. The problem is that segregated social realities reinforce bias, prejudice, and distrust.

An American Values Survey conducted by PRRI, which assessed the scope and diversity of Americans' social networks, brought these challenges into stark relief.[22] In the study Americans were asked to name people with whom they had "discussed matters important to [them]" in the previous six months, regardless of the nature of the relationship or the frequency of interaction. Among white Americans, 91 percent of the people composing their social networks were also white, while 5 percent were identified as some other race.[23] Fully three-quarters of white Americans reported that the network of people with whom they discussed important matters was entirely white, with no minority presence, while 15 percent reported having a more racially mixed social network. This is a bipartisan challenge: white Republicans (81 percent) are about as likely as white Democrats (78 percent) to have social networks that are entirely composed of white people. These survey results signal a deficit of relationship with people of other races and ethnicities. Worse, this lack of relationship makes us much more liable to hold on to our prejudices and fall prey to dehumanizing the other.

As the parent of two young sons, I have spent the last few years avidly watching almost every animated and kid-friendly film that comes out. Date nights are few and far between, and seeing a new movie that the entire family can enjoy, whether in the theater before COVID or at home, feels like a welcome reprieve. It is ironic that at the same time as our culture has seen a resurgence of white supremacy and nationalism, we have the most racially inclusive messages found across cinema and television. It would be difficult for my childhood self to imagine the options that my two Black sons have now to see themselves reflected in a range of positive characters on film and television, such as superheroes like Black Panther, Spider-Man (in *Into the Spider-Verse*), and Black Lightning. We have well-written television shows such as *This Is Us* and *Black-ish* that provide social commentary on race relations in ways that are humorous, disarming, and thought-provoking. Even in the realm of animated film, movies such as *Zootopia* strongly promote themes of e pluribus unum.

While important, films and television obviously aren't sufficient to change mindsets enough to enlist everyone as antiracists. We need much more hands-on and intense training and engagement that confers real skills, creates the space for brave dialogue, and leads to actionable commitments. We need to accelerate the growth of the antiracism movement. One important way is through allyship.

Allyship—both a concept and a commitment—is increasingly important for building the Beloved Community. One of the most effective trainings around allyship was developed by Whitney Parnell, of Service Never Sleeps. For Parnell, the Beloved Community is built through realizing our shared humanity, signifying a world in which "we are all able to be embraced for who we are, we are all able to thrive, and everyone is able to reach our highest potential."[24] Since its inception in 2015, Service Never Sleeps has led more than 3,500 allyship trainings around the country with a broad range of companies and nonprofit organizations.[25] In 2019, I had the privilege of experiencing allyship firsthand when Parnell led the staff of my organization, Sojourners, through the allyship training.

"We all have a responsibility to serve as an ally with people who are oppressed and marginalized, particularly in situations in which we enjoy privilege of various forms," Parnell explains. "Allies serve as bridge builders and courageous interrupters who ensure that everyone is valued, heard, and can realize their full potential."[26] The beauty of allyship is that everyone can be an ally. Everyone possesses privilege in some part of their life and identity, whether because of their gender, able-bodiedness, race, sexual orientation and gender identity, or something else. But becoming an ally requires moving beyond our often negative associations with privilege and becoming more self-aware about all the ways we enjoy privilege. Instead of stigmatizing privilege, allyship flips the script, giving those who are privileged the responsibility to interrupt discrimination and injustice in ways that take the burden off the marginalized and in the process help to build the Beloved Community.

Historically, society has usually forced the responsibility of dismantling injustice on the marginalized. But the privileged are often in a stronger position to interrupt and dismantle injustice. "To do this work we must overcome our own sense of fragility, guilt, and the desire to be a savior rather than an ally," says Parnell. "We must be willing to embrace that we all have work to do and that allyship is an ongoing journey of shedding the harmful ways we misuse and hold onto our privilege rather than putting love into action by using our privilege to dismantle injustice."[27]

The true spirit of e pluribus unum also engages in courageous and transformational bridge-building across our differences. Recently, the community-organizing group PICO California (part of the Faith in Action national network) launched an initiative called the Belong Movement. The initiative provides a curriculum over four sessions equipping members of congregations and community organizations to build deep solidarity across difference through story sharing, learning about the structural drivers of exclusion, and creating a shared vision for what "communities of belonging" look like. The Belong Movement is rooted in a commitment to "radical kinship and exquisite mutuality," explains the organization's director, Joseph Tomás McKellar. "Radical kindship holds that we maintain our sacred identities even as we embrace a more expansive identity. This requires counteracting the narrative that we are safer when we are segregated from each other." Exquisite mutuality is tied to the understanding that our full liberation and wholeness are inextricably linked to those of others, particularly the most marginalized.[28]

According to McKellar, "The Belong Movement was built on Dr. King's belief that power is the ability to achieve purpose, and that power is a product of the quantity and quality of our relationships. However, it's not enough to simply preach to the choir and engage those who already see themselves as 'woke' to the struggle for racial justice and building the Beloved Community. The 'still waking' must also be included in a journey of encounter, learning, and visioning across difference." PICO California hopes that its "Belong Movement initiative offers a template for congregations and organizations to overcome the polarization and division that characterizes this era and contributes to the sacred work of becoming a new people with an expansive shared identity and purpose—a new people who are standing with and for each other as they build power for Beloved Community."[29] This can be achieved by cultivating a deeper sense of belonging through engaging people across different backgrounds. The participants commit to four sessions helping them build deep relationships and educating them about the forces driving exclusion. When the commitment to engage diverse communities grows, a shared vision develops for what a country of belonging looks like.

Among those building the Beloved Community and developing exquisite mutuality are organizations such as Kindred, founded by Laura Wilson Phelan. Kindred cultivates and mobilizes the power of diverse coalitions of elementary school parents to work in partnership with school leadership to drive improved outcomes for all students. Since achieving diversity in itself isn't solving the opportunity gap, it is necessary to build rich, authentic parent networks to surround all children with the support they need to thrive. Further, children who grow up surrounded by people of different identities and backgrounds go on to choose to live in diverse communities as adults. Research shows that the social networks of families play a significant role in helping their children to build the skills and knowledge to fulfill their potential.

Kindred begins with safe dialogues among parents of different backgrounds about race, equity, and their hopes for their children. As parents realize how their interactions at school affect the opportunities children receive, dialogue leads to parent-driven initiatives that make meaningful differences for better student learning and more equitable access to in-school and extracurricular opportunities. Kindred's complex theory of change draws from more than fifty studies in the fields of sociology, psychology, education, and behavioral economics. Three central themes emerged from this research and inform Kindred's model. A longitudinal study of more than five hundred Chicago schools found that family involvement in schools to improve education mattered *as much as* school leadership, teacher quality, safety, and curricular rigor.[30] Without family involvement, the odds of success in turning a school around fell from 40 percent to 10 percent.[31]

A separate study by Robert Putnam of Harvard explored the role of social networks on student outcomes.[32] His research found that social networks, more than any other factor—including poverty—predict test scores and dropout rates. He also looked at the impact of segregation and isolation. Increasing isolation causes people of different backgrounds to interact less with one another, and thereby to have less likelihood of influencing one another's ideas or building empathy. In turn, these issues affect how people vote on important matters related to school funding and access to resources.

Kindred's founder, Phelan, explains: "We are hard-wired as human beings to create connection and community with one another. Yet the ways that racism and classism have been socialized in our country can lead to fear, shame, and guilt that get in the way of our building relationships across lines of difference. People need spaces where it feels safe to unpack what we've been socialized to believe so that we can replace our fear and assumptions with connection and love."[33]

Dialogue groups create space for people of different backgrounds to engage in deeper introspection about the community they want to build together. One of Kindred's first exercises uses an "identity star," which asks parents to identify five things that form their identity and then discuss patterns that come up. These dialogue circles create shared meaning and significant bonds of love and connection that then often lead parents to feel a deep sense of outrage about the disparities that exist in their schools.[34] The statistics surrounding kids in their community become real people, a shift that then increases the commitment to advancing racial equity and diversity. "It takes all of us to achieve collective well-being and collective liberation," Phelan believes, "and when we treat other people inhumanely, it dehumanizes us." To Phelan, the Beloved Community is one in which "we would care for each other's children as if they are our own. We would look out for each other and operate from a position of empathy and solidarity, expecting that in return."[35]

As we embrace mutuality and our diversity as defining strengths, one of the most challenging aspects of building the Beloved Community is repenting and making amends for the deep wounds and injustices of the past. This necessarily includes intentional amends through some form of reparations for the legacy of slavery. Ta-Nehisi Coates's provocative 2014 essay in the *Atlantic* on "The Case for Reparations,"[36] as well as the 2020 racial awakening over police violence and systemic racism, has led to an upsurge of attention to reparations. This dialogue is long overdue, even though the call for reparations is often misunderstood and sometimes elicits a shrill and defensive reaction.

At the very least, a national dialogue around reparations will shed new light on the connections between our past and our present, generating greater social and political will to ensure that every American can realize their full potential and to guarantee that the American creed applies to everyone equally. The conversation can also galvanize greater urgency to address long-standing inequalities and injustices that continue to disproportionately impact people of color, particularly Black and Native American people.

The case for reparations is often tied to all the ways in which 246 years of legal slavery served as the backbone in building America's wealth, as well as to the specific promise made by General William T. Sherman at the end of the Civil War to grant "forty acres and a mule" to every surviving family of slavery, a promissory note that was quickly reversed by President Andrew Johnson after the assassination of President Lincoln.[37] The four hundred thousand acres of land that were promised and then later denied have resulted in an estimated $6.4 trillion in lost revenue to descendants of slaves in present-day dollars.[38] While finding a way to make amends for this grave injustice represents the right starting point, it is important not to reduce reparations solely to financial payments, particularly since these payments would likely be legally tenuous and difficult to administer. A financial payment alone would inadequately address the systemic issues that continue to reproduce racial disadvantage and injustice. As Kelly Brown Douglas argues, "For faith communities, reparations must not be only an effort to compensate for past harms, they must also chart a pathway to a just future. . . . It is left for faith communities to 'repair the breach' between present injustice and God's just future. Reparations must not simply look back, but most importantly must push forward."[39]

To more fully right past wrongs is to strengthen our resolve and redouble our collective efforts to eliminate lingering racial disparities and dramatically expand opportunities to those who have been historically shut out due to mutating forms of white supremacy, from slavery to the present. On a practical level, doing so will allow us to overcome both the privileges and the burdens that continue to accompany race in America. This will require significant review of and transformations in public policy and the criminal justice system.

While important, reparations are not only some form of payment—reparations require a system change. If, among other changes, reparations took the form of more radical efforts to level the playing field in public education, making it a true priority to ensure that every Black child received a quality education, it would serve as a catalyst to change the overall system. This could include the government offering substantial debt forgiveness to African Americans who are carrying onerous student loan debt. And if reparations included significant housing assistance through access to low-interest, government-backed loans and cash assistance for down payments for African Americans seeking to purchase a home, it could change the racial geography of America. Reparations need to also include bolder reforms and real transformation in our criminal justice system, including exonerating inmates who have been the victims of unjust or overly punitive sentences, particularly inmates caught up in the so-called war on drugs and crime. Reparations could also include every African American child receiving a savings bond when they are born, which would help close the shameful wealth gap between Black and white Americans.

For some advocates of reparations, these approaches may seem insufficient. But pursued at a significant enough scale, they could have a great impact on the lives of African Americans, and they would provide building blocks for what an even more holistic form of reparations could look like. On a pragmatic level, this initial approach is also more likely to garner support from most Americans, which at least for the near future will be a prerequisite for moving any serious form of reparations forward.

An important starting point to explore and build support for these and other measures is H.R. 40, a bill originally introduced by Representative John Conyers in 1989 in the House of Representatives. The bill seeks to address "the fundamental injustice, cruelty, brutality, and inhumanity of slavery in the United States and the 13 American colonies between 1619 and 1865 and to establish a commission to study and consider a national apology and proposal for reparations for the institution of slavery, its subsequent de jure and de facto racial and economic discrimination against African Americans, and the impact of these forces on living African Americans, to make recommendations to the Congress on appropriate remedies, and for other purposes."[40]

Another hopeful sign has been the explosion of local Truth, Racial Healing, and Transformation commissions across the country seeking to unearth and redress issues of racial injustice. For example, in 2020 "nearly twenty commissions focused on truth telling and racial healing were established at the local level by state legislatures, county supervisors, town councils, and community leaders. Most of these initiatives take the form of a committee of representative local leaders with a mandate to examine the state of racial relations in their city or state, through a variety of sources, including testimony, honoring the memory of victims of abuse, and making policy proposals."[41] Similar to what some communities have done on a local level, a resolution in Congress Proposed by Congresswoman Barbara Lee, H.R. 100, seeks to establish a US Commission on Truth, Racial Healing, and Transformation "to properly acknowledge, memorialize, and be a catalyst for progress toward jettisoning the belief in a hierarchy of human value, embracing our common humanity, and permanently eliminating persistent racial inequities."[42]

Before we can better arrive at concrete policy proposals and solutions, these mutually reinforcing proposals to establish a commission represent an obvious and vital next step to help spark a national dialogue and build consensus around concrete and actionable remedies to the historical and present-day impacts of systemic racism. We need to begin with understanding the human cost and harm that slavery and all of its mutated forms of Jim Crow segregation, mass incarceration, and beyond have imposed on Black Americans.

"Out of many, one" is not inevitable. We have seen the dire consequences of words and actions by people in positions of power who benefit from dividing us, encouraging us to fear one another, and convincing too many of us that we should value some while ignoring and even dehumanizing others. America can never fully thrive as an idea or a shared political, social, and economic project without us *choosing* to become one people. In the Christian tradition, some of the earliest images from the biblical book of Acts offer profound examples of a people choosing to become "out of many, one." The early witness of Jesus's first disciples is a beautiful expression of oneness and mutuality: "All the believers were one in heart and mind. No one claimed that any of their possessions was their own, but they shared everything they had. With great power the apostles continued to testify to the resurrection of the Lord Jesus. And God's grace was so powerfully at work in them all that there were no needy persons among them. For from time to time those who owned land or houses sold them, brought the money from the sales and put it at the apostles' feet, and it was distributed to anyone who had need" (Acts 4:32–35).

Out of many, we can become one nation. And that one nation must be increasingly built by one diverse people who see, celebrate, value, and respect our glorious and increasing ethnic and racial diversity as a defining strength and not a weakness—a strength central to our national character. Our commitment to e pluribus unum must also include the urgent work of combating sexism, Islamophobia, anti-Semitism, homophobia, ableism, and more—all of which are antithetical to the Beloved Community.

E pluribus unum is a hallmark of building the Beloved Community. It requires the hard work of identifying and overcoming bias and prejudice within ourselves and serving as an ally to people marginalized in those spaces in which we enjoy privilege. This is no easy commitment, and it will require significant discomfort and humility, but ultimately our liberation and wholeness depend on the liberation and wholeness of everyone. By taking this journey together, we as a people will be made free and more whole.

Chapter Four

REIMAGINING THE BELOVED COMMUNITY

The Beloved Community is a realistic vision of an achievable society, one in which problems and conflict exist, but are resolved peacefully and without bitterness. In the Beloved Community, caring and compassion drive political policies that support the worldwide elimination of poverty and hunger and all forms of bigotry and violence. The Beloved Community is a state of heart and mind, a spirit of hope and goodwill that transcends all boundaries and barriers and embraces all creation. At its core, the Beloved Community is an engine of reconciliation. This way of living seems a long way from the kind of world that we have now, but I believe it is a goal that can be accomplished through courage and determination, and through education and training if enough people are willing to make the necessary commitment. —Coretta Scott King

I GREW UP IN THE SHADOW OF THE CIVIL RIGHTS MOVEMENT, BELIEVING THAT I WAS born in the wrong era. The conviction that my generation had inherited the unfinished business of that movement was instilled in me by my parents. More than two decades before the birth of the Black Lives Matter movement, I came of age with the hope that the animating vision of the civil rights movement was still alive and simply needed to be recast and revitalized. But when a nation loses sight of shared values and ideals, and lacks a shared spiritual and moral foundation to bind us together, that nation will become a house irrevocably divided—and as Jesus foretold, a house divided against itself cannot stand (Mark 3:25). What is required to capture the moral imagination and hopes of subsequent generations, including my own, is the vision of this book and my life work.

It is easy to freeze-frame and sanitize the bold vision and aspirations of the civil rights movement as only being something from a bygone era. And many of us have seen that vision derailed and overshadowed by the culture wars, a rapacious form of capitalism, and political schism. We have seen many aspects of civil rights history erased or altered to make the past more palatable. We are often quick to embrace the Dr. King of Montgomery and Selma but tend to ignore his broader vision of dismantling the triplets of racism, militarism, and materialism. When we romanticize or whitewash the civil rights movement's vision, we become blind to the movement's far-reaching call for transformation, which is still relevant and powerful today.

When I look back over American history and at other movements pushing for real change, the Beloved Community stands out as the most holistic and transformational moral vision capable of uniting a severely divided nation. Coined in the early days of the twentieth century by philosopher-theologian Josiah Royce, the term was used by him and then by other leaders of the Fellowship of Reconciliation, an interfaith organization founded in 1915. Martin Luther King Jr., who was also a member of the Fellowship of Reconciliation, popularized the term. Historian Fred Smith writes, "For King, the Beloved Community is the actualization of an inclusive human community. It is a mutually cooperative and voluntary venture of humans to assume a semblance of responsibility for their brothers and sisters. King describes the Beloved Community as a vision of total interrelatedness. It is the solidarity of the human family. Because, people are dependent upon each other and are knitted together in a single garment of destiny, caught in an inescapable network of mutuality."[1]

To King, the Beloved Community wasn't a belief in a utopian dream but, according to the Martin Luther King Jr. Center for Nonviolent Social Change, "a realistic, achievable goal that could be attained by a critical mass of people committed to and trained in the philosophy and methods of nonviolence." The King Center emphasizes that "the core value of the quest for Dr. King's Beloved Community was agape love. He said that 'Agape does not begin by discriminating between worthy and unworthy people. . . . It begins by loving others for their sakes' and 'makes no distinction between a friend and enemy; it is directed toward both. . . . Agape is love seeking to preserve and create community.'" Furthermore, "Dr. King believed that the age-old tradition of hating one's opponents was not only immoral, but bad strategy which perpetuated the cycle of revenge and retaliation. Only nonviolence, he believed, had the power to break the cycle of retributive violence and create lasting peace through reconciliation."[2]

As I began to study historic leaders who believed that building the Beloved Community could change history, I looked at those who arose from within the movement, including the Southern Christian Leadership Conference, the Student Nonviolent Coordinating Committee, the Congress for Racial Equality, the Mississippi Freedom Party, and others. Within the civil rights movement, the Beloved Community served as a meta-narrative and North Star. The more I studied, the more I was humbled by the moral courage and sacrifice I met. Movement leaders, both well-known and unsung, demonstrated a resilient dedication to dismantling Jim Crow segregation and replacing it with the Beloved Community. I think of the moral fortitude required to sit at a "whites only" lunch counter in resistance, to face down hoses and dogs, to risk being brutalized and imprisoned indefinitely to defy segregation, all while people hurl racial epithets and physically attack you.

A few years ago, the fiftieth anniversary of King's assassination gave us the opportunity to reflect on his vision for our nation. Somehow that vision has lost its urgency. But it has not lost its ability to capture the moral imagination and hearts of new generations. In the 1960s, King and other civil rights leaders often referenced the pursuit of the Beloved Community in their speeches, writings, and public pronouncements. Yet the concept was rarely fully defined, beyond signature quotes that spoke to a commitment to nonviolence, reconciliation, equality, brotherhood and sisterhood, and agape love as keys to its construction. A first-order principle and commitment, it was almost as if King and other leaders presumed that people understood what they meant by "the Beloved Community."

One of the earliest and most authoritative speeches King gave that referenced the Beloved Community was in 1956. He spoke at a victory rally following the announcement of a favorable Supreme Court decision desegregating the buses of Montgomery, Alabama. Even in a moment in which King and other activists sacrificed so much while making what may have seemed at the time like small gains, he saw the glory of the bigger picture and the ultimate goal: "The end is reconciliation; the end is redemption; the end is the creation of the Beloved Community. It is this type of spirit and this type of love that can transform opponents into friends. It is this type of goodwill that will transform the deep gloom of the old age into the exuberant gladness of the new age. It is this love which will bring about miracles in the hearts of men."[3]

Later, when Dr. King gave his famous speech at the Lincoln Memorial during the 1963 March on Washington, he shared a dream of the Beloved Community that he had long envisioned and fought to achieve: "I still have a dream," King famously exclaimed. "It is a dream deeply rooted in the American dream. I have a dream that one day this nation will rise up and live out the true meaning of its creed: 'We hold these truths to be self-evident, that all men are created equal.'"[4]

Building on this vision, our task today is to reinterpret and contemporize the Beloved Community for our own cultural and political moment. Reenvisioning the Beloved Community calls us to draw on foundational religious and civic ideals. It means that we live into deeper commitments that allow us to build that community today. It means we recognize key markers of the Beloved Community and build on these, including equality rooted in *imago dei* (the image of God in everyone), radical welcome, *ubuntu* interdependence, restorative stewardship, nonviolence, and dignity for all.

This oft-neglected narrative still has the power to unite us and bridge our deep divisions, in part because it hasn't yet been co-opted or politicized. The pursuit of an expanded and reimagined Beloved Community combines civic humanitarianism with deep spiritual and religious values. It's a vision that resonates across religions and with the nonreligious. And it's a vision with the ability to disarm the myths and divisive forces that haunt our nation.

For King, the Beloved Community was inextricably linked to nonviolence and reconciliation. In his 1959 Palm Sunday sermon on Mahatma Gandhi, King elaborated on the effects of choosing nonviolence over violence: "The aftermath of nonviolence is the creation of the Beloved

Community, so that when the battle's over, a new relationship comes into being between the oppressed and the oppressor."[5] This conviction is at the center of our nation's need for the vision of the Beloved Community today. We must cast a big enough vision so that white Americans—particularly those in red states, rural areas, and conservative churches—can see a place for themselves, too, in that vision, all without compromising a clear commitment to truth-telling and justice. At the same time, we must cast a vision that repents for our painful history with racism and other isms. As King taught, the lie and idolatry of racism disfigures the image of God and harms both the oppressor and the oppressed.

While the civil rights movement helped to change the moral narrative around segregation, the movement failed to sustain a vision that could weather the crisis of the Vietnam War, as well as the rise of Black Power and the Religious Right as two countervailing narratives. When parts of the movement abandoned its spiritual and religious underpinnings and lost sight of the moral vision behind the Beloved Community, the movement lost momentum and fractured. For example, the rapid demise of the Student Nonviolent Coordinating Committee (SNCC) came after a pivotal election in 1964 in which Stokely Carmichael defeated John Lewis to become the new chair. Historian Charles Marsh explains in his book *The Beloved Community*, "Black power shirked the discipline and focus that the commitment to nonviolence engendered and sustained."[6] As SNCC moved away from being an interracial movement committed to nonviolence as a way of life and as a form of resistance and adopted a more militant and cosmic commitment to Black Power, its spiritual underpinnings began to fall apart. The group became a shell of its old self, buffeted by disputes between factions loyal to different movement leaders.

The deep spiritual and theological roots of the civil rights struggle are often ignored or understated. But without its deep religiosity and spirituality—the fuel and inspiration that so often made great sacrifice and moral resistance possible—there is no movement. While America is less religious that it was in the 1950s and '60s, it is still a deeply religious and spiritual nation. Secular arguments alone, I believe, will not be compelling and resilient enough to catalyze the depth of change necessary to defeat the lie of white supremacy and build the Beloved Community.

Since faith leaders can become intoxicated with the pursuit of power and co-opted by those same powers, we must resist politicizing religion to advance overly ideological or purely partisan agendas. But just like the civil rights leaders of the past, we must find ways to shake apolitical Christians out of apolitical hibernation and help them recognize that the pursuit of the Beloved Community is at the heart of the work of the church and is an essential manifestation of discipleship. This is true for Jews, Muslims, and people of other religions or no religion as well.

During the civil rights struggle, the pursuit of the Beloved Community was often handicapped by deep-seated patriarchy and homophobia within the Black church and the leadership structure of the civil rights movement. Thus, the vision for the Beloved Community needs to be recast to include the full contributions of women and of lesbian, gay, bisexual, and transgender people. The Black Lives Matter (BLM) movement provides a powerful contemporary example of this commitment. The stark reality of racialized police violence gave birth to the BLM movement, which is the closest parallel we have today to the spirit of the Student Nonviolent Coordinating Committee. In 2013, three Black women organizers—Alicia Garza, Patrisse Cullors, and Opal Tometi—created a project called #BlackLivesMatter, aimed at increasing political will and movement-building, in response to the acquittal of Trayvon Martin's murderer, George Zimmerman. Garza describes how BLM differentiated itself from traditional perceptions of Black activism: "It goes beyond the narrow nationalism that can be prevalent within some Black communities, which merely call on Black people to love Black, live Black, and buy Black, keeping straight cis[gendered] Black men in the front of the movement while our sisters, queer and trans and disabled folk take up roles in the background or not at all."[7] This commitment to avoid replicating harmful practices that excluded and marginalized so many in past liberation movements is imperative for the movements of tomorrow.

Since the civil rights movement started to dissipate at the end of the 1960s, our nation has taken many, albeit painfully uneven steps in the journey to realize the Beloved Community. While the ultimate goal must be a just and equitable society, one important indicator of that journey is the societal lurching toward fuller integration. We feel more empathy and solidarity with people who live or work close to us and are in direct relationship with us, and the book *Moving toward Integration* shows a substantial improvement in residential integration between 1970 and 1980.[8] Since then, however, racial segregation has dropped more slowly, with the "dissimilarity index" standing at seventy in 2010 compared to ninety-three in 1970. Furthermore, the research finds that Black people living in racial enclaves suffer unusually high rates of unemployment, mortality, and single parenting. This racialized geography continues to suffocate opportunity. Another chief indicator in the Beloved Community "CT scan" is trend lines in school segregation, including by class. Alarmingly, between 1991 and 2012, segregation of poor pupils rose by 40 percent.[9] Since 2000, the number of Americans living in extremely poor neighborhoods has nearly doubled, from seven million to fourteen million.[10] Furthermore, data based on research conducted by the Public Religion Research Institute (PRRI) in 2014 shows that a full 75 percent of white Americans have "entirely white social networks without any minority presence."[11] The same holds true for slightly less than two-thirds of Black Americans.[12]

The Beloved Community cannot be reduced to a bumper sticker or defined through a single slogan. But my summary of a new vision for the Beloved Community—my remix, as it were—is to build a nation in which neither punishment nor privilege is viciously attached to one's race, skin color, gender, ethnicity, nationality, or sexual orientation and gender identity.

Ensuring that punishment and privilege are no longer tied to any of these central identities represents a standard for the Beloved Community that poses a high bar, but this must become a barometer by which we measure our life together and public policy. Living up to these standards would mean that every person, all of whom are made in the image of God, would be equally valued and respected and that their dignity would be affirmed. Modern-day America is alarmingly far from achieving these commitments, because the legacy of oppression and discrimination continues to show up in the present, which is compounded by ongoing systemic injustices and inequality. Repairing this inequity will require closing what Dr. Eddie S. Glaude Jr. describes as "the value gap," which places different values on human life, treating some lives as much more valuable and worthy than others.[13]

Punishment continues to be tied to race in America, as evidenced by egregious racial disparities in police stops and arrests and judicial sentencing for similar crimes. Until Black lives are presumed innocent rather than so often guilty and there is truly equal justice under the law, we have urgent work to do to achieve this first standard. Privileges also remain starkly entrenched, with deep-seated racial disparities in wealth, income, education, employment, and housing—all tied to the legacy of the past and to the continuation of discriminatory policies, systems, and attitudes.

The Beloved Community cannot be defined only around what *shouldn't* happen—it must also be defined around a positive vision of the preferred future. Imagining together what ought to be requires a deeper unpacking of the qualifier "beloved." The word *beloved* signifies what we most value and cherish. Beloved starts from a standpoint of steadfast love, which involves mutual regard and mutual concern. It requires a commitment to empathy. In a spiritual and religious sense, beloved starts with an understanding and a belief that we are beloved by God—that God knows everything about us, including our vices, shortcomings, and contradictions, and loves us anyway. In Beloved Community, radically inclusive and resilient love is the norm. It is a community in which we are constantly seeking to build and restore right relationships. In Beloved Community, the needs of the most vulnerable are recognized and prioritized, because the moral test of our society centers around how the most vulnerable people, including children and the elderly, are faring. In Beloved Community, our differences stemming from ethnicity, race, gender, and sexual orientation and gender identity are not feared or scapegoated but are celebrated and embraced. In Beloved Community, a commitment to honor and protect human dignity becomes a sacred and shared responsibility.

You can't simply describe the Beloved Community in words. It also must be felt and experienced. In 2018, I had the privilege of participating in an intensive, weeklong immersion leadership program called True North Leadership, hosted at the 1440 Multiversity in California. The program is based on Bill George's book *Discover Your True North*[14] and engages in topics that include exploring your life story, your self-awareness and emotional intelligence, crucible moments, and the purpose of your leadership. During the first day, we were put into small groups, which became our leadership circles to reflect together on the concepts and ideas introduced in plenary. I was amazed at how deep you can go and how vulnerable you can be with six strangers in such a short period of time. In many ways, I soon felt closer to these very diverse men and women than I did to many of my own organization's staff, with whom I had worked for years. This was made possible in large part by building an environment with the right expectations and conditions in which Beloved Community could flourish. In these conversations, which often took place around a firepit in the beautiful redwood forest, I got glimpses of how quickly we can build Beloved Community and what that feels like.

Michelle Maldonado, one of my group members, put it this way: "Sometimes the Beloved Community is quiet and contemplative, where quiet is not feared or uncomfortable and you can simply be. At other times it may be loud and high-energy, full of co-creative movement like a dance through life." Our small group built strong and lasting bonds as we shared our deepest hurts, hopes, and dreams in a space filled with curiosity and a loving embrace of self and others, laced with wisdom and discernment to allow for individual and collective growth and transformation. Another member of our group, Joslyn Johnson, echoed this sentiment, saying, "Beloved Community is like extended family, where unconditional love resides. It is a safe place to be seen, heard, and loved." While it was arguably much easier to build Beloved Community in what felt like an almost ideal bubble, detached from the pressures and stresses of the real world, the week showed me the power of authenticity and vulnerability in building community among a group of diverse strangers who, by the end, had become friends who didn't want to part company.

Stephen Lewis, one of the coauthors of *Another Way*,[15] in a conversation with me provided a compelling road map for building the Beloved Community, saying it is "how we get a glimpse of what it means to be fully seen and to give our best potential. It is how we create the kinds of space that we all long for where we can be fully human and humane with one another." Lewis believes that we will achieve the Beloved Community when the so-called least among us—the invisible, the marginalized—can experience and pursue human flourishing, their full potential for living, and be a designer of solutions that confront their problems.[16]

While my point of reference for the Beloved Community is tied to the civil rights movement and the lived theology of the Black church, a similar moral vision is expressed in other religions, cultural communities, and movements. While the words *beloved* and *community* are not always used, the meaning behind them shows up across many cultural and religious traditions.

Dr. Grace Ji-Sun Kim explains another way of understanding the Beloved Community through the Korean term *jeong*, which permeates Korean culture and "is part of what gives joy, attachment, and meaning to many people's lives. *Jeong* is a difficult word to translate into English, but on a simple level it can be understood as love. However, the term *jeong* also includes affection, attachment, compassion, kindness, sharing, connection, and sympathy to people and even objects. Jeong captures the essence of love and affection between people that is sticky and inseparable, like honey between our fingers." Kim explains further, "Jeong is located in one's heart as well as between individuals. This feeling between individuals may be related to the Eastern notion of collective emotion and the deep-rooted sense of community, as jeong diminishes the 'I' and the confines that are attached to it and blurs the boundaries between people."[17]

Author and activist Kathy Khang describes how this sticky kind of love is "difficult to untangle or separate oneself from, and thus makes us stay connected to one another. Even though you may argue or fight with your friend, spouse, or family member, jeong will bring you back together. The experience of jeong flows out of you to the other to cause connectedness, affection, and love. There is no logical reason or validation of why one experiences jeong; it just happens."[18]

The Beloved Community finds expression across religions. When I led the Faith Initiative at the World Bank, I had the privilege of working with a broad range of religious leaders, scholars, and thought leaders. It was truly an immersion into global religions. One of my first projects involved gathering a small group of interreligious leaders to identify the common threads that bind together the world's largest religions in a shared commitment to combat extreme poverty around the world.

This was an ambitious task, particularly given the diversity of the group and the challenge of finding shared language across religious traditions, including those outside of the Abrahamic faiths.

The group produced a groundbreaking statement titled *Ending Extreme Poverty: A Moral and Spiritual Imperative*, which provided a moral and religious narrative behind the goal of ending extreme poverty by the year 2030, which later became a cornerstone of the Sustainable Development Goals. The statement read, in part: "We in the faith community embrace this moral imperative [to end extreme poverty] because we share the belief that the moral test of a society is how the weakest and most vulnerable are faring. Our sacred texts also call us to combat injustice and uplift the poorest in our midst . . . No one, regardless of sex, age, race, or belief, should be denied experiencing fullness of life."[19]

In the process of drafting and building consensus around this statement, I further learned to appreciate the differences and similarities between the world's religions. From the Jewish concept of *tikkun olam*, found in the Mishnah body of classical rabbinic teachings, we gain an understanding of how acts of kindness can be performed to perfect or repair the world. The phrase tikkun olam is tied to humans' responsibility for fixing what is wrong with the world. Rabbi Jonah Pesner, director of the Religious Action Center of Reform Judaism, ties the Beloved Community to an ancient conversation between Rabbi Hillel and Shammai. Shammai asks Hillel to explain all of Judaism while he's standing on one foot. Hillel responds, "What is hateful to you do not do to any person. The rest is commentary and go and learn."[20]

The emphasis in Islam on affirming dignity and respect connects with building Beloved Community. The Islamic Relief Worldwide organization explains, "At the core of Islamic teaching about development is the innate dignity conferred by God on every man, woman, and child. The Qur'an unambiguously declares: 'We have bestowed dignity on the progeny of Adam . . . and conferred on them special favours, above a great part of Our creation' (al-Isra, 17:70). Thus everyone has the right to live a life worthy of dignity and respect simply by virtue of being human; regardless of race, religion, gender, ability, age, or economic status."[21] According to Islamic Relief, "The Islamic principle at the core of preserving the dignity of human beings is justice. . . . This is evidenced from the Qur'anic injunction: 'Be just, for this is closest to God-conciousness [*sic*]' (al-Ma'idah, 5:8)."[22]

Eboo Patel, founder of the Interfaith Youth Core, describes how the Prophet Muhammad, twelve years into his ministry, "while teaching monotheism and mercy, is hounded out of the city of Mecca for choosing the path of cooperation. The Prophet then goes to Medina in 622 and creates the Constitution of Medina, a pact of cooperation between the Jews and Muslims."[23] Dr. Mohamed Elsanousi, executive director of the Network for Religious and Traditional Peacemakers, also cites the Medina constitution as the most prominent example in Islam of the Beloved Community, because "the community that the Prophet Muhammad created in Medina calls everyone to *umma*, or a sense of community regardless of ethnicity or religion. The pact forms a bond of mutual cooperation between the different religious and ethnic tribes." According to Elsanousi, "How Muslims live their moral values in public is another marker of the Beloved Community." The ethos and ethic behind the Medina constitution were also the ethos and ethic behind the Marakesh Declaration, which in 2017 united prominent Muslim scholars and leaders around a commitment to protecting religious freedom across the Muslim world. In the Beloved Community, Elsanousi says, "no one should be left behind and everyone should be included."[24]

From the biblical prophets through Jesus and the earliest disciples, the Bible has a great deal to say about what the Beloved Community looks like, even if the two words *beloved* and *community* never show up together. Jesus's frequent references to the kingdom of God and God's reign, and the biblical prophets' emphasis on *tsedeq*, *mishpat*, and *hesed*, which translate to "righteousness," "justice," and "steadfast love," provide the very essence of the Beloved Community. In Mark's gospel, Jesus begins his public ministry proclaiming that the "the kingdom of God is at hand" (1:15). Thus, the way Jesus lived, taught, healed, and transformed lives offers us windows into what the Beloved Community looks like and how we should go about achieving it.

In scripture there are countless glimpses into God's preferred future. In Acts 2 and 4, the Apostle Paul paints a picture of the Beloved Community in the early church, where resources are shared, everyone is cared for, and multiethnic, multilingual, and multinational community takes shape (Acts 2:42–47 and 4:32–37). We also see this vision in the book of Revelation, which promises a new heaven and a new earth in which there is no pain, conflict, or enmity and where all things are made new in the midst of God's glorious and everlasting presence (Revelation 21:1–6).

In the Hebrew Bible, references to the Promised Land provide a poignant glimpse into all that relates to the Beloved Community. The prophet Isaiah offers one of the most powerful visions of the Beloved Community. From the midst of widespread misery, injustice, and inequity, Isaiah paints a picture of "new heavens and a new earth" (65:17–25) in which the tragedies of this world will not need to be repeated. In this new earth we see community, harmony, tranquility, rejoicing, abundance, long life, productivity, and blessings. It will be a world filled with a holistic justice characterized by right relationships between people and God, neighbor with neighbor, and people with all of God's creation—the Beloved Community.

Dr. John Kinney, the former dean of Virginia Union Proctor School of Theology, where I attended seminary, says we must be so filled with God's promises that the brokenness of what is starts getting replaced by the pregnant possibility of *what ought to be*. Living out the call in the Lord's Prayer that proclaims, "Thy kingdom come, . . . on earth as it is in heaven," Christians are called to yank pieces of heaven and bring them down to earth, generating glimpses of what heaven will look like based on the Beloved Community we build in the here and now.

I love how the concept of Beloved Community combines a commitment to treating every person as beloved with a commitment to affirming and strengthening the bonds of community. In many ways this taps into the conventionally progressive emphasis on rights and justice as well as the conventionally conservative emphasis on community and freedom. Unlike the term *social justice*, the term *Beloved Community* hasn't been overly politicized, misappropriated, or co-opted. A commitment to an enlarged sense of community protects us from the dangers of feeling isolated and retreating into rigid and narrow tribes. In embracing the power of an enlarged community, we must understand the distinction between community and nation; nations are defined by borders, communities by relationships—including, in our digital age, ones that are built virtually. In an increasingly interconnected and interdependent world, the Beloved

Community must encompass global realities and a global worldview. It is not by any means a solely American project. Among the reminders of this interdependence are the overwhelming global impact of the COVID-19 pandemic and the ongoing crisis of climate change.

Building the Beloved Community also involves an intersectional understanding and approach to identifying and combating injustice. The term *intersectionality*, coined in 1992 by Columbia University law professor Kimberlé Crenshaw and often misunderstood and unfairly maligned, is, according to Crenshaw herself, an important "lens through which you can see where power comes and collides, where it interlocks and intersects."[25] This lens is critical for understanding how the various isms of racism, sexism, heterosexism, and ableism, which all serve as enemies of the Beloved Community, interlock and reinforce each other. This lens must inform how we envision the Beloved Community and how we go about building it.

Imagine what it would look like if America sought to embody the Beloved Community. Feelings of isolation, loneliness, resentment, and contempt could be replaced by a deep sense of belonging rooted in a shared moral vision that offers inclusion, that welcomes and values everyone. The Beloved Community can't be reduced to an abstract, amorphous concept or utopian dream. As we will explore, it is a practical vision, made real through lived expressions and replicable commitments that are contagious and liberating.

My journey in understanding the Beloved Community accelerated when, at the end of my sophomore year of high school, my mom was offered a job at the University of Arizona as the vice president of student affairs. Before I knew it, our family was moving from the temperate Pacific Northwest to the blazing heat of the Arizona desert. I did my best to embrace the change as a challenge and a new adventure. I had lived a blessed but sheltered life in Bellingham, Washington, a place lacking in socioeconomic and racial diversity. In Tucson, it turned out, there was no high school in the neighborhood where my parents bought a house. I was given the freedom to enroll in any school in the city. This felt like a loaded decision, one that would shape my path into college and beyond. Ultimately, I decided on Amphitheater High, one of the most racially and socioeconomically diverse schools in the city, with large percentages of Black, Latino/a, and white students.

I quickly realized there were really two high schools coexisting within Amphitheater. The advanced track was almost entirely white and was more competitive and better resourced, while most Black and Latino/a students were on the general track. Outside of sports and clubs, the tracks operated in almost two separate academic worlds with profoundly different expectations. The advanced track was college bound, while the primary goal for students on the general track was simply graduation. This two-tiered system created a self-fulfilling prophecy: it further disadvantaged students who came from more challenging backgrounds and privileged students who came from more affluent backgrounds.

What I saw led me to get involved in a program called APEX, run by the University of Arizona to provide additional support and resources to students of color in public schools across Tucson. APEX provided mentoring, test preparation, and, most important, a space in which students of color could support each other, expand their ambition, and better realize their potential. In my senior year I became president of my high school chapter, which afforded me the opportunity to work to equalize the playing field. APEX helped to build the Beloved Community by nurturing the hopes and aspirations of students the school system often overlooked.

These were some of the first experiences that enabled me to work on building the Beloved Community in a tangible way. At the time, I didn't have a full grasp of what *Beloved Community* meant, but I was inspired by the civil rights struggle and understood that building a more just and inclusive world required concrete commitments, actions, and sacrifices at every level—from the personal to the economic, social, and political.

The pursuit of the Beloved Community has served as a moral compass, a way of living into and expanding the work that the prophets and those in the early church began and that King and other civil rights leaders courageously continued. If this moral vision resonates with you, explore with me how we can become co-creators and co-architects of the Beloved Community.

Part Two

BUILDING BLOCKS OF THE BELOVED COMMUNITY

WHERE THERE IS NO VISION, THE BOOK OF PROVERBS SAYS, THE PEOPLE PERISH (29:18). It has long been one of my favorite proverbs, and it inspires me to participate in communicating a bold and more hopeful vision for our nation and world. It also speaks to how this book is structured. In Part I, I offered a vision of what the Beloved Community means and what it might look like today. But I would add an addendum to the proverb's timeless wisdom: Where there is a lack of sound strategy to build that vision, the people also perish. So in Part II, I seek to unpack the strategies—the building blocks—necessary to actualize that vision of the Beloved Community.

Each chapter names an obstacle to building the Beloved Community and discusses the building-block strategy for overcoming it. These obstacles include the myths we have believed that have shaped and distorted the ethos of the nation; the falsehoods and omissions that so often characterize our misunderstanding of American history; the impact of toxic polarization on our body politic; and a corrosive form of nationalism that many often confuse for patriotism. The building-block strategies for change must include telling the truth about damage done in the false name of God, patriotism, politics, or history—rationales that have so often fueled our toxic polarization. They also include critiquing and holding America accountable when it falls short of its ideals, which is imperative for the health of our democracy. Lastly, building the Beloved

Community requires we must unmask the myths that have shaped America and combat the ways these myths have been absolutized to justify exclusion and oppression.

While these obstacles are not exhaustive, overcoming each of them serves as an essential building block for building the Beloved Community and creating a radically more just, equitable, and inclusive America.

Chapter Five

UNMASKING AMERICA'S MYTHS

Very often, histories of nation-states are little more than myths that hide the seams that stitch the nation to the state. —Jill Lepore

The tough mind is sharp and penetrating, breaking through the crust of legends and myths and sifting the true from the false. —Martin Luther King Jr.

THE UNITED STATES HAS BEEN PROFOUNDLY SHAPED BY A SERIES OF SHARED MYTHS regarding the meaning of the nation and its creed. For most Americans, these myths continue to function at an unconscious level. We investigate these myths in a course on comparative religion and politics that I teach at Pepperdine University's Washington, DC, campus. Most prominent are the myths of America as a chosen nation, a Christian nation, and an innocent nation. All these myths have propped up the founding myth of white supremacy, which remains a principal fault line in American politics. For the sake of building the Beloved Community and forming a more perfect union, it is imperative that we better understand the origins and ongoing impact of these myths and how they have undergirded the primary myth of white supremacy.[1]

The pervasiveness of these myths helps explain why Americans have such divergent and often colliding versions and understandings of the nation's story, a reality that exacerbates deep social divisions and polarization. These myths are often distorted stories of our history that have created chasms in our sense of who we are and who we claim to be. It's urgent that we unmask and debunk these myths to cast a more inclusive and unifying vision. Building the Beloved Community requires that we better understand how our nation's history has been distorted, misappropriated, or erased in ways that undermine America's promise, betray many of our central ideals, and stifle our collective potential.

In his book *Myths America Lives By*, Richard T. Hughes writes, "The English word *myth* derives from the Greek word mythos, which literally means 'story.' Contrary to colloquial usage, a myth is not a story that is patently untrue. Rather, a myth is a story that, whether true or false, helps us discern the meaning and purpose of our lives and, for that reason, speaks truth to those who embrace it."[2] Hughes identifies the challenge to us all: If Americans in significant numbers conclude that the American story is false and bankrupt, we fear the nation will be in danger of disintegration. This often leads to what Hughes calls the absolutist response, in which people respond to critiques of the country with uncritical affirmations of the nation's righteousness and tell those they see as dissidents to either love America or leave it.

Hughes identifies five myths that emerged in specific periods of American history; to varying degrees, each flourishes today, often in combination with others. While most of these myths hold a kernel of truth and offer the potential for good, in the absolutizing and distorting of them, Americans have often undermined the potential virtues that otherwise stood at their respective cores. Consciously and unconsciously, these myths form the DNA of America. But, to use the terminology of my faith tradition, they have too often degenerated into sinful idols.

Hughes highlights the myths that have shaped America:

- The Myth of a Chosen Nation—the notion that God Almighty chose the United States for a special mission in the world.
- The Myth of Nature's Nation—the conviction that American ideals and institutions are rooted in the natural order, that is, in God's own intentions first revealed at the dawn of civilization.
- The Myth of the Millennial Nation—the notion that the United States, building on that natural order, will usher in a final golden age for all humankind.

- The Myth of a Christian Nation—the claim that America is a Christian nation, consistently guided by Christian values.
- The Myth of the Innocent Nation—the conviction that, while other nations may have blood on their hands, the nobility of the American cause always redeems the nation and renders it innocent.[3]

A combination of these myths generated the doctrine of Manifest Destiny, which has shaped our national psyche and has been used to oppress and dominate different peoples, but especially the Native American population. Over time these myths have morphed and mutated to profoundly shape our understanding of America. Take, for example, the danger and appeal of the "America First" slogan. If we fail to understand the history behind this slogan, we will be unable to address the harm it perpetuates. "America First" was first used as a slogan in 1917 by the publishing magnate William Randolph Hearst to voice opposition to US involvement in World War I. Similarly, to understand the slogan "Make America Great Again," we must turn back to the time it was coined during Ronald Reagan's 1980 presidential campaign and see how it was marshaled in a time of economic distress to awaken a sense of patriotism. Referring to America's inherent and lost greatness feeds the myths—among them the myth of the US as a chosen and innocent nation—that continue to divide us.

The myth that Americans are a chosen people provides the religious foundation for the notion of American exceptionalism.[4] The myth emerged among the Puritans in the colonial period. At its best, the myth summoned the Puritans to "bear one another's burdens" (Gal 6:2) and to take great risks and make sacrifices to establish a new community rooted in Christian values. At its worst, the myth filled the Puritans and other early American settlers with a sense of God-ordained "chosenness" that justified oppression and hostility toward the Native population and led to a triumphalist and insular posture. John Winthrop, the first governor of the Massachusetts Bay Colony, popularized this myth with his sermon delivered on the ship *Arbella* just before arriving to the colony, saying, "For we must consider that we shall be as a city upon a hill. The eyes of all people are upon us. So that if we shall deal falsely with our God in this work we have undertaken, and so cause Him to withdraw His present help from us, we shall be made a story and a by-word through the world."[5] Winthrop and the Puritans believed that by purifying their version of Christianity and building a model Protestant community in the New World, they would serve as an example to the Old World. Accordingly, America represented the new Promised Land, the new Israel that God granted to the Puritans so they could prosper. "In the Puritan imagination," Hughes explains, "England became Egypt, the Atlantic Ocean the Red Sea, the American wilderness their own land of Canaan, and the Puritans themselves became the new Israel."[6]

Even as early white Americans increasingly embraced the Myth of the Chosen Nation as a sign that God had favored them with power, dominion, and control, enslaved Africans in response devised alternative narratives to survive in a hostile and alien culture. For example, slaves also identified with the saga of ancient Israel and the exodus narrative. But in their version, Hughes writes, "the white South became Egypt, the land of oppression, and the North became the Land of Canaan, flowing with milk and honey. Building on this redeemed version of the chosen nation myth, Harriet Tubman acquired the designation 'Black Moses' for smuggling slaves to freedom in northern states."[7]

Out of the First and Second Great Awakenings, religious revivals in the eighteenth and nineteenth centuries, emerged the Myth of the Christian Nation. Despite the nation's nonsectarian founding, this myth promulgated the notion that America was fundamentally a Christian nation and tried to transform the country in that image. Hughes reminds us that "outside of Maryland, Rhode Island, and Pennsylvania, there were virtually no significant models of the separation of church and state when the nation was born, either in Europe or in the United States." He continues, "Shortly after the nation's birth, Christians throughout the country launched a massive revival designed, in part, to achieve through persuasion what they could no longer achieve through coercion or force of law. Through that revival, they sought to transform America into a Christian nation."[8]

In 1739, a series of isolated revivals converged into a general spiritual awakening that swept the colonies from New England to Georgia.

Rev. George Whitfield, who was one of the most prominent preachers at the time, helped to spark these revival fires. Another prominent preacher, Jonathan Edwards, wrote a treatise in 1742 titled "Some Thoughts Concerning the Present Revival of Religion in New England," in which he makes a bold prediction: "It is not unlikely, that this work of God's Spirit, so extraordinary and wonderful, is the dawning, or at least a prelude of that glorious work of God, so often foretold in scripture, which, in the progress and issue of it, shall renew the world of [humankind]."[9] Evangelist Charles G. Finney played an instrumental role in the Second Great Awakening, leading revivals that began in the 1820s in towns and communities across the US. Finney also "funneled hundreds and perhaps thousands into a moral crusade," inspiring new converts to work for prison reform, temperance, and, most prominently, the abolition of slavery.[10] Both the First and Second Great Awakenings were successful in democratizing faith, leading to the explosive growth of Christianity across the new country, particularly of a more evangelical brand through the growth of Methodist and Baptist churches.

While the US was founded on the separation of church and state, the Myth of a Christian Nation has led many parts of the American church to believe and act as though Christianity represents the nation's established religion, often conflating the cross with the flag and promoting versions of Christian nationalism. As Katherine Stewart chronicles in her book *The Power Worshippers: Inside the Dangerous Rise of Religious Nationalism*, the modern Christian nationalist movement is driven by a "dense network of think tanks, advocacy groups, and pastoral organizations embedded in a rapidly expanding community of international alliances and united not by any central command but by a shared, antidemocratic vision and a common will to power." The movement "does not seek to add another voice to America's pluralistic democracy but to replace our foundational democratic principles and institutions with a state grounded on a particular version of Christianity, answering to what some adherents call a 'biblical worldview' that also happens to serve the interests of its plutocratic funders and allied political leaders."[11] The modern Christian nationalist movement is grounded in the pervasive Myth of the Christian Nation, which helps to obscure the movement's danger to our democracy.

While many early Christians in the US were inspired by their faith to oppose slavery, far more twisted the Bible to justify the institution of slavery and the lie of white supremacy. Sadly, the Bible has been misused and abused to justify slavery, Jim Crow, the disenfranchisement of women, and many other evils. Dr. Eddie S. Glaude Jr. explains, "The people who settled the country had a fatal flaw. They could recognize a man when they saw one . . . but since they were Christian, and since they had already decided that they came to establish a free country, the only way to justify the role this chattel was playing in one's life was to say that he was not a man. For if he wasn't, then no crime had been committed. That lie is the basis of our present trouble."[12] Slaveholders dealt with this irreconcilable contradiction by creating their own version of the Bible, often referred to as the Slavery Bible, which took out every reference to God's commitment to justice and freedom. Yet the good news is that the same Bible—and even, in some cases, the same verses—that were used to justify evil were also used by abolitionists and later civil rights leaders to challenge and ultimately dismantle these and other ills.

Many of the founders, including Thomas Jefferson, were deists and never intended to create an explicitly Christian nation. They were deeply committed to the separation of church and state, which became codified into the US Constitution through the First Amendment. The notion of America as a Christian nation also contradicts the plain fact of growing religious pluralism.

The Myth of the Innocent Nation emerged in the twentieth century, drawing strength from the other myths. America's innocence, according to this myth, is rooted in its sense of being "chosen" or exceptional and in its supposed favor by God as a Christian nation. Consequently, America naturally stands for what is good and righteous and can do no wrong. American rhetoric in World War I established the pattern to which the myth of innocence would conform itself for the rest of the century. President Woodrow Wilson described the imperial German government as one "which has thrown aside all consideration of humanity and of right and is running amuck." Shortly after America entered the war, Wilson presented the American cause as righteous, innocent, and free of self-interest in a speech to the Senate in 1917. "American principles and

American policies," Wilson proclaimed, "are the principles of [humanity] and must prevail." The American experience in World War I prepared the country to imagine itself an innocent, disinterested participant in the conflicts of the world.[13]

After World War II, communism filled the enemy role previously played by Nazi Germany. To counteract the Soviet threat, Americans routinely juxtaposed their "deeply felt religious faith against godless and atheistic communism." For many years, this theme was a prominent feature of evangelist Billy Graham's preaching. Graham said, "Only as millions of Americans turn to Jesus Christ at this hour and accept him as their Savior can this nation possibly be spared the onslaught of a demon-possessed communism." A more recent example of the influence of this myth was the inability of many people to answer the question "Why do they hate us?" after the horrific 9/11 terrorist attacks. While the attacks were heinous and indefensible, President George W. Bush went on to label North Korea, Iran, and Iraq as the "axis of evil" while placing America unambiguously on the side of right. This myth also shows up in political rhetoric that asserts that America is the greatest democracy or best country in the world. While our democracy has often served as a model and an inspiration for many other countries, these assertions can hide ways in which our nation has backtracked in its democratic norms and commitments, whether through the erosion of trust, gerrymandered congressional districts, or pervasive voter suppression against minority communities, just to name a few deeply troubling trends. There's a danger in dividing the world into rigid categories of good and evil as it can blind us to the evil that lies within ourselves and the good that can be redeemed in even the evilest person or nation.[14]

What's more, our presumed innocence can blind us to the harmful consequences of our actions, even if such consequences are unintended.

Fifteen years after the 2004 publication of *Myths America Lives By*—and after receiving critical feedback from both friends and other scholars—Hughes produced a second edition of the book, this time framing the myths in the context of what he now calls the primal myth: white supremacy. Even though the first edition was filled with quotes from African American leaders, including Frederick Douglass,

Malcolm X, and Martin Luther King Jr., who forcefully critiqued and challenged these myths, white supremacy was not named as a myth in its own right. Hughes illustrates just how easy it is for Americans to take the myth of white supremacy for granted. I admire his candor and vulnerability when he reflects back on his first edition: "I began to see that whites like me—whites who strongly reject racist ideology—can escape the power of the white supremacist myth only with extraordinary effort, if at all. That is because assumptions of white supremacy are like the very air we breathe: They surround us, envelop us, and shape us, but do so in ways we seldom discern." In the second edition, Hughes writes that "the Myth of White Supremacy is the primal American myth that informs all the others and, second, that one of the chief functions of the other five myths is to protect and obscure the Myth of White Supremacy, to hide it from our awareness, and to assure us that we remain innocent after all."[15]

I conclude my religion-and-politics class by engaging my students in a provocative conversation on whether there is anything positive about these myths and whether they can be redeemed. I agree with Hughes that some of the myths have some positive truths within them, particularly elements associated with the idea that America is a chosen and Christian nation. For example, if being "chosen" means a responsibility to advance human dignity and model representative democracy, that is worth preserving and celebrating. It is also both ahistorical and counterproductive to ignore the ways in which America's founding and Constitution were heavily influenced by Christian beliefs and values. The best of these Christian values can be affirmed and universalized in ways that don't exclude or undervalue non-Christians for their contributions to America. Dr. Martin Luther King Jr. and the Southern Christian Leadership Conference modeled how to do this as they were rooted in and appealed to their Christian faith while advancing the civil rights struggle, not to create a Christian nation but to build a radically more just nation.

Regardless of where you land on the question of whether any of these myths can be redeemed, they can serve as a valuable "decoder ring," helping us to better identify and resist ways in which distortions of our history and self-identity betray our fundamental values and can be used to perpetuate injustice. We must be conscientious and vigilant in rejecting the ways these myths derail the project of forming a more perfect union and building the Beloved Community by contributing to exclusion, oppression, blindness, or triumphalism.

Chapter Six

TELLING THE WHOLE TRUTH TO SET US FREE

Jesus said, "If you hold to my teaching, you are really my disciples. Then you will know the truth, and the truth will set you free." —John 8:31–32

We know, in the case of the person, that whoever cannot tell himself the truth about his past is trapped in it, immobilized in the prison of his undiscovered self. This is also true of nations. —James Baldwin

History, despite its wrenching pain, cannot be unlived, but if faced with courage, need not be lived again. —Maya Angelou

Until the lion tells the story, the hunter will always be the hero. —West African proverb

"WE HOLD THESE TRUTHS TO BE SELF-EVIDENT," DECLARES THE DECLARATION OF Independence, that all people "are created equal, that they are endowed by their Creator with certain unalienable Rights, that among these are Life, Liberty, and the pursuit of Happiness."[1] These ideals, of course, were deeply compromised at the nation's founding as they excluded women and people of color and only initially applied to land-owning white men, but these truths, this story of America, can still be redeemed.

Our national stories—our stories of us—convey what we value, what has shaped us, and where we have been. While telling the whole story about our history can be uncomfortable and painful, it is necessary and ultimately redemptive. Telling the whole story is a prerequisite to constructing a more hopeful and unifying shared story that plants and waters the seeds of the Beloved Community. If we choose the path of denial or amnesia, we will remain captive to our past and liable to repeat the cruelty and inhumanity contained in it.

At the root of America's story is the lie of white supremacy, which profoundly shaped our past and persists in our present. No one tells this story better than Bryan Stevenson and the Equal Justice Initiative (EJI). Stevenson often speaks to the way in which memory is a powerful force in how a country evolves. In the case of the United States, our memory is haunted—we are in a post-genocidal society struggling with the effects of buried traumas tied to our history. Few of us have experienced the freedom of telling the whole truth of this history. This is the call of the Beloved Community. When the Beloved Community is willing to tell the whole truth, we find healing for all of us.

In 2018 I had the honor of first visiting the then-new Legacy Museum and the National Memorial for Peace and Justice in Montgomery, Alabama. The museum and memorial, both constructed by EJI, serve as poignant reminders of the imperative to tell the whole, unvarnished story of America—because only the whole truth will set us free.[2] In 2018 and again in 2019, I joined hundreds of Christian clergy and other leaders participating in the annual Samuel DeWitt Proctor conference in Birmingham and then the Christian Churches Together conference in Montgomery. I had learned about plans to build the memorial when I was part of a gathering of faith leaders meeting with Stevenson, who became famous through his *New York Times* bestselling book and blockbuster movie *Just Mercy*.[3] Later, I experienced the jarring but stunning manifestation of EJI's work in the memorial, which identifies and memorializes the more than four thousand African American men, women, and children who were lynched between 1877 and 1950.[4] Eight hundred steel monuments, each one representing a US county where at least one or more racial lynchings took place, hold the victims' engraved names, documenting the too-often-untold story of the lynching of Black Americans.[5] Prior to the public opening of the memorial, we faith leaders participated in a sacred ceremony in which we dug up and put in a jar a portion of the earth from a site near Montgomery where a Black man had been lynched.

As we dug the earth and filled the jar, we prayed over the soil and prayed for the man's descendants. These jars of sacred earth, from states across the country where documented lynchings took place, are now housed at the memorial. A plaque there captures the purpose and mission of the memorial:

> At this memorial, we remember the thousands killed, the genera-
> tions of black people terrorized, and the legacy of the suffering
> and injustice that haunts us still. We also remember the countless
> victims whose deaths were not recorded in news archives and can-
> not be documented, who are recognized solely in the mournful
> memories of those who loved them. We believe that telling the
> truth about the age of racial terror and reflecting together on this
> period and its legacy can lead to a more thoughtful and informed
> commitment to justice today. We hope this memorial will inspire
> individuals, communities, and this nation to claim our difficult
> history and commit to a just and peaceful future.

EJI also built, as a companion to the national memorial, the Legacy Museum, located in downtown Montgomery. The museum takes visitors on a visceral journey through some of the stories of the twelve million people kidnapped and forcibly brought to the Americas as slaves, the nine million people terrorized by various forms of violence (including lynch-ing), the ten million people segregated under the system of Jim Crow, and the nearly seven million people who today remain under the control of the criminal justice system. The museum connects the dots between the seen and unseen ways in which racial oppression has mutated throughout our nation's history—from the shackles of slavery to indentured servi-tude in the post-Reconstruction era, from the reign of terror that took place through lynching and the stark injustices of segregation in the Jim Crow South to the criminalization of Black bodies through the war on crime and drugs and up to today's era of mass incarceration and racialized police violence. Many museums, despite their best intentions, tell history through a distinctly biased lens, some more slanted than others. I am grateful that the Legacy Museum tells the truth about white supremacy in an uncensored and uncompromising way.

An hour and a half north, in Birmingham, you can find a somewhat more sanitized version of this history at the Birmingham Civil Rights Institute.[6] The institute is situated across the street from the 16th Street Baptist Church, where four girls were viciously killed in a racist bombing attack in 1963. While the two museums cover some of the same history, I was struck by how differently they tell this story. Some of the most moving aspects of the institute include a walk through a replica of segregated Birmingham, remnants of one of the Greyhound buses firebombed during the Freedom Rides, and the opportunity to witness the story of civil rights leaders such as Rev. Fred Shuttlesworth. The Birmingham museum is certainly worth visiting, but it feels like a step inside a time machine, as though the brutal history of slavery and Jim Crow segregation were just a ghost of the past and not something that profoundly shapes our present reality.

In contrast, EJI's Legacy Museum and National Memorial tell this story within a longer narrative arc that connects the dots to our present, making a convincing case that we can't fully move forward unless we come to terms with our brutal past. At the Legacy Museum you can peer into a slave cell and watch as a slave woman pleads with you to help her find and reunite with her children. You can pick up a phone and listen to prison inmates tell their stories; in one case the heartbreaking story is told by a woman, raped by a corrections officer while in prison, whose baby was taken away from her after it was born. You can watch a video of former convicts telling about surviving heart-wrenching violence in Alabama's St. Clair prison, one of the most dangerous prisons in the US. The museum shows how the criminal justice system remains the institution least impacted by the civil rights movement and how our nation's endorsement of racially biased narratives has never been fully confronted.

As I left the memorial in tears after my initial visit, I couldn't help but wish a replica could be built on the National Mall in Washington, DC, so that far more Americans would be confronted with the stories told there. The museums in Montgomery and Birmingham are both treasures, but they reveal two fairly different ways of telling our history. Unfortunately, many of the most painful parts of our history are taught to us with the approach of the Birmingham Civil Rights museum. I am also a big fan of the Smithsonian's National Museum of African American History and Culture in DC because it covers such a sweeping breadth of Black history and culture. Even as it does, though, the specific history of how white supremacy and racism have evolved and mutated into the present can sometimes get buried.

The history of Black Americans also gets lost in the approach many schools, including many colleges and universities, take in teaching US history. In a courtroom, witnesses swear to "tell the truth, the whole truth, and nothing but the truth, so help me God." Tragically, what is required in court rarely has been applied to our education system. My education is a case in point. I was mesmerized by the civil rights movement at an early age and voraciously read historical accounts of the movement, yet I was still underinformed until college about the history of Reconstruction or of the Southern Strategy, which I believe are essential for understanding how we have gotten to where we are now. I often use the Pepperdine class I teach as an informal focus group and have seen that even students from one of our elite colleges are woefully unfamiliar with many of the truths that this chapter seeks to illuminate.

Truth-telling is good for the soul, but it often comes with a price tag on our reputation. That is one reason people often resist and even seek to discredit efforts at historical truth-telling. A recent example of this unfortunate trend manifested in the reactions to the groundbreaking 1619 Project of the *New York Times Magazine*. To mark the four-hundredth anniversary year of the first twenty slaves arriving on American shores off Port Comfort, Virginia, the magazine published a series of articles, interviews, and videos that brought to life the history of slavery as well as its continued impact on our nation. The project aimed "to reframe the country's history by placing the consequences of slavery and the contributions of black Americans at the very center of our national narrative."[7] The magazine was met with backlash, primarily from conservative academics, politicians, and think tanks.

When publications like the *Times* and places like the National Memorial for Peace and Justice speak the truth, they often meet backlash. But they also inspire others to speak the truth. Speaking out, we inspire others to speak the truth. The National Memorial was inspired, in part, by observing the way post-war Germany made the courageous decision to memorialize the true story about the horrific atrocities committed by the

Nazis under the Third Reich by building hundreds of public memorials to the victims of the Holocaust. The memorials can be found across Germany and ensure that these atrocities are never forgotten by subsequent generations of Germans, helping them have an ingrained understanding of the whole story and inspiring a deeper commitment to never allow such a horrific tragedy to happen again.

Prior to the creation of civil rights museums and more recent memorials, America largely ignored the history of slavery and Jim Crow segregation. Adding insult to injury, states across the country, particularly in the South, instead erected monuments to Confederate generals and soldiers, particularly after the period of Reconstruction. These monuments were designed to strike fear into the Black population as those symbols of white supremacy often stood in town and city centers, under the guise of Southern heritage and pride.

The next phase of the National Memorial's truth-telling work invites every county in which a documented lynching took place to display a replica bronze column in their local courthouse or in a prominent public space. These replica columns, with the names of every documented victim of lynching etched into them, aim to help these communities remember and honor the lives lost. They also serve as a physical witness to the whole story, engendering a greater commitment to resist any future forms of racial terror.

I can't help wonder what the next set of memorials will be that our nation will need to create. What will the Beloved Community inspire and require of us? Will my two young sons' generation construct memorials to the Black men and women slain by racialized police violence in the era in which they grew up?

At this pivotal moment in the story of us, we need that brave kind of Legacy Museum framing and storytelling, telling us the whole story, connecting the past to the present. This echoes the whole, unvarnished truth that Jesus said "will set you free" (John 8:31–32).

The National Memorial for Peace and Justice and the Legacy Museum are powerful reminders of the imperative to ensure that every American knows a series of basic truths about our nation's history. It is the only way to realize a lasting, more perfect union and a resilient Beloved

Community. More and more people are telling these truths. And we need to pay attention.

In cases where a more accurate and comprehensive version of our history is taught, we are challenged to unlearn the omissions, revisionist histories, and deeply biased renditions of the American story that so many all of us were given. While history is always told from a particular vantage point, if every American were able to receive a more accurate and honest baseline understanding of our nation's history, our conversations around who we are, what we value, and who we want to be would have common ground and be much less contentious. But until we can tell the whole story about our history—from slavery to current racism, from the brutal treatment and extermination of Native Americans to the subjugation of women, from detention camps for Japanese Americans during World War II to violence and discrimination against the LGBTQ community—our country will fail in reaching its full potential, and attempts to build the Beloved Community will take place on an unstable foundation.

A few key moments in our history provide foundational truths for our nation's rebirth. These important events have been explained and interpreted in much greater detail in many other books, among them one of my recent favorites, *These Truths*,[8] by Harvard professor and historian Jill Lepore, whom I've cited in earlier chapters. The examples that I share here are only meant to be illustrative of how we can and must relearn the truth of what has been so often erased or misrepresented in our public memory.

Telling the whole truth is not about guilting, shaming, or seeking national self-loathing. Instead, it is about learning so that we can avoid repeating the mistakes of the past and be better informed and equipped to repent for and rectify present injustices that are so often inextricably linked to the past. This historical truth-telling does not take away from the goodness, valor, and courage of countless Americans throughout our history who have defended and advanced our most sacred ideals. Instead, it offers a corrective so that we lean into telling the liberating whole truth.

Most traditional renditions of American history begin with the American colonies. But a more honest history of America must start with

Indigenous peoples, who inhabited this land for millennia. A true history must consider the barbaric mistreatment and annihilation of the Native American population by European newcomers in the name of discovery, trade routes, and profit. This history is almost always glossed over or distorted by stories of the early pilgrims exchanging food with the Native Americans for the supposed first Thanksgiving or with dehumanizing images of Indigenous communities' barbarism toward the early settlers. What is often untold is the degree to which Native populations were decimated by disease and warfare due to land-grabbing by settlers and then later by federal and state authorities, who often engaged in treaties and then violated them. Rarely told are the stories of Indigenous valor and dignity in their resistance. In an earlier chapter, we looked at how the doctrine of Manifest Destiny "sanctified" abuse, violence, and displacement of Native Americans. This brutal history includes the forced removal of tribal peoples through a policy enacted by President Andrew Jackson. In 1838 and 1839, the policy forced the Cherokee nation to give up its land east of the Mississippi River and migrate to present-day Oklahoma. More than four thousand of the fifteen thousand Cherokee people died along the way due to hunger, disease, and exhaustion. David Treuer's *The Heartbeat of Wounded Knee* gives a compelling and honest counternarrative documenting the nation's betrayal and brutality toward Indigenous peoples—and their resilience—since that 1890 massacre.[9]

Better known and more often told is the history of American slavery. Even so, most Americans have been exposed to or have accepted a fairly sanitized version. Films such as the groundbreaking *12 Years a Slave*[10] have helped open the eyes of many to the sheer brutality and inhumanity of the slave system, retelling the history and correcting the record. Within that corrected record is the unfolding truth about the degree to which the Bible and Christianity were misused to justify the system of slavery. The corrected record must include the degree to which the system of slavery provided the free labor and collateral that built so much of the nation's wealth.

Many historically important moments are often misunderstood or ignored entirely in our history books and collective memory. A few examples include the demise of Reconstruction, the emergence of the Southern Strategy, and the birth of the Religious Right. The first involves the period just after Reconstruction. We easily forget just how short-lived the period of Reconstruction after the end of the Civil War was—and the role an insidious political compromise played in reversing the gains of that era. The Emancipation Proclamation freed African slaves, and the passage of the Thirteenth, Fourteenth, and Fifteenth Amendments,[11] fostered a short-lived rebirth or second founding of the nation after the Civil War, extending and protecting the rights of all citizens. However, it also resulted in a significant backlash, particularly in the South, culminating in the Compromise of 1877, in which Republican presidential candidate Rutherford Hayes struck a deal with Southern Democrats to settle the highly contested 1876 election. As a bipartisan congressional commission debated the outcome, allies of Hayes met in secret with moderate Southern Democrats to negotiate acceptance of Hayes's election. The Democrats agreed not to block Hayes's victory on the condition that Republicans withdraw all federal troops from the South. This consolidated Democratic control over the region. As the withdrawal of federal troops from the South commenced, Southerners reimposed new forms of enslavement under the guise of sharecropping and later through the system of Jim Crow segregation.[12] Imagine how our nation's history might have evolved differently without this bitter betrayal of Black freedom.

A second historically significant truth that is often ignored is the impact of the Republican Party's ongoing embrace of the "Southern Strategy," which has profoundly shaped and influenced our nation's politics ever since, culminating in many respects in the election of President Trump. To understand the Southern Strategy, we must look at a pivotal moment: when President Lyndon Johnson signed the Voting Rights Act of 1965. President Johnson, who defied Southern Democrats in pushing this watershed legislation to guarantee Black Americans the right to vote, predicted that his support for this bill would cost the Democratic Party a generation of voters in the South.

President Johnson's prediction proved right. Through the 1960s and '70s, the nation went through a significant political realignment due to an exodus of white Southern Democrats to the Republican Party. This was solidified by an overt plan that leaders in the GOP used to stoke racial fear and grievances in what has come to be called the Southern Strategy.

The Southern Strategy started with Barry Goldwater's 1964 presidential campaign. Angie Maxwell explains, "Originally called 'Operation Dixie,' the strategy aggressively championed Sen. Goldwater's vote against the 1964 Civil Rights Act." Largely because of this strategy, despite Johnson's landslide overall victory, Goldwater carried five Deep South states, including 87 percent of the vote in Mississippi. His blunt appeal turned off many other voters, as these states and his native Arizona were the only ones Goldwater won. Yet others took note of the strategy and its success in Southern states.[13]

Taking lessons from Goldwater's overt and strident racist appeals, the next election cycle brought Nixon's team, which employed more coded language. This included his calling for the restoration of "law and order," which signaled his support for an end to protests, marches, and boycotts. And it foreshadowed his declaration of a "war on drugs," which played on racialized fears about the rise of crime. During his 1980 presidential bid, Ronald Reagan expanded Nixon's racial code to include supposedly "colorblind" appeals for economic justice, according to Maxwell. Reagan encouraged Americans to "move past race," even as he invoked the image of the "welfare queen," a stereotypical, caricatured Black woman Reagan described as having "'80 names, 30 addresses, [and] 12 Social Security cards,' resulting in a tax-free income of $150,000." Through this scapegoating and stereotyping, Reagan portrayed racial minorities as undeserving "takers," while ignoring the institutional racism that is so often at the heart of economic inequity. To lower-income and middle-class white Southern voters, according to Maxwell, his message was clear: "African Americans were to blame for their own standing in society and . . . government programs aimed at alleviating racial inequities would disadvantage white Americans." Through these and other efforts, Maxwell points out, "the GOP successfully fused ideas about the role of government in the economy, women's place in society, white evangelical Christianity and white racial grievance, in what became a 'long Southern strategy' that extended well past the days of Goldwater and Nixon," setting the stage for Trump's presidential run in 2016.[14]

Likewise, Michelle Alexander, a visiting professor at Union Theological Seminary and author of *The New Jim Crow: Mass Incarceration in the Age of Colorblindness*, writes in the *New York Times*,

Contrary to what many people would have us believe, what our nation is experiencing is not an "aberration." The politics of "Trumpism" and "fake news" are not new; they are as old as the nation itself. The very same playbook has been used over and over in this country by those who seek to preserve racial hierarchy, or to exploit racial resentments and anxieties for political gain, each time with similar results. Back in the 1980s and '90s, Democratic and Republican politicians leaned heavily on the racial stereotypes of "crack heads," "crack babies," "super predators," and "welfare queens" to mobilize public support for the War on Drugs, a get-tough movement and a prison-building boom—a political strategy that was traceable in large part to the desire to appeal to poor and working-class white voters who had defected from the Democratic Party in the wake of the civil rights movement.[15]

It is impossible to understand the evolution of American politics without understanding the impact of the Southern Strategy—in all its guises and iterations—on both political parties and ultimately on all Americans.

A third example of an important but often misunderstood or unknown aspect of our history involves the Religious Right, which has had a significant impact on the nation's politics, perceptions of the church, and the Republican Party. In a 2014 article titled "The Real Origins of the Religious Right," Dr. Randall Balmer explains,

One of the most durable myths in recent history is that the religious right, the coalition of conservative evangelicals and fundamentalists, emerged as a political movement in response to the US Supreme Court's 1973 *Roe v. Wade* ruling legalizing abortion. But the abortion myth quickly collapses under historical scrutiny. In fact, it wasn't until 1979—a full six years after *Roe*—that evangelical leaders, at the behest of conservative activist Paul Weyrich, seized on abortion not for moral reasons, but as a rallying-cry to deny President Jimmy Carter a second term. Why? Because the anti-abortion crusade was more palatable than the religious right's real motive: protecting segregated schools.[16]

Before the creation of the Moral Majority, the Christian Coalition, and more recent organizations such as the Family Research Council, the Religious Right was birthed through an agreement between Weyrich and other Republican political operatives and televangelist Jerry Falwell. Together they formed an alliance to convert the then largely apolitical evangelical community into a loyal political bloc, exploiting the divisive matter of the desegregation of Christian schools. The federal government's threat to take away the tax-exempt status of Christian schools that refused to admit Black students, most prominently Bob Jones University, generated outrage among many white evangelicals and helped build the political momentum they were looking for.

Years later the Religious Right embraced issues such as abortion, religious liberty, and opposition to gay marriage, but the movement's racist origins continue to resound today. These roots help to explain the seemingly unconditional support most conservative evangelicals gave to Trump despite the alarming narcissism, immorality, mendacity, and racism he displayed. The public perception of evangelicals and Christians more broadly as an overly politicized, intolerant, and nationalistic movement overly tied to the Republican Party represents a direct threat to the cause of evangelism and the integrity and witness of the church.

Telling the whole truth will also require us to acknowledge the truths of the long struggles for women's rights and gender equality. This history and unfinished business undergird the demands and urgency of the #MeToo movement. Susan B. Anthony and Elizabeth Stanton are familiar to most because they served as pioneers in the suffrage movement. But the degree of resistance and violence that so many of the suffragists faced is often glossed over or forgotten. In the seventy years following the 1848 women's rights convention in Seneca Falls, New York, which is often considered the birth of the movement, suffragists worked to educate the public about the validity of women's suffrage by circulating petitions and lobbying Congress to pass a constitutional amendment to enfranchise women. In 1920, through the tireless campaigning of the National American Woman Suffrage Association and the National Woman's Party, the Nineteenth Amendment, enfranchising women, was finally ratified. While tragically excluding women of color, this victory is considered the most significant achievement of women in the Progressive Era—and the single largest extension of democratic voting rights in our nation's history.

Another milestone in the long journey for women's rights and equality was the passage of Title VII of the 1964 Civil Rights Act. Title VII prohibits employment discrimination on the basis of sex as well as race, religion, and national origin. While the category "sex" was included as a last-ditch effort to kill the bill, it still passed. With its passage, the Equal Employment Opportunity Commission was established to investigate discrimination complaints. According to the National Women's History Alliance,

> Within the commission's first five years, it received 50,000 sex discrimination complaints. But it was quickly obvious that the commission was not very interested in pursuing these complaints. Betty Friedan, the chairs of the various state Commissions on the Status of Women, and other feminists agreed to form a civil rights organization for women similar to the NAACP. In 1966, the National Organization for Women was organized, soon to be followed by an array of other mass-membership organizations addressing the needs of specific groups of women, including Blacks, Latinas, Asians-Americans [sic], lesbians, welfare recipients, business owners, aspiring politicians, and tradeswomen and professional women of every sort.[17]

The Equal Rights Amendment (ERA) marked another seminal moment. The ERA languished in Congress for almost fifty years, finally passed in 1972, and was sent to the states for ratification. The act simply read, "Equality of rights under the law shall not be denied or abridged by the United States or by any state on account of sex." To many women's rights activists, its ratification by the required thirty-eight states seemed almost a given, as many underestimated the pushback by men and many conservative women. While the campaign to ratify the act ultimately fell three states short of the thirty-eight needed before the congressionally set deadline, the process galvanized millions of women across the nation to become actively involved in the women's rights movement in their own communities and led to the creation of the National Organization for Women. Seventy-five percent of the women legislators in those three pivotal states supported the ERA, but only 46 percent of men voted to ratify.[18] The imperative to make the ERA the Twenty-eighth Amendment continues, particularly after Virginia became the thirty-eighth state to ratify it in January 2020.[19]

While great strides have been made in the context of women's access to higher education and participation in the workplace, significant work must be done to address unequal pay, insufficient women's representation in politics, and the alarming pervasiveness of gender-based violence, among many other challenges to ensure that women can enjoy their full rights and realize their full potential. Judging by the indicator of political representation, our nation has a very long way to go toward women's equality. As the National Women's History Alliance documents, "Jeannette Rankin was the first woman elected to Congress, in 1916. By 1971, three generations later, women were still less than 3 percent of our congressional representatives. Today women hold only 11 percent of the seats in Congress, and 21 percent of the state legislative seats."[20]

America also often suffers amnesia about its controversial history around immigration. There have been many dark periods in which our immigration policy has been blatantly racist and ethnocentric, followed by intermittent eras in which the country has welcomed and embraced a rich diversity of immigrants. For most of American history, the vast majority of the world's peoples were ineligible for US citizenship due to their race, origin, or sex.[21] Many people of Irish, Italian, and Eastern European descent were at points considered not white enough and were summarily restricted from immigrating. The cost of forgetting these histories is that the nation will continue engaging in such practices, rather than facing them. American Catholics can easily forget the degree of religious persecution Catholics experienced for decades. In the 1840s, many Americans opposed to a new wave of immigrants, chiefly Irish and German Catholics, founded a new political party, the Native American Party, also known as the American Party or the Know-Nothings. The Chinese Exclusion Act of 1882 was passed to prevent Chinese workers from entering the US in response to fears of declining wages and economic ills blamed on Chinese workers on the West Coast and to assuage concerns about maintaining white "racial purity."[22]

In 1924, Congress passed a two-part Immigration Act, banning immigration from anywhere in Asia, vastly restricting immigration from Europe, and sorting out European immigrants by their national origins. Less eugenically desirable southern and eastern Europeans—Italians, Hungarians, and Jews—were all but barred entry.[23] Then, in 1965, in the shadow of the Statue of Liberty, President Lyndon Johnson signed the Immigration and Nationality Act. With that signature, he announced in his 1964 State of the Union address, that "in establishing preferences, a nation that was built by the immigrants of all lands can ask those who now seek admission: 'What can you do for our country?' But we should not be asking: 'In what country were you born?'"[24]

The push and pull between a history filled with exclusion—often fueled by religious, racial, and ethnic prejudice—and moments of deep inclusion and welcome continue to tug at the very meaning of who America has been and who it will be.

Setting our nation free also requires truth-telling about our mistreatment of Mexican immigrants and other people from Central America and beyond. America's history of racial subjugation and discrimination is not simply a Black and white one; it includes brutality and racism directed at people from Mexico and across Latin America. Latinos/as in the United States now number 56.5 million, a full 18 percent of the population. Almost two-thirds are native-born. By 2050, Latinos/as will account for a third of this country's residents. Sandy Ovalle, a colleague at Sojourners, captures the ongoing impact of these often-untold truths with searing clarity: "Although we come from a multitude of identities, histories, skin colors, and cultures, we are united by so many beautiful things. We are also united by the perceived threat that we are to this nation. This threat of extermination lives in our bones and now feels much more real. We are not OK."[25]

Ovalle retells the history that "in 1848, when the US took over Indigenous and Mexican lands in the Southwest, Mexican people living in those areas were given a choice to become US citizens or leave. . . . Those who have been unable to assimilate were harassed, intimidated, or violently eliminated. For [Latino/a] people in the Southwest, particularly in Texas, this first came in the form of lynchings," beginning in the mid-nineteenth century and occurring well into the twentieth. People of Mexican descent were often accused of witchcraft, deception, cheating, or theft and lost their lives at the hands of vigilantes, local police, or the Texas Rangers, a statewide law enforcement group. "During the period of La Matanza (The Massacre) of 1915, violence against Mexican Americans and Mexicans in border towns escalated, leaving hundreds and possibly thousands of ethnic Mexicans dead." During the Great Depression, close to two million Mexicans were deported to Mexico even though roughly half were US citizens. "They were 'sent home' without due process," victims of false narratives, as many white Americans blamed them for taking jobs and benefits that "should" have gone to white Americans—never mind that the United States was the deportees' home.[26]

All of these stories—and so many others—call for a clear-eyed acknowledgment of the truth. Each calls us to correct, refute, and address biased or ahistorical teachings that whitewash our history. The only way we can move to a true Beloved Community is in telling the truth about what this country has done, including, notably, the intense racism against Asian Americans, such as that against Chinese immigrants and later the dark period of the internment of Japanese Americans during World War II. We need to tell the whole truth about persecution, discrimination, and violence toward the LGBTQ community, which includes the initial denial and resistance by President Ronald Reagan and other politicians in addressing the AIDS crisis, as well as far too many religious leaders who responded with condemnation and stigma rather than compassion and love.

Seeking the whole truth requires interrogating the histories that we have been given, requiring us to think critically and seek the truth behind what we are told. The political, religious, ethnic, and racial drivers that so often twist our histories into destructive and ahistorical narratives—whether overt or encoded—poison the pursuit of a more perfect union and just America. The Beloved Community teaches us that only by understanding, sharing, insisting on, and advocating for the whole truth can we cocreate the America we hope for.

Chapter Seven

OVERCOMING TOXIC POLARIZATION

Judging others makes us blind, whereas love is illuminating. By judging others, we blind ourselves to our own evil and to the grace which others are just as entitled to as we are. —Dietrich Bonhoeffer

Every kingdom divided against itself will be ruined, and every city or household divided against itself will not stand. —Jesus, Matthew 12:25

"FOR HEAVEN'S SAKE, 'WEAR A DAMN MASK'" WAS THE TITLE OF A PIECE I WROTE, with a heavy dose of personal exasperation, at the height of the COVID-19 pandemic. I'm not one to be profane, but I felt a sense of desperation in making the case that wearing a mask was a test of our commitment to living out the Golden Rule by protecting and loving our neighbors, as well as a civic test of advancing the common good.[1]

Recall that stretch of pandemic months. How did the act of wearing a mask become a partisan and polarizing issue in American life and politics when it was a fundamental issue of public health and, particularly for many communities of color, a matter of life and death? The simple but somehow controversial act of wearing a mask became yet another weapon in our culture wars and exposed just how polarized our nation has become along partisan and racialized lines. Hubris, denial, and selfish individualism led far too many Americans to reject public-health advice as they refused to wear a mask in public. I often wondered, If white Americans were dying at such a disproportionate rate as Black

Americans, would the resistance to mask-wearing have been so fierce in some parts of the country? Only in a hyper-polarized and partisan climate could a public-health commitment to protect ourselves and our neighbors by the simple act of masking up be transformed into a partisan issue and a statement of personal freedom.

Like many others, at the height of the pandemic I felt daily outrage and at times powerlessness in the face of the colossal failure of leadership by the Trump administration's negligent response to the coronavirus, as well as exasperation at a president failing to lead by example. According to research by the Pew Research Center, by summer 2020 mask-wearing had become a significant partisan issue. Democrats and Democratic-leaners were more likely than Republicans and Republican-leaners to say they personally wore a mask all or most of the time (76 percent vs. 53 percent).[2] But the virus didn't care about our politics or our party loyalties. And the stark reality is that universal mask-wearing could have saved thousands of lives and accelerated the reopening of schools, businesses, and the rest of the economy.

Partisan and cultural division over mask-wearing and practicing social distancing is just the tip of the iceberg of rising polarization. Polarization—so often driven and exacerbated by distrust, anger, grievance, contempt, and vitriol—has poisoned our politics and public discourse. It has become one of the greatest threats to our democracy and civic health. It tears away at the social fabric that holds our nation together and lends itself to self-perpetuating cycles that are hard to reverse. An extreme form, which I refer to as toxic polarization, is a process by which entire societies devolve and unravel. That means it is also one of the greatest threats both to a more perfect union and to building the Beloved Community. But polarization is not inevitable, and it can be reversed. The good news is that we already possess many potent antidotes and treatments.

The organization More in Common offers a clear diagnosis of the problem: "Societies are fracturing as the forces of division grow stronger, driving people apart. We are losing trust in each other and in the future. Feelings of frustration, powerlessness, and a loss of belonging are making us vulnerable to 'us versus them' stories, which turn us against each other.

Social media is magnifying the loudest and most extreme voices. A generation ago, experts claimed the forces of democracy, freedom, and progress were unstoppable. Instead, we are entering the 2020s with many of the most established democracies feeling weakened, unstable, and under increasing threat."[3]

The *Atlantic* focused its December 2019 issue on our nation's dangerous divisions; its featured article was headlined "How to Stop a Civil War." Under that provocative title, Jeffrey Goldberg provided a sobering examination of the forces working to divide the nation:

> The structural failures in our democratic system that allowed a grifter into the White House in the first place—this might be our gravest challenge. Or perhaps it is the tribalization of our politics, brought about by pathological levels of inequality, technological and demographic upheaval, and the tenacious persistence of racism. Or maybe it is that we as a people no longer seem to know who we are or what our common purpose is. . . . We don't believe that conditions in the United States today resemble those of 1850s America. But we worry that the ties that bind us are fraying at alarming speed—we are becoming contemptuous of each other in ways that are both dire and possibly irreversible.[4]

Polarization is the close cousin of division. Division in this country is the byproduct of vastly different perspectives of life in America, how we access and understand truth, and what America means and how it is experienced. Not all forms of division are negative or the same, but in polarization we meet a particularly dangerous schismatic form. Polarization is often fed by zero-sum and us-vs.-them thinking and tends to be supercharged by fear, uncertainty, and a sense of grievance. Polarization morphs into a more toxic form when cultural norms such as civility, decency, integrity, solidarity, and shared purpose atrophy and when dislike and distrust metastasize into hate or contempt for the "other." A recent American Values Survey found that eight in ten Democrats believe the Republican Party has been taken over by racists, and that eight in ten Republicans believe the Democratic Party has been taken over by socialists.[5] Harmful caricatures like these, even ones that contain some truth, make it difficult to foster dialogue, build relationships, and seek common ground.

Over time parallel and dissonant realities are bound to collide. The result will be destructive to our nation's soul. Constructing echo chambers in our media and social media shelters us from opposing points of view, which often only reinforces our own misperceptions and biases. For instance, investigative reporting by the *New York Times* has shown that local newspapers, which in the past served as a bastion of more balanced and nonpoliticized news for many Americans, are being replaced by much more partisan and propaganda-heavy alternatives. One alarming example is Maine Business Daily, founded by Brian Timpone, which the *Times* reports "is part of a fast-growing network of nearly 1,300 websites that aim to fill a void left by vanishing local newspapers across the country. Yet the network, now in all 50 states, is built not on traditional journalism but on propaganda ordered up by dozens of conservative think tanks, political operatives, corporate executives, and public-relations professionals."[6] While at first glance these sites appear to be ordinary local-news outlets, many of the stories are directed by political groups and corporate PR firms to promote a Republican candidate or a company or to smear their rivals. The *Times* reports, "While Mr. Timpone's sites generally do not post information that is outright false, the operation is rooted in deception, eschewing hallmarks of news reporting like fairness and transparency."

As a father of two sons who in just a few years will be in middle school, I'm deeply worried about the power and pull of technology and social media. I have seen firsthand the addictive and corrosive impact of misuse and overuse. I'm even more worried about the destructive impact and even existential threat that these powerful tools pose to our democracy if misused; they represent an almost ubiquitous force in supercharging toxic polarization. As the 2020 movie *The Social Dilemma* starkly reveals, we have gone from the information age to a disinformation age. In the documentary, former Google employee Tristan Harris argues that social media competes for our attention through a business model designed to keep us addicted, gathering data and using complex algorithms to predict our behavior and increase our use. The film argues that, in essence, social media has become a drug whose benign and even beneficial origins have been eclipsed by a business model driven by the profit motive and focused on advertising. Social media is designed to fuel a vicious cycle of wanting more, leaving people more anxious and fragile. Since 2011, as social media use exploded, there has been an alarming increase in depression and suicide, particularly among preteen and teenage girls. This does not seem coincidental. According to the documentary's website, a 2017 *American Journal of Epidemiology* study involving five thousand people found that "higher social media use correlated with self-reported declines in mental and physical health and life satisfaction."[7]

The danger is that the misuse of social media is fueling polarization corrosive to our democracy and detrimental to building the Beloved Community, enabling 2.7 billion users to construct their own reality and reinforce their worldview in ways that are often hard to contradict. It often amplifies hearsay, gossip, and disinformation so we don't know what is true. For instance, in the 2016 election, Russia applied the tools of social media for the nefarious purpose of sowing division and chaos into the election with the goal of bolstering one candidate and fomenting a culture war.

If everyone is entitled to their own "facts," there's no shared understanding of reality, which suffocates our ability to find common ground and break out of an us-vs.-them mentality. At worst, we could be moving toward a world in which most people believe that nothing is objectively true and no one can be trusted.

It is not easy to quantify exactly how divided and polarized America has become, though almost all surveys of these trends point in alarming directions. A recent Pew report, based on nearly ten thousand interviews, underscores the raw antagonism that now exists across political lines, despite broadly expressed desires for civility. The only common ground seems to be agreement that things are bad and getting worse. Here are a few trends reported by Pew:

- Overwhelming majorities in both political parties say that the extent of polarization is growing worse—and half of them say this is cause for concern.

- More than seven in ten Democrats and more than three in four Republicans say that disagreements with those in the other party go beyond policy differences.
- That same set says there is no longer agreement about "basic facts."
- Because politics is often carried out in alternate and competing media universes, the gulf is widening.
- Beyond facts are the lack of shared values and goals—55 percent of Republicans say Democrats are "more immoral" when compared with other Americans while 47 percent of Democrats say the same about Republicans.
- Majorities in both parties say those in the opposing party do not share their nonpolitical values and goals.[8]

The schism isn't only about differences of opinion. It's about a deficit of hope. According to the 2019 Public Religion Research Institute (PRRI) / the *Atlantic* Pluralism Survey mentioned in chapter 3, Americans are also substantially more pessimistic than in the past about the country's ability to heal its political divisions.[9] Nearly six in ten Americans say they feel pessimistic about whether Americans who hold different political views can come together and solve the country's problems. The survey also found that Americans possess extremely divergent opinions about what issues even matter.[10] As a result, elections increasingly represent a clash of worldviews rather than a contest over which party and candidates have the best ideas for addressing shared concerns and priorities.

"We the people," the aspirational union indicated in the nation's founding premise and promise, must be reimagined. It must be expanded beyond existing factions and beyond all identity groups that vie for our loyalty and attention. "Crosscutting identities—such as religious affiliations or strong ties to a location—help people come together around identities that are not polarized," says Rachel Kleinfeld, senior fellow at the Carnegie Endowment for International Peace. "Social trust is a nation's immune system. When it weakens, countries are less able to fend off or recover from all manner of ills."[11]

But there is no identifying the antidotes to toxic polarization unless we commit ourselves to better understanding what drives it. The more we consume one-sided news sources, according to More in Common, the more our views about the other side become exaggerated and mis-informed, particularly regarding those holding opposing political and ideological views.[12] Even with the vicious feedback loop between what many Americans find entertaining or informative and what is currently being offered as news or entertainment, we have far more power than we realize to short-circuit and reverse this vicious cycle. It's a power we have a responsibility to use. Affecting every area of life, this feedback loop is in politics, religion, and culture.

Toxic polarization has also infected our politics. Politicians and political parties often manufacture and exploit division to fuel their fundraising campaigns, distinguish themselves from their opponents, and gener-ate greater degrees of loyalty. Our seemingly broken two-party system increasingly favors the extremes, in part due to the growth of gerry-mandered districts and the influence of money in politics. Many mem-bers of Congress have come to distrust the motives of the other side and often show contempt for dissenting opinion. As a result, politicians too often refuse to build upon shared values and aspirations. Compro-mise has become almost taboo, with immense pressures to maintain par-tisan loyalty. Compromise—often a necessity for progress—has been cast as surrender or betrayal. Moderate Democrats and moderate Republicans have grown increasingly scarce within our political system.

These and other alarming trends are noted in *Building U.S. Resilience to Political Violence*, a gathering of insights from the field of international nonviolence and peacebuilding, which "reveals that much can be done to prevent violence and increase resilience—if leaders with influence and resources are ready to face these challenges squarely now." The study, pub-lished in December 2019, highlights "four risk factors for violence: elite factionalization, societal polarization, a rise in hate speech and rhetoric, and weakening institutions." The study notes that elite factionalization "occurs when a country's politics devolve into distinct groups engaging in winner-take-all competition to promote their own interests at the expense of the other group or the overall collective. Goldstone et al. (2010) note this is 'often accompanied by confrontational mass mobilization . . . and by the intimidation or manipulation of electoral competition . . .' further explaining that it is this 'relationship among political elites—a polarized politics of exclusive identities or ideologies, in conjunction with partially democratic institutions— . . . that most powerfully presages instability.'"[13]

Summarizing similar insights from social and political science research, Kleinfeld argues that whereas polarization was once more defined by policy differences, it has increasingly become tied to in-group or tribal identities. "Through this phenomenon, often referred to as affective polarization," Kleinfeld explains, "we change our policy views to fit those of our in-group and at worst demonstrate disgust for the other tribe. While our nation has been divided by racial animus and grievance since our nation's founding, and more starkly since the culture wars of the 1960s, these differences are not immutable. Toxic polarization has been accelerated by the rise of entrepreneurial politicians who have exploited and amplified our distrust and hatred for the other for perceived political gain, often using warlike and even violent rhetoric and eroding public confidence in democracy and truth itself."[14] President Trump was the quintessential political entrepreneur of affective polarization.

In order to combat toxic polarization, we must understand the science behind it. Over the past few years, I have come to better understand many of the ways in which our brains are hardwired for polarization. Social psychologists and neuroscientists have long known that the human brain is a powerful engine for divisions, tied in part to our innate fight-or-flight impulse and our basic needs for survival, security, and belonging. I have gained a much deeper appreciation for these insights from Andrew Hanauer, founder and CEO of the One America Movement. The organization combats polarization and builds the Beloved Community by uniting Americans from across significant religious, socioeconomic, and racial differences to work together to solve common concerns. The One America Movement responds to growing research showing that our divides are increasingly defined by *who we are*, and *not what we believe*. "While in the past forty years, our ideologies have hardly changed, we hate and distrust each other a lot more. To do this transformational work," Hanauer says, "we need to be working for redemption and reconciliation all the time." He believes that "polarization is an attack on this commitment because it leads people to believe that the only way to build the Beloved Community is to defeat the other side rather than building relationships with them."[15]

Hanauer explains that "paradoxically, identity-based conflict is much more difficult to resolve and to bridge because it is so often nonnegotiable. When identities get stacked into one mega-identity, societies move in a dangerous direction." And when everything becomes all about one identity rather than a healthy mix of identities, Hanauer notes, we increasingly feel as though we need groups to protect us. Hanauer compares combating toxic polarization to *The Matrix*, one of my favorite films, in which once you are made aware of these cognitive malfunctions, you start to see the world in a new way and begin to depolarize the way you think and act. Amid pressures and trends reinforcing singular identities, we must increasingly wrestle with how we can positively shape the norms for groups of which we are a part. Courage is required to speak out when our own side errs and fuels toxic polarization.

Disagreement on issues is common and natural and should leave room for respectful dialogue. But polarization becomes harmful when it says, "I don't know you, or you are a part of another group, so I assume the worst about you and act accordingly," says Hanauer. In this vein my actions then cause you to hate and distrust me back. As a result of this vicious cycle, instead of trying to persuade or convince people who disagree with us, we become motivated to defeat or marginalize them. Winning becomes the ultimate goal, and we grow more focused on protecting our group identity than on advancing policy goals or a set of core values.

We must actively resist the temptation to hate our enemies, particularly those who have harmed us or the ones we love. That is in part why people such as Nelson Mandela and Martin Luther King Jr. were so transformational. Mandela had twenty-seven years of his life stripped away in prison, yet upon his release he helped broker a peaceful democratic transition in South Africa while promoting reconciliation through both forgiveness and truth-telling about the atrocities committed under the system of apartheid. Dr. King, who almost lost his life when he was stabbed, was constantly under threats to his life and endured numerous days in prison—and yet he refused to let these injustices turn into hate as he preached that "love is the only force capable of transforming an enemy into a friend."[16]

Neuroscience shows that we are hardwired for polarization by various brain functions—perhaps more aptly called malfunctions. These include meta-perception,[17] motive attribution asymmetry,[18] sacred values,[19] and the halo effect[20]—key concepts that Hanauer describes in an accessible and compelling way: "Meta-perception, for instance, is how people understand external views of themselves. We are built to key in to how others perceive us. If they don't like us, our defense mechanisms jump into action and in turn we don't like them back. The problem is in degree. We often think that other groups dislike us far more than they do. As a result, we ascribe a more monolithic and extreme viewpoint to others."[21]

Motive attribution asymmetry, or misattribution, is also an issue of perception and degree. We perceive that "our side" acts only out of love and the other side acts out of hate. Once we allow ourselves to think this way, it is increasingly difficult to engage the other side. To illustrate this, Hanauer asks us to imagine our initial reaction when someone cuts us off suddenly in traffic. We will likely assume the person is mean, rude, or texting, rather than assigning a more benign motive, such as that it was a genuine mistake or that the driver is trying to get to the hospital. Two political examples of misattribution are that the other side is "trying to take away our guns" or wants to "take away our health care." Misattribution can also feed the notion that when our side messes up, we excuse it as an anomaly, but when the other side messes up, it is who they are.

Former American Enterprise Institute president Arthur Brooks, in his book *Love Your Enemies: How Decent People Can Save America from the Culture of Contempt*, also cites "motive attribution asymmetry." In Mona Charen's review of the book, she writes, "Brooks argues that Americans today are as alienated, as willing to assume the worst about the other side, as are Israelis and Palestinians. As a result, reaching solutions on matters such as gun control, health care, and religious liberty is as likely as getting to a resolution of the Israeli-Palestinian conflict." Charen quotes from Brooks's book: "While anger seeks to bring someone back into the fold, contempt seeks to exile. It attempts to mock, shame, and permanently exclude from relationships by belittling, humiliating, and ignoring.

So while anger says, 'I care about this,' contempt says, 'You disgust me. You are beneath caring about.'" Charen goes on to explain that "what Brooks calls the 'outrage industrial complex'—cable news, social media, and entertainment—feeds this mutual hostility and profits handsomely by it. For the rest of us, this diet of disdain is like acid eating away at the bonds of community."[22]

Regarding sacred values, Hanauer explains, "All of us have things we hold sacred. According to neuroscience, sacred values are processed in a different part of our brain. An extreme illustration of this would be if someone were to offer me $1,000 in exchange for my child; I would be offended and would immediately reject the proposition because my child is sacred to me. Sacred things in our lives become almost impossible for us to negotiate around. When we apply these values to politics, and as politics hinge increasingly on our identity, we tend to treat more and more things as sacred and therefore nonnegotiable." For example, if respecting the American flag is core to your identity, Hanauer argues, then Colin Kaepernick kneeling during the national anthem can feel incontrovertibly wrong, regardless of his motives or ultimate cause.[23]

"Our brains make assumptive leaps that we don't even realize we are making," says Hanauer, describing the halo effect. "If we like something or someone, our brain assumes that things related to that person or thing are compatible. When we vote for and support a politician, our brains want to believe that what the politician does is in line with our values. Subsequently, if we hear that politician being attacked, it can feel as though that attack is a personal one on us."

By paying attention to how our brains function—and so often malfunction—we are able to avoid the ways we are wired for division and the inadvertent spread of toxic polarization. While it is true that we are deeply divided as a nation and that toxic polarization seems to be getting worse, there is still good news based on many things that unite us.

Before the 2020 election, More in Common conducted polling research that was reported in *American Fabric: Identity and Belonging*.[24] The pollsters interviewed a broad and diverse cross section of Americans about their perceptions of the country, sense of belonging, trusted sources of information, and conceptions of responsibility to the country. The poll found that "Americans [felt] divided and concerned, but they [did] not feel powerless." Fully 94 percent of Americans said that the country was very divided politically, and 92 percent were worried for the future. However, just 21 percent said they believe that citizens' decisions and actions have little influence on how society works. And while 70 percent said that "some" or "major changes" are needed to "live up to the principle that all people are created equal," ultimately most reported feeling glad to be from the United States. Fully 74 percent said they are proud and 80 percent grateful to be American—majority views that held across genders, races, regions, parties, and education levels. The study also found that 70 percent of respondents believe that significant progress remains necessary in order to live up to America's aspired principle of equality. However, the clear majority—Americans across races—said they believe that this country is freer than any other country and that voting, tolerance of others' beliefs, and learning our history are important to being a good American. The report concluded,

> This sense of shared values and beliefs is so central to American identity that historians have described America as a "creedal nation." As More in Common's research found in 2018, Americans are united in believing that commitment to freedom and equality is important for being American, with more than nine in ten recognizing the relevance of those values. But as the United States enters 2021, it feels far from fully realizing this vision. . . . Entrenched polarization has left us feeling that we share less in common with each other and that ever more parts of our national fabric are stretched and worn thin. After a pandemic, a historic movement against police brutality, and a contentious presidential election, the country feels exhausted—not least because each event appeared to inflame rather than abate existing political conflict.

In this context, forging a more shared American identity feels daunting, yet possible—and necessary.

One place where I've been able to engage in powerful connections around both a shared American and a shared Christian identity has been the Great Objects Gathering. Begun in 2009 by Clapham Group principal Mark Rodgers, the gathering has brought together Christian leaders from across the political spectrum for conversations around the intersection of faith and social concern. My sense is that these deep conversations and fellowship are made possible because the diverse participants are more committed to their mutual identity in Christ than to their party affiliation or ideological leanings. The gathering of influential leaders is meant to be a continuation of the legacy of William Wilberforce, a leader of the movement to end slavery in England. In the eighth Great Objects convening, held in Alexandria, Virginia, in 2019, the group engaged in a candid discussion around polarization, exploring to what extent we have contributed to it, have been affected by it, and can play a more proactive role in combating it. After two days of rich and often intense dialogue, we chose partners from the group, making a commitment to pray for them and reach out to check in on them in the future. We also engaged in corporate worship. While the gathering only lasted two-and-a-half days, it fostered deep bonds built on a shared love for Jesus and a desire to be more faithful in our Christian walk and witness.

A growing number of cross-partisan initiatives are also working to bridge the chasm of partisanship and polarization. Since 2020, I have participated in one such effort called Patriots and Pragmatists (P&P). Mike Berkowtiz, one of P&P's cofounders shared with me that "In early 2017, recognizing a gap in cross-partisan convening spaces devoted to the underlying challenges facing American democracy and a lack of networks for individual funders interested in engaging on these issues, he and Rachel Pritzker launched P&P." The effort "organizes funders, organizational leaders, and opinion influencers across the political spectrum whose allegiance to American democracy supersedes their partisan identities. P&P creates the convening space for such individuals to build strong relationships, learn together, and take common actions." What began as an experiment has evolved organically to become a vital network and convening space for the democracy movement and a crucial piece of infrastructure for this emerging field.[25]

P&P's statement of principles provides a blueprint for democratic principles and governance. Berkowitz shared,

P&P members hail from across the political spectrum. We call ourselves Republicans, Democrats, and independents, progressives, moderates, and conservatives. We cherish our right to disagree about the issues of the day, but we put our country and its ideals ahead of party affiliation or political identity. We are united by a concern about the future of our democratic republic, and we are willing to work together to preserve, revitalize, and reimagine threatened democratic norms and institutions. We treasure the Constitution of the United States and the inalienable rights it guarantees. . . . We are citizens, not subjects; to build a more perfect union we must participate purposefully in civic life. P&P members debate with ideas, not insults, and know that no one has a monopoly on the truth. These are the beliefs that unite us and that together we pledge to defend.

These are the very ground rules and norms that could help depolarize our politics at every level, particularly in Congress, where the challenges of toxic polarization have been most acute. While I have sometimes disagreed with other P&P members, I have appreciated the participants' deep commitment to disagree without impugning other participants' motives or character and to engage in ways that enable us to learn from and be changed by each other's perspectives, expertise, and convictions. I've been impressed by several of the conservative participants, many of whom were part of the Never Trump movement at great personal risk to their reputations, careers, and safety. It takes integrity and fortitude to resist the contradictions and immorality that you see within your own group or tribe, in this case your own ideological movement and political party. This type of courageous dissent serves as an important antibody to the rise of toxic polarization within the bloodstream of our body politic.

One of the most potent antidotes to toxic polarization is an intentional journey together to solve common problems. When we work together to advance a shared moral vision, we gain an understanding of how we might go forward as a nation. In 2018, for example, the One America Movement brought together a conservative evangelical church in West Virginia with a synagogue and a mosque in the Washington, DC, area. Many people in DC feel as though they live in a bubble and that a rural West Virginia town just ninety minutes away represents a different world. Joel Rainey, lead pastor at Covenant Church in Shepherdstown,

West Virginia, and Aaron Alexander and Lauren Holtzblatt, co-senior rabbis at Adas Israel Congregation in DC, reflected on this work. "With our politics today often defined by our opposition to or support of this one individual [Trump], it's hard not to feel that the divide here may be too wide to bridge. But we disagree," they wrote in an op-ed published in the *Washington Post*.[26] Not only do our divides harm us in terms of civil dialogue, they explained, but

> overall, life expectancy [in the country] is going down, thanks almost entirely to our devastating opioid epidemic. So rather than talk about our differences, demonize each other, or ignore each other, we have decided to take a different path. We're going to act together. In partnership with community leaders, health officials, other faith communities in Washington and West Virginia, and the national organization the One America Movement, our two communities are rolling up their sleeves to work together to fight opioids in West Virginia's Eastern Panhandle. West Virginia leads the nation in overdose death rates . . . [which] was nearly triple the national average. . . . While opioids thrive on shame and stigma—each family is afraid to admit to their community that their child or loved one is addicted—polarization thrives on the unspoken fear of being stigmatized by our own "tribe" for daring to reach out across divides.

Together these leaders and their congregants visited clinics, cared for people suffering from opioid addiction, and built deep relationships through interaction and exchanges. "Acting together isn't important only because we have much to act on," the faith leaders wrote. "It also helps us create new identities together. The teamwork instills a sense of 'we' where before there was only 'us' and 'them.'"

Our faith traditions provide potent antidotes to toxic polarization. We are reminded by faith leaders such as Father Richard Rohr that we can overcome toxic polarization only when we are willing to break out of overly dualistic or binary thinking. Rohr, founder of the Center for Action and Contemplation, notes that dualistic thinking often sees the world, including our politics and our faith, in black and white terms that often lend themselves to all-or-nothing thinking. "One reason we have failed to understand so much of the teaching of Jesus, much less follow it, is because we try to understand with dualistic minds," Rohr explains.[27] Rohr calls Jesus "the first nondual religious thinker of the West," and said that Jesus "modeled and exemplified nonduality more than giving us any systematic teaching on it." Rohr posits that "the dualistic mind . . . knows by comparison, opposition, and differentiation. It uses descriptive words like good/evil, pretty/ugly, smart/stupid, not realizing there may be a hundred degrees between the two ends of each spectrum. Dualistic thinking works well for the sake of simplification and conversation, but not for the sake of truth or the immense subtlety of actual personal experience."

We tend to settle for easy answers, Rohr says, leaving deep perception to poets, philosophers, and prophets. Yet Rohr argues that "depth and breadth of perception should be the primary arena for all authentic religion. How else could we possibly search for God?"

Jesus continually talks about mercy, forgiveness, and grace. As each of these is truly experienced, Rohr explains, they succeed in breaking down dualism. If we experience being loved when we are unworthy, being forgiven when we've done something wrong, we are moved into nondual thinking.[28] You move from what Rohr calls "meritocracy, quid-pro-quo thinking, to the huge ocean of grace, where you stop counting, you stop calculating." Rohr says: "That for me is the task of much of the entire spiritual life of a mystic or a saint—they fall deeper and deeper into that ocean of grace, and stop all the dang counting of 'how much has been given to me,' 'how much I deserve.'" Entirely too much focus is paid to counting and deserving and earning—what Rohr calls entitlement thinking. When you're trapped inside the counting mind, Rohr says, "you're going to have the kind of angry country we have today, where you're just looking for who to blame, who to hate, who to shoot. It's reaching that level."

In politics, there have long been debates around purism and pragmatism, moderation and extremism, incrementalism and revolutionary change. These can serve as healthy tensions. But false binaries that prevent us from engaging the other and seeking common ground and, where necessary, compromise are false choices that often keep us from building bridges. "We have no permanent enemies or friends, only permanent interests" is a mantra often attributed to the grandfather of community organizing, Saul Alinsky. What's missing from this analysis is that we also have resilient values that factor into the equation for how we pursue change. When we start with shared values, we open new possibilities for identifying shared interests. This helps us to calibrate and de-escalate our real and perceived divisions.

I witnessed these principles in action early in my career. In the early days of HIV/AIDS, the disease was associated almost exclusively with the gay community. As a result, it stirred strong ideological differences around the use of condoms and sexuality. Later, as AIDS became an increasingly global crisis, most acutely in southern Africa, I worked alongside others to build a big-tent coalition to help transform America's response to the AIDS pandemic. During this time I observed that many progressive organizations had reason to distrust the George W. Bush administration, including over the decision to go to war in Iraq, which I had also opposed. Despite this polarized political environment, many of us sought to build common ground, enlisting and working alongside conservative allies to help persuade the Bush administration to launch a groundbreaking initiative, which later became the President's Emergency Plan for AIDS Relief—one of the defining achievements of US global leadership, which has helped to save more than 13 million lives and reverse the AIDS pandemic in Africa. If leaders and organizations had become overly entrenched in their positions and refused to compromise around prevention measures, the enterprise would have failed. What resulted was a joint commitment to support abstinence and faithful monogamy where possible and culturally appropriate, while increasing access to condoms for those who chose to engage in sex.

It would be an understatement to say that ACT UP, Health GAP, World Vision, and the Catholic Church—let alone Franklin Graham and Samaritan's Purse—did not see eye-to-eye on response to these and other issues. And while not all of these organizations worked closely together, they did agree on a détente and on taking a big-tent approach that helped mobilize broad political support behind bold US leadership from both sides of the aisle. This was made possible in part because they didn't impugn the motives behind those who had different approaches—which allowed a moral imperative to save lives to supersede many other sharp differences, including around contraception and homosexuality.

People of faith possess powerful spiritual resources to combat toxic polarization. In these chapters, we've already met some people and organizations who have derived tools for this work from the Hebrew Bible and the Christian scriptures. In the pages to come, we'll meet more of those seeking to apply the concept of *imago dei*—the declaration that every person is made in the image of God. We'll encounter those who look to the New Testament and Jesus's call to love God and love our neighbors. And we'll explore the letters of the apostle Paul, who taught that in Jesus there is no division, no toxic polarization—because in Christ there is neither Jew nor gentile, neither slave nor free person, neither male nor female (Galatians 3:28).

Our identity as people of faith should eclipse every other identity we have—partisanship, ideology, race, gender, and more. Those of us who understand ourselves to be saved by grace recognize that our salvation is not in any group identity but through our relationship with Christ. As people of faith and conscience, we have the tools to combat and overcome the toxic polarization that is too often fueled by manufactured divisions, false binaries, and us/them thinking.

In one of my favorite sermons of Martin Luther King Jr., he preaches from the apostle Paul's call "Do not conform any longer to the patterns of this world, but be transformed by the renewing of your mind" (Romans 12:2). According to King's remixed version, "If our world is to be saved from its pending doom, it will come not through the complacent adjustment of the conforming majority but through the creative maladjustment of a nonconforming minority."[29] Being creatively maladjusted to toxic polarization is increasingly a test of faith and of our commitment to preserving our democracy. We too must be creatively maladjusted to the seductive and addictive forces that fuel toxic polarization. In so doing, over time there is the promise of bridging and healing so many of our nation's most intractable and bitter divisions. The question for us now is whether we will courageously engage our faith and our wills to do so and, in the process, create essential space for building the Beloved Community.

Chapter Eight

REDEEMING PATRIOTISM

Patriotism is when love of your own people comes first; nationalism, when hate for people other than your own comes first.
—Charles de Gaulle

It's been said that racism is so American that when we protest racism, some assume we're protesting America. —Beyoncé Knowles

THE QUESTION "DO YOU LOVE YOUR COUNTRY?" CAN BE USED BOTH AS A BADGE OF honor and as a cudgel for division. Patriotism, or love of country, can be a glue that contributes to a more perfect union or it can be a cancer that kills the very cells that make the union possible. Patriotism comes in many forms. Its most destructive, often nationalistic forms erode the very foundation upon which the Beloved Community is built and suffocate efforts to form a more perfect union. As a result, redeeming patriotism represents a vital part of creating the atmosphere in which a more perfect union and the Beloved Community can breathe.

Soon after its release in 2015, the Broadway musical *Hamilton* became a smash hit and a cultural phenomenon. Even though the story of our nation's founding is more than two hundred years old, the themes of the musical are timeless and relevant. In brilliant fashion, writer and producer Lin-Manuel Miranda managed to recast the story of America's birth through the life of one of the nation's most unsung founding fathers, Alexander Hamilton. With the lyrical power of hip-hop and the spoken word, the musical retells the story of our nation's founding in a way that resonates with Americans of all backgrounds. The broad popularity of *Hamilton* signals that many Americans yearn for a more honest and inspiring rendition of our history told in a contemporary fashion.

In 2018, I had the opportunity to see the musical when it premiered in Washington, DC. By this time, I had already listened to the soundtrack enough that I had almost every song memorized. Finally attending the live musical was riveting—in particular, seeing a cast that mirrored the racial diversity of modern-day America play our nation's founders, who were almost entirely white and male. In a thought-provoking way, *Hamilton* inspires a deeper pride in America without triumphalism, and with edifying truth-telling. It brings to life the long-standing fights and paradoxes of our nation's past that persist in our present. Daveed Diggs, the actor who played Thomas Jefferson in the original cast, captures this. "Putting brown people at the center of the story, you are saying we built this country too," Diggs said. "If you watch this musical and you feel a sense of pride inspired by the America that you see, you should be inspired to take action to make what you see become true in real life."[1]

For America to realize its fullest potential, the musical reminds us, we must redefine and reclaim a healthier version of patriotism that must always be tied to the project of building a more just and inclusive America. This requires overcoming the temptations of nationalism and embracing a more honest rendition of our history.

Nationalism is an unhealthy and often dangerous perversion of patriotism. When patriotism starts to bleed into nationalism, it becomes poisonous and destructive. A healthy patriotism is animated by a love for one's country and an ongoing commitment to realize the country's deepest ideals. In the context of the United States, this includes an abiding belief in equal justice under the law and a commitment to liberty and justice for all. In contrast, nationalism is often animated by a hatred for and fear of the other. Any "patriotism" that is based on a hierarchy of human value, viewing and treating some lives as more valuable than others, easily devolves into destructive nationalism.

Destructive nationalism is often promulgated through fearmongering and mistruth, conflating patriotism with xenophobia and a tolerance of or appeals to white supremacy. A patriotism that is blind and ahistorical poisons us all and, at worst, reasserts the lie that some Americans are the "true Americans" and that some Americans are worth more than others.

For example, on Independence Day 2020, then president Trump casti-
gated people who sought the removal of Confederate flags and monuments as left-wing extremists who are not "trying to better America, but
to end America." Later, in his speech at the Republican National Convention, Trump inveighed, "In the left's backward view, they do not see
America as the most free, just and exceptional nation on earth. Instead,
they see a wicked nation that must be punished for its sins. . . . If the left
gains power they will demolish the suburbs, confiscate your guns and
appoint justices who will wipe away your Second Amendment and other
constitutional freedoms."[2] These incendiary comments exemplify how
Trump dipped into the deep well of white resentment, fear, and anxiety,
equating critique of America's faults and sins as a betrayal of patriotism
rather than an affirmation of the ideals that bind America together.

When patriotism is based on a claim to "soil"—an entitled connection to land—and "blood"—which so often shows up in normalizing and
privileging whiteness—it easily devolves into a destructive nationalism.
By its very nature, an appeal to soil and blood rests on exclusion and
superiority. The lonelier and more isolated people become, the stronger the allure of destructive nationalism becomes, as does the absolute
embrace of America's myths of being a chosen, innocent, and Christian
nation. This leads to increasingly exclusionary and self-righteous forms
of nationalism, relying on falsehoods and distortions that blind us to our
faults while exacerbating a mentality that finds fault in others.

According to Jill Lepore, "In the context of nationalism, protecting
national pride is paramount. Thus, any criticism of the nation's abuses or
shortcomings, particularly those that are directed at the dominant group,
immediately become a personal attack on national pride and identity. In
a similar fashion, in identity politics, protecting identity groups becomes
paramount, thus any criticism of a particular identity group becomes an
attack on all. When pitted against the politics of identity, our country
risks further devolving into a contest of blame and grievance."[3]

The rise of destructive nationalism is not just an American phenomenon; it has become a global contagion. "The end of the Cold War
didn't kill nationalism," notes Lepore. "Global trade didn't kill nationalism. Immigration reform didn't kill nationalism. The internet didn't
kill nationalism. Instead, arguably, all of these developments only stoked

nationalism."[4] And the COVID-19 pandemic further fanned the flames of nationalism as many countries became more nativist, protectionist, and xenophobic in response.

In recent decades, destructive nationalism combined with ethnic or tribal hatred ravaged Bosnia and incited a genocide in Rwanda. More recently, leaders stoking destructive nationalism have grown into positions of greater influence and power, including Vladimir Putin in Russia, Recep Tayyip Erdoğan in Turkey, Viktor Orbán in Hungary, Jaroslaw Kaczynski in Poland, Jair Bolsonaro in Brazil, and Rodrigo Duterte in the Philippines, among others.

For Christians, the cross wrapped in the American flag, or any flag, is dangerous. Many Christian theologies in America promote a "God is on our side" mentality that conflates and confuses the aims of the church with the aims of the state, just as across the globe heretical religious ideologies have undergirded and fueled nationalism. We must resist trying to co-opt God into a political party or into our narrow national interests. We are a nation under God; we sometimes act as though we are a nation in which God is under us. We are called to always remember our source. As the Gospel of John puts it, "for God so loved the world that he gave us his only begotten Son" (3:16). Nowhere in scripture can we find justification for a nationalistic version of "for God so loved America." Faith also can't be reduced purely to politics. As Jim Wallis regularly puts it, "Our faith should inform our politics, and not the other way around." Nor can or should faith be completely apolitical, as our faith has profound social, political, and economic implications for our lives.

For many in America, part of what has made Christian nationalism so seductive is its long history. Since the time of the Roman emperor Constantine, there has been a deep history of fusing church and state. Christians are still trying to fully recover our prophetic zeal and independence, compromised when in 312 CE Constantine converted to Christianity, then issued an edict legalizing Christianity in the Roman Empire. In the process, Constantine co-opted the church and fused the aims and vices of the Roman Empire with the Christian movement, initiating the transition to the era of "Christian Empire."[5] Christianity moved from its marginalized status as a persecuted countercultural movement to occupying a central place in the corridors of power. The closer Christians got to Rome, the further they moved from Jesus, who had been crucified by Roman authorities for treason. Since that time, the temptation for Christians has remained to conflate religious power with political power.

The call to the Beloved Community is a steadfast resistance to blind allegiance to any particular political ideology or party and a return to embracing the radical and transformational social and political implications of following our faith. In his seminal 1949 book, *Jesus and the Disinherited*, theologian Howard Thurman points out what he calls "the three hounds of hell" that track the disinherited: fear, hate, and hypocrisy.[6] Through these three forces, Thurman—a great mystic and a mentor to Martin Luther King Jr. and other civil rights leaders—presciently named the foundation of destructive nationalism. Rooted in a fear of the other, nationalism mutates into hatred that justifies and reinforces fear. The combustible combination of fear and hate leads to a dangerous phenomenon that French philosopher René Girard calls the scapegoating mechanism.[7] Scapegoating "resolves" conflict by uniting against an arbitrary other who is excluded and blamed for political and national chaos around us. In our current context, this can be seen in immigrants being blamed for people's economic hardship and sense of dislocation. Data points to another story: Statistically, immigrants make positive contributions to the economy, rarely take jobs that others seek or covet, and often take jobs that many see as less desirable. Despite evidence to the contrary, scapegoating mechanisms often lead people to blame the poor for their own predicament, as though there must be poor choices or character deficiencies that led to their poverty. This scapegoating and the biases and false assumptions behind it have directly led to Black and brown Americans being targeted, considered violent, treated as threats, overincarcerated, and murdered at the hands of police. These are just some examples of the scapegoating mechanism at work.

A passionate commitment to living out our nation's best ideals and fulfilling our nation's most sacred promises is built on something entirely different from nationalism. Rather than blind loyalty to a nation that is rooted in fear, redeeming patriotism starts from a posture of steadfast love for community and country. This is not a demeaning love requiring superiority to others or a sentimental love that ignores people's hurts and pain. What makes a nation strong and worthy of pride is an aspirational and resilient love that values and celebrates the pursuit of shared ideals for the common good.

Redeeming patriotism must be rooted in a love, to borrow from the words of Paul, that seeks to "overcome evil with good" (Romans 12:21). Love of country must be resilient and mature enough to identify and celebrate what is good while not denying those parts of our history or within our present reality that are harmful and evil.

Redeeming patriotism understands and even celebrates that those who protest and critique America are often demonstrating the deepest expression of patriotism. In helping to lift up a mirror to force this country to confront and correct its own contradictions and shortcomings, they offer America the opportunity to right wrongs and to more fully realize its promise and ideals. Thus, a healthy form of patriotism insists on both critique and correction for a country to grow and change as we strive toward a more perfect union. Theodore Johnson echoes this sentiment in a *New York Times Magazine* article about Black patriotism, arguing, as the subtitle puts it, that "for Black Americans, loving the country and criticizing it have always been inseparable." He writes, "For a people who loved a nation that did not love them back, a new brand of patriotism was required—expansive enough for anger and questioning of the nation as well as adoration and respect. Political psychologists refer to this as constructive patriotism, and have found that it leads to increased civic participation, at times in demonstration of dissatisfaction with the country and at times in reclamation of its principles."[8]

The More in Common research finds that the real gap in patriotism is not among the races but between political ideologies. Overall, the study finds that conservatives tend to define America by its perceived strengths and that progressives tend to emphasize its perceived weaknesses.[9] Johnson rightly points out that "Black Americans, of course, do both. Black patriotism does not hold that America is irredeemably racist—it asks if America is interested in redemption. It is forward-looking and informed by history, meshing optimism about the nation's prospects with a realism about its struggles with racial equality."[10] Yes, Black Americans have long practiced redemptive patriotism as a matter of both pride and survival, and all of America can learn from this inspiring witness.

Redeeming patriotism requires moral courage. When Colin Kaepernick first took a knee in protest of police brutality and the murder of Black lives, he did so alone. Soon, other athletes took a knee as well. And in 2020, after protests erupted across the country and around the world in response to the gruesome murder of Floyd, NFL commissioner Roger Goodell experienced a change of heart and publicly embraced the Black Lives Matter cause. He was joined by NASCAR, which banned Confederate flags at its events after the lone Black driver, Bubba Wallace, spoke out with courage and clarity. Major corporations including Amazon and Walmart embraced the mantra, along with millions of white people, seemingly for the first time. But imagine what could have happened if Goodell had exercised greater moral leadership much earlier in response to Kaepernick and others who took a knee. Imagine if a beloved American sport had generated honest dialogue about racialized policing and policy brutality. In the absence of moral leadership from the league and so many other organizations, the focus turned to whether players had the right to kneel, rather than to a courageous dialogue with fans about why so many players felt compelled to protest in this public way.

Redeeming patriotism also requires putting the common good and one's oath of office to work in service of the Constitution over the narrow pursuit of purely partisan agendas or interests. Civil servants and political appointees who served as whistleblowers under the Trump administration or who were willing to defy a president of their own party to protect the Constitution and defend the legitimate election results exhibited a redeemed patriotism. This included Chris Krebs, the director of the Cybersecurity and Infrastructure Security Agency, who was fired by Trump after acting with integrity by contradicting the baseless claims of widespread fraud in the 2020 election, stating in a press release that the election was "the most secure in American history. . . . There is no evidence that any voting system deleted or lost votes, changed votes, or was in any way compromised."[11] A redeemed patriotism was also shown by Brad Raffensperger, Georgia's Republican secretary of state, who, despite inordinate pressure by Trump and other Republican leaders to discredit and overturn the narrow Biden victory in his state, defended the legitimacy of Georgia's electoral process.

To counteract and cure the cancer of destructive nationalism, we must become more vocal about our love for America even alongside our critique. In 2020, with the coronavirus crisis and the police murders of Breonna Taylor, George Floyd, and others, this became an exceptional challenge—as communities of color and Indigenous communities were infected and killed by the virus at a disproportionate rate and the whole world witnessed the sheer depravity of Derek Chauvin's white knee crushing the breath out of Floyd's life for over nine excruciating minutes. And yet even in the face of these and other struggles, love for America and its ideals is something I embrace and try to share.

America, with its vibrancy, ingenuity, and grit. This country, with the resiliency of the American spirit. America, where at our best we have defended human rights and sowed seeds of democracy around the world—even if at times done unevenly or counterproductively. America, I love your multiculturalism and diversity, where you can see almost the entire world reflected in so many of our cities. America, I love that you have provided refuge and solace for some of the world's most persecuted and oppressed people, even if this commitment has been halting. America, I love the genius of your entrepreneurship and inventiveness, the scholarship and excellence of American higher learning. America, I love the beauty and breadth of your landscapes—from the rugged alpine mountains of the Pacific Northwest to the sandy, sun-scorched beaches of California and Florida to the awesome grandeur of Yellowstone and the Grand Canyon to the breathtaking glory of the Rockies and the bustling cosmopolitan cities of the Midwest and Northeast. America, I love the music and art forms you have invented, the brilliance of jazz, hip-hop, rock-and-roll, country, and Go-Go—the often-unheralded music out of my own Washington, DC. America, I love your pioneering democratic system of checks and balances, divided government, and constitutional rights. And despite your major setbacks, I love your onward march toward forming a more perfect union and becoming a more inclusive and just democracy. These are just some of the reasons to preserve this country, to celebrate it, to strengthen it.

In building the Beloved Community, one way to redeem patriotism is to look at that which holds primacy in the Christian tradition, the sacrament of communion. There we are offered some timeless insights.

Communion is a shared sacrament that unites Christians across a vast diversity of denominations and doctrines. Those who take communion are instructed by the words of Jesus, who taught his followers to first search themselves and repent for anything that has separated them from being in right relationship with God, one another, and creation. Communion calls us to remember who we are and whose we are as we engage in corporate repentance and rededication to God's word and will.

In a similar vein, for a country that has fallen woefully short of its ideals and promises, acknowledgment and repentance for past wrongs forms a crucial starting point for transformation and for developing right relationship with one another. This is not about navel gazing or national self-loathing, but instead it is an ever-present call to strive to form the Beloved Community. Repenting for our failures allows us to create more authentic space for that more perfect union to be realized, to celebrate the ideals that make America worth loving and honoring.

Redeeming patriotism requires communicating our love for the best of America's ideals and aspirations. It requires understanding that the right to critique America is part of the brilliance of America. It requires making America's ideals become real for all. It requires that which communion offers: repentance, restoration within one's community, and a willingness to change. Redeeming patriotism requires greater willingness to have courageous and civil conversations about the very ideals that make us love America. It refuses pointless arguments over who loves America more. Redeeming patriotism requires rejecting the false and dangerous idol of destructive nationalism and its often-seen companion of Christian nationalism, which feed on our attachment to blood and soil rather than to shared ideals and the common aspiration to build an America in which everyone is valued and respected and can thrive.

Part Three

BEATITUDES OF THE BELOVED COMMUNITY

IN THE SERMON ON THE MOUNT, JESUS CAPTURES WHAT CHRISTIAN DISCIPLESHIP requires and how Christians are to stand out from the rest of society. He offers a set of timeless and countercultural values and commitments known as the "beatitudes" that call on his followers to be salt and light for the rest of the world. The beatitudes come from the Christian tradition, but they resonate with the teachings from other faith traditions as well. Each beatitude starts with the words "Blessed are," such as "Blessed are the meek," "Blessed are the poor in spirit," and so on. In other words, as a result of living out these core values, we will be blessed and we will bless others.

In a similar fashion and with the aim of building on these values, I offer a series of beatitudes central to building the Beloved Community. Together they form a more holistic vision of what a preferred future for the nation and world would look like if the Beloved Community became our core operating system.

In the first part of the book, we looked at our need for the Beloved Community and how it represents a unifying and transformative moral vision for the country and even the world. In the second part, we explored the things that stand in the way of building that vision and building blocks for how to overcome them. In Part III, we turn to how we can build and realize that vision practically. Each chapter details a fundamental value of the Beloved Community. Each beatitude chapter also describes the spiritual lies and distorted narratives that must be replaced by new, redemptive narratives and truths.

Each chapter also highlights people and organizations that have applied that chapter's beatitude to some of the most pressing issues we face. It's important to see illustrative and real examples of how the Beloved Community is being enacted in creative, courageous, and transformational ways in communities across the nation. I hope these stories help supercharge a growing movement of sharing, adapting, and scaling up the Beloved-Community revolution that is already underway.

We are in what feels like a "kairos" time, a propitious moment for decision or action that opens the door to transformational change. Kairos moments often begin with widespread awakening, which opens the door to a deeper reckoning with long-standing, entrenched injustices. The challenge and opportunity in front of us is to catalyze often disconnected and small-scale efforts into stronger movements that generate what Malcolm Gladwell famously calls a tipping point—in public opinion, personal behavior, community practice, and ultimately public policy.

In my Pepperdine course, the final assignment I give my students is to interview religious and faith-based organizations working on opposite sides of a contemporary public-policy issue. In the process, they tackle pressing wedge issues in American politics, including abortion, climate change, immigration, criminal justice, domestic poverty, and health care. In their presentations they analyze policy issues through lenses such as the founding myths shaping America, insights on biblical justice, religious freedom, and church-state issues. At the close of the presentation, they offer prescriptions around how religious actors can best play a leadership role in building common ground to advance concrete policy solutions.

In many ways this is an overly ambitious assignment, and asking college students to "solve" these issues may seem unfair. Still, the students rise to the challenge, and I'm impressed with their insights and prescriptions. I end each class by reminding them how religious actors have so often played a transformational role in changing public opinion and fueling social movements that have changed society and politics. Each time I listen to student visions and reflect on the campaigns and movements in my life, I realize how much faith I still have in the incredible power people of faith and conscience possess to bridge many of the divides in our nation and to co-create a radically more just and inclusive

America. I'll share some of those stories in the chapters ahead, providing glimpses of the Beloved Community breaking through.

Building the Beloved Community is as much about the journey as about a destination and a preferred future. Let's journey to that future, that destination, together.

Chapter Nine

EQUALITY: THE IMAGO DEI IMPERATIVE

Will the US ever be us? Lord willing! / For now we know, the new Jim Crow. / They stop, search, and arrest our souls. / Police and policies patrol philosophies of control. A cruel hand taking hold. / We let go to free them so we can free us. / America's moment to come to Jesus. —Common

[Blacks] have proceeded from a premise that equality means what it says, and they have taken white Americans at their word when they talked of it as an objective. But most whites in America in 1967, including many persons of goodwill, proceed from the premise that equality is a loose expression for improvement. White America is not even psychologically organized to close the gap—essentially it seeks only to make it less painful and less obvious but in most respects to retain it. Most of the abrasions between [Blacks] and white liberals arise from this fact. —Martin Luther King Jr.

We hold these truths to be self-evident, that all men are created equal, that they are endowed by their Creator with certain unalienable Rights, that among these are Life, Liberty, and the pursuit of Happiness. —Thomas Jefferson

JEFFERSON'S TIMELESS WORDS FROM THE DECLARATION OF INDEPENDENCE ENCOMPASS both the beautiful promise and the ugly betrayal of America. We can easily forget that when these words were written, they applied only to white, landholding men. Since then, America has been engaged in an ongoing struggle to redefine the "we" in this promise and extend the full meaning of these words to everyone—including women, African Americans, Native Americans, and other people of color, and most recently to lesbian, gay, bisexual, and transgender people. Despite the painful ways we have fallen tragically short of living up to this creed, the creed is still profoundly inspirational and aspirational, capturing the depth and breadth of what equality means and requires. The word *equality* takes on many different meanings and definitions. As with the term *social justice*, our interpretations of *equality* can be so heavily loaded that the word generates confusion and controversy. Equality can also be so misunderstood and watered down that it becomes almost meaningless as a concept. Foundational to the Beloved Community is a newfound understanding of what equality means and what building a radically more equal America will require. In chapter 4, I offered a baseline goal for equality in which neither privilege nor punishment is tied to race, ethnicity, gender, religious belief, or sexual orientation and gender identity—a goal I believe most Americans would embrace. While a high bar, this goal helps us to actualize America's creed for all Americans. It also serves as a guiding star for shaping policy and political decisions the nation needs to make.

The Black Lives Matter movement galvanized a cultural shift, a potential breaking point in our nation's history. George Floyd in many ways became our generation's Emmett Till, a fourteen-year-old who, in 1955, became a symbol of racial terror when he was brutally killed after being falsely accused of whistling at a white woman in Mississippi. Coverage in Black magazines and newspapers, including *Jet* magazine's photo of Till's open casket and mutilated body, sparked outrage and moral courage to resist the evils of Jim Crow segregation and racial oppression. In a similar fashion, the brutal police murder of Floyd, and subsequent mass protests in the midst of the coronavirus pandemic, laid bare in stunning and stark terms to the world what the Black community and others have known in struggle—that liberty and justice are not and never have been equal for Black people or other people of color.

Despite this partial awakening, one of the greatest challenges remains changing perceptions of whether there is even a problem with racial injustice and systemic racism. These perceptions continue to be heavily tied to our social location, racial background, and partisan leanings. According to the Public Religion Research Institute (PRRI) / the *Atlantic* Pluralism Survey,[1] 42 percent of Americans believe that "discrimination against whites is as big a problem as discrimination against blacks," with approximately two-thirds of Republicans agreeing with this statement. The battles over civil rights and advances that were attempted in past decades to equalize the playing field, most visibly through affirmative-action programs, generated a backlash among many white Americans, particularly among conservatives. But I'm confident that if we asked those 42 percent of Americans whether they would rather be Black than white, if they were honest with themselves they would quickly balk, as they unconsciously recognize that opportunities and privileges still tilt heavily toward white America.

Sadly, recent nationwide protests over racial injustice have had very disparate impacts on shaping public opinion. A PRRI survey found that "in the wake of the killing of George Floyd by a police officer, the attitudes of Democrats and religiously unaffiliated Americans have shifted significantly, but there has been no movement among Republicans and white evangelical Protestants." For example, as of June 2020, approximately eight in ten Republicans and seven in ten white evangelical Protestants continue to say that the recent killings of Black men by police are isolated incidents, rather than part of a pattern of how police treat African Americans—views that were roughly the same as in 2018.[2] A Barna survey echoed these results, finding that self-identified Christians who say their faith is very important in their lives are no more likely to acknowledge racial injustice than they were before Floyd's murder. The survey actually found a significant increase in the percentage of practicing Christians who say race is "not at all" a problem in the US.[3]

Part of the reason for this alarming disconnect is the lack of real relationship between Black and white worlds. It is also due to a sense of grievance and economic insecurity gripping many disaffected white working-class and middle-class Americans. Many white Americans feel left behind, misunderstood, and resentful about being stuck in the quicksand of stagnant wages and vanishing economic mobility. Those gripped by grievance and a false sense of entitlement must be inspired and persuaded to see that an America in which neither punishment nor privilege is tied to factors such as race or ethnicity is an America more aligned with their values and where they can also thrive.

President Trump's "Bible photo op" on June 1, 2020, during the nationwide protests against systemic racism and police violence following George Floyd's brutal murder made a deep impression on me. That night I experienced fitful insomnia. I couldn't get the image out of my mind of Trump's sacrilegious and offensive publicity stunt as he stood with an uncomfortable smile, holding up a Bible in front of St. John's Episcopal Church, in Washington, DC. The violent removal of peaceful protesters by police in Lafayette Park to enable this photo op felt like the action of an authoritarian strongman, not an American president. Early the next morning, I took my family down to the White House to pray and to allow my then seven- and nine-year-old sons to show solidarity with the protests that were taking place in cities around the country. Sojourners was cosponsoring a solidarity vigil that the Episcopal Diocese of Washington had planned for that day, and I wanted to help reclaim that sacred space before the event. When we arrived, we were confronted by a phalanx of police officers in military gear who had blocked off access to the entire block leading to St. John's Church. I knelt in front of the police, my own Bible in hand, and prayed for the safety of every protester and police officer and that our demands for an end to police violence and systemic racism would be heard at every level of government, including by the president. This took place just days before DC mayor Muriel Bowser renamed the intersection between St. John's Church and the White House "Black Lives Matter Plaza" and had "Black Lives Matter" painted on the street in large, bright letters.

What is equal justice, and what does it require? Most people understand equality either as striving toward equal outcomes in life for everyone or as ensuring equal opportunity. Reality falls woefully short of either of those definitions. While a noble goal, absolute equality of outcome is unobtainable in a capitalist system, with market forces naturally rewarding some people more than others. But even with this reality built into our economic system, we should not tolerate or be complacent about the alarming growth of extreme inequality, particularly given the ways in which these disparities remain so racialized and tied to both past and present injustice. At the height of the COVID-19 pandemic, our nation faced the jarring contrast between a record stock market surpassing thirty thousand for the first time and severe hardship with record food lines and dire unemployment.

While many of the benefits of a capitalist system are worth preserving, the growing inequality in the US and around the world has reached absurd and indefensible levels, largely because the rules of capitalism are often rigged. The inordinate power of many big businesses and the super-rich is fueling an inequality crisis in part by dodging taxes, stagnating wages, and corrupting our politics. While there have been some positive shifts such as the growth of the B-Corps movement, which certifies companies for their social and environmental impact, among others, maximizing shareholder profit still serves as the primary focus of most big business. Instead the focus should increasingly be on the pursuit of the so-called triple bottom line that seeks to maximize benefit to employees, shareholders, and the larger society. Because of this, our economic system needs revamped rules and a revitalized ethic. Oxfam's report *An Economy for the 99 percent* puts this in stark relief, showing that the gap between rich and poor has reached astronomical proportions, with the world's eight richest men possessing more wealth than half of the world's population combined.[4] Americans in the top 1 percent averaged over forty times more income than the bottom 90 percent. According to the Census Bureau, in 2019 income inequality in the United States hit its highest level since the bureau started tracking it more than five decades ago.[5] In particular, the racial wealth divide has been one of the most stubborn and intractable forms of inequality and injustice. Dr. King had the foresight to see that the next phase of the civil rights movement had to focus on economic justice and poverty, which is why he was organizing the Poor People's Campaign prior to his assassination in 1968.

Fortunately, there is a great deal of room between achieving equality of opportunity and equality of outcome, and both can be pursued in ways that are mutually reinforcing. What enables us to go deeper and build greater urgency around the project of realizing a radically more equal society is a new narrative, which I believe should be tied to the concept of *imago dei*. Imago dei—the understanding that every person is made in the image and likeness of God—is a foundational conviction within Judaism and Christianity. This shared belief has profound implications for how we understand equality, which from a religious and spiritual vantage point is inextricably tied to protecting human dignity and the sacred worth of every human person. From a religious perspective, imago dei means that the spark and image of the divine lies within every person. Thus, when we stare into the eyes of another person, we are staring into not only God's creation, but into God's very image. When we oppress or treat another person with contempt or hate, we reject and denigrate God.

While studying in South Africa, I had the opportunity to learn a bit of both Zulu and Xhosa. I've forgotten most of what I learned, but a few words left an indelible impression, including the Zulu greeting *Sawubona*, which doesn't just mean hello. In a deeper sense it means, "I see you. I see your humanity. I see your dignity and respect." Akin to the concept of imago dei, it means "I see the God that is in you." The response is *Sihkona*, which means "I am here." It suggests that "Until you see me, I do not exist." This greeting and the response signify that we can only experience our full humanity through affirming the humanity of other people.[6]

While our nation's founders didn't explicitly mention imago dei, they appealed to the concept in the Declaration of Independence and the Constitution. Despite the glaring prejudice of the founding fathers in confining full personhood and rights to only white men, they enshrined in our nation's founding documents an abiding belief in and commitment to equality—that all "men" (persons) are "created equal" and "endowed by their Creator with certain unalienable rights," including life, liberty, and the pursuit of happiness. Historian Jill Lepore goes deeper, arguing that "the American experiment rests on three political ideas—'these truths,' Thomas Jefferson called them—political equality, natural rights, and the sovereignty of the people."[7] Within these, political equality is arguably the most revolutionary, foundational, and elusive of "these truths."

The commitment to equality is particularly critical in the context of the struggle to overcome attitudes and systems steeped in white supremacy and racial bias. We've seen how punishment continues to be tied to race in America. As a result, one of the most important places to begin this level of change is in our criminal justice system, which continuously betrays our nation's foundational promise of "equal justice under the law." Black and brown people are often criminalized and presumed guilty, even if the standard of law presumes innocence. This trend shows up in the significant disparities in arrests, sentencings, and convictions between white, Black, and brown Americans for the same crimes. The Equal Justice Initiative has also convincingly documented that "racial disparities persist at every level of the so-called justice system: from misdemeanor arrests, police brutality and killings, to executions."[8] The criminal justice system is the greatest test of equality, particularly because it's the place where we sanction the coercive use of force, including lethal force, in the name of public safety and the common good.

The struggle to transform policing and the criminal justice system has a long and halting history. "In 1967, the Kerner Commission, appointed by Lyndon B. Johnson to investigate the causes of uprisings and rioting that year, recommended ways to improve the relationship between the police and black communities, but in the end it entrenched law enforcement as a means of social control," wrote the *New York Times* in a June 2020 discussion on how to reform policing.[9]

In a passionate speech at the Black Entertainment Television Awards in 2016, activist and actor Jesse Williams captured the urgency behind transforming the nature of policing: "Now, what we've been doing is looking at the data and we know that police somehow manage to deescalate, disarm, and not kill white people every day. So what's going to happen is we are going to have equal rights and justice in our own country or we will restructure their function and ours."[10]

To understand how we got here, we must go all the way back to when the concept of race was invented. The construct of race originated with Gomes de Zurara, an adviser to the Portuguese King Afonso, who grouped peoples from Africa into a single race to create hierarchy and defend the lucrative commerce in human lives. The slave trade became justified through the construction of a Black race, an invented group upon which de Zurara hung racist ideas. As Ibram X. Kendi explains, "This cause and effect—a racist power creates racist policies out of raw self-interest; the racist policies necessitate racist ideas to justify them—lingers over the life of racism." In 1735, Swedish botanist Carl Linnaeus "locked in the racial hierarchy of humankind in *Systema Naturae*," Kendi writes, and "color-coded the races as White, Yellow, Red, and Black. . . . The

Linnaeus taxonomy became the blueprint that nearly every enlightened race maker followed and that race makers still follow today."[11] This twisted and pernicious logic was embraced by whites in the Americas—including many of the founding fathers—to justify what was clearly morally indefensible. Only such logic could result in the Three-Fifths Compromise, counting enslaved Black people as three-fifths of a person and excluding them from all rights and privileges. Dr. Eddie S. Glaude Jr. writes that Americans have "believed that the color of one's skin determined the relative value of an individual's life and justified the way American society was organized. That belief and justification had dehumanized entire groups of people. White Americans were not excluded from its effects."[12]

Thus, racial disparities in our criminal justice system and beyond are rooted in a narrative of racial difference and inferiority constructed initially to justify the enslavement and subjugation of Black people. This pernicious belief survived the formal abolition of slavery and mutated to include the current all-too-common belief associating Black people with danger and criminality. The "tough on crime" policies that helped lead to mass incarceration are rooted in the belief that Black and brown people are inherently guilty and dangerous. That belief still drives excessive and unjust sentencing and policing policies today. Putting this in context, the US has more prisons, jails, and detention centers than it does degree-granting institutions.[13] We have more incarcerated people than any country in the world,[14] disproportionately people of color, the majority of whom are serving time for nonviolent offenses.[15] Many are people who need medical interventions, not incarceration. Many of our schools are over-policed but lack social workers—leading to racial and class disparities in what is called the school-to-prison pipeline. Private prisons have become a multibillion-dollar industry, incentivized to maintain quotas, with their stock becoming one of the most bought and sold on Wall Street.

Mass incarceration is not a humane, effective, or sustainable way to reduce violent crime. And using prisons to deal with poverty and mental illness makes these problems worse. People often leave overcrowded and violent prisons more traumatized, mentally ill, and physically battered than when they went in. Today, nearly ten million Americans—including millions of children—have an immediate family member in jail or prison.

More than 4.5 million Americans—disproportionately Black and brown people—can't vote because of a past conviction. And each year we lose $87 billion in Gross Domestic Product due to mass incarceration.

"Each of us is more than the worst thing we've ever done."[16] These iconic words of Bryan Stevenson are a critical reminder that Beloved Community requires seeing and affirming the imago dei that is within everyone, including people who are currently or were formerly incarcerated. I have been inspired by the witness and work of Marlon Peterson, an author, speaker, and change agent who spent his entire twenties inside New York state prisons for his involvement in a crime as a teenager. During that time, he earned an associate degree in criminal justice, and he spent the last five years of his incarceration as head of the Transitional Services Center, where he created curricula for men returning from prison.

Peterson believes that the stories of the seventy million people in America with a criminal conviction need to be heard, including their journeys of success. He now produces the *Decarcerated* podcast to highlight the spirit of resilience and transformation that defines these stories. As he puts it, "My life's work is an un-telling of all the things I was taught to tell myself . . . that I am undeserving; that I am unable to love; that my past mistakes are the limitations of my present; that I'm nothing."[17] Peterson believes that "the Beloved Community is not static, it is constantly evolving; it's us expanding who we include and value." He told me the poignant story of how, while he was in prison, many of the older guys would refer to each other as "beloved"; they would greet each other with the words "How ya doing, beloved?" or "Hey, what's up, beloved?" This greeting was both a way to create safety in a volatile environment and to affirm each other's humanity in an environment that often seeks to strip it away. "It doesn't require a lot of work to see the humanity in someone who is innocent," Peterson says, "but what about someone who is guilty, even of a violent crime? It's not about absolving them, but instead about still seeing their humanity."[18] Peterson's story reminded me of how, like many other Black preachers, I often refer to the congregation as "beloved" when I'm preaching. The imago dei imperative should inspire all of us to see every person as beloved and call them so. It also requires sacrifice.

"How much are you willing to sacrifice for full freedom and justice?" I was asked this question at a retreat with activists and other faith leaders near Ferguson, Missouri, just months after the tragic police killing of Michael Brown Jr. It is a question that has stuck with me in the struggle to transform our racialized and broken criminal justice system. German theologian Dietrich Bonhoeffer spoke about cheap grace, which he described as "grace without discipleship, grace without the cross, grace without Jesus Christ, living and incarnate."[19] These activists challenged us to consider the meaning of cheap justice. It wasn't enough that as faith leaders we were writing, speaking, and preaching against police violence and racial injustice. The deeper question was whether we were willing to put our reputations and bodies on the line. This new generation of activists was reinventing the rules of social change while building on the legacy of the Student Nonviolent Coordinating Committee and the civil rights movement. I saw how much they were willing to sacrifice to realize a society where punishment is no longer tied to race.

Much of the media coverage of the protests in Ferguson painted a misleading picture of aimless and angry youth or, at worst, hooligans and criminals. The night the grand jury announced that no charges would be brought against white police officer Darren Wilson, the media's overly reality-TV coverage fixated on a small minority of protesters who burned buildings and looted stores in a fury of rage. This slanted coverage obscured another, more inspirational story of a much larger cadre of young people willing to sacrifice everything so that they and future generations could be truly free. These new freedom fighters fought for a future free of excessive and racialized policing—a future in which their humanity and dignity is respected and affirmed. We've repeatedly seen that kind of jaundiced coverage of Black Lives Matter protests over the years, including after the murders of George Floyd, Rayshard Brooks, and so many others. A study by the Armed Conflict Location and Event Data Project found that about 93 percent of the racial justice protests that swept the United States in summer 2020 remained peaceful and non-destructive, while only a small portion led to the property destruction and violence that often dominated the headlines.[20] In times when oppression against the Black community reaches a breaking point and boils over into protest, focusing on rare acts of violence has been a long-standing political tactic for many politicians to stoke white fear, ignoring the root causes behind why people are protesting and blaming the protesters for threatening "law and order."

That summer of sustained record-breaking protests shifted the public narrative and helped people see that long-overdue police reforms simply aren't enough. These overdue reforms range from the banning of choke-holds and no-knock warrants to new standards on the use of force to the mandatory use of body cameras and strengthening civilian review boards. Other reforms will require leadership by Congress, including a national registry of police misconduct and an end to qualified immunity, a doctrine that shields police from civil lawsuits when they kill someone in the line of duty. But while all of these changes are important, we can't simply reform our way out of this crisis. Instead, we must transform the nature of policing itself.

The mantra of some protesters to "defund the police" sparked a great deal of controversy, partly because it was often mischaracterized by opponents. The deeper importance of this demand is that it forces us to reevaluate the role of police and reframe how we understand the larger goal of public safety, of which the police are a central piece but not the totality. This demand can also lead to an overdue evaluation of police budgets and practices, with the goal of reinvesting resources into more effective and holistic ways of promoting public safety. Instead of treating the police as the only solution to public-safety concerns, we must have a more holistic understanding of the broader forces that lead to public safety, including access to mental health services and affordable housing, the role of social work, the impact of our education system, forms of restorative justice and conflict prevention, and more—in other words, the presence of both opportunity and dignity. The pursuit of the Beloved Community requires embracing this broader and more holistic understanding of what real public safety requires.

Part of the problem is that most police forces are currently being asked to do far too much, from responding to domestic disputes to dealing with mental health issues to enforcing discipline in schools. As a result, police are often overstretched and undertrained, and are ill-equipped to deal with all that is being asked of them. Many current police functions, such as enforcing speeding tickets and traffic violations, simply do not require the lethal use of force. Problems with policing are compounded by a system and culture that protects police misconduct, in part due to the partial immunity protections for police officers and the inordinate power of police unions, who have so often resisted reforms that would lead to greater accountability.

It's important to view contentious issues from multiple vantage points and perspectives, and this is true concerning the transformation of policing. I've learned a great deal about the complexities of policing and public safety from Ryan Zuidema, the Lynchburg, Virginia, chief of police. Ryan and I met through the Aspen Civil Society Fellowship. While we often see things through different political lenses, we share a deep commitment to upholding equal justice under the law and just policing. Following the killing of Floyd and in response to local protests, Zuidema organized a series of six listening sessions to better understand the outrage and unease in his community. At the first hearing, he said, "We're here to listen to what you have to say. . . . We truly want to hear the good, the bad, and the ugly." In at times emotional and personal moments, more than a dozen speakers detailed run-ins with police, criticizing the department for aggressive tactics and for profiling racial minorities. Zuidema compiled the comments at each of the listening sessions and developed an action plan to address the concerns raised.[21] Zuidema says, "This continued collaboration is critical for strengthening the bonds already established between our department and those we serve as we partner with and protect all Lynchburg residents and visitors."[22] While there are no quick fixes to transforming policing, many evidence-based policy reforms and best practices have been known for quite some time. What has often been missing is the trust to foster honest dialogue between the community and the police and the political will to enact serious and sweeping reforms.

My time in Ferguson led me to envision a program to equip and mobilize clergy and church leaders to serve as change agents to transform policing and the criminal justice system. The program would require building relationships of greater trust and accountability with the police as well as policy changes to restructure policing. This idea was also inspired by my experiences with the Boston TenPoint Coalition,[23] which exposed me to the importance of community policing and to the power of clergy to improve public safety and police accountability.

Rev. Terrance McKinley had played a key role in launching a DC-area program called Make the Covenant that echoed these ideas. McKinley, an elder in the African Methodist Episcopal Church and the racial justice mobilizing director at Sojourners, helped launch what we called the Matthew 25 racialized policing program—a partnership between Sojourners, the Christian Community Development Association, and Howard University Divinity School—to transform policing and build safe and thriving communities. Sojourners recruited fifty clergy and next-generation leaders from across the greater Washington area to participate in an intensive six-month cohort training program. Through the program, the cohort learned about the criminal justice system and how directly addressing racialized policing can help lead to thriving ministries and communities. Utilizing a scorecard based on the recommendations in the 21st Century Policing Report,[24] we measured precincts' level of commitment to proven best practices leading to more just policing and better public safety. The program also focused on the root causes of violence in police forces and justice systems, which include implicit bias, corruption, broken systems of accountability, distrust, and a culture of impunity for bad actors, among others. The cohort weathered the COVID-19 pandemic and wrapped up amid the nation's reckoning with police violence and systemic racism.

Dr. Harold Dean Trulear, associate professor of applied theology at Howard Divinity School, serves as the unofficial dean of the cohort program. Trulear has considerable expertise as well as his own experience of having served a year in prison. He reminded the cohort that one in twenty-three Pennsylvanians (and one in forty-eight people nationally) are under parole. He noted the role people of faith have played in criminal justice reform efforts. Historically, the first probation officer was a Catholic priest in a system originally designed to foster rehabilitation. Probation and parole have gone from social support to an extension of policing in a larger criminal justice system that is primarily punitive, framed by retribution. Trulear explained that proximity to the criminal justice system is found throughout scripture. For example, Jesus was crucified after a sham trial, Moses was a fugitive after killing an Egyptian solider, and after his conversion Paul wrote many of his letters to the church from his own prison cell.

The cohort program is focused on transforming policing, even as it works to ensure that offenders see themselves as fully human and that churches offer support and love to offenders from the moment of arrest through their reentry. Prior to his own release from prison, Trulear wrote of his deep yearning for the church to increase its advocacy on behalf of all affected by crime and incarceration:

> Although I will not be for much longer, today, at the moment that I write this, I am inmate #10002648, George W. Hill Correctional Facility, Delaware County, PA. Not the Rev. Trulear who pastored a church, not Dr. Trulear who commanded the attention of seminary students at Howard Divinity School, but an inmate with a number, sitting in a discharge cell at the end of a year of jail, furloughs, and work release. . . . So many with me feel forgotten, because they are. In the past they were even forgotten by me, a one-time pastor not far from this jail who purported to shepherd a church which included five women whose sons served time with me this year. I don't know which is worse—the shame of my incarceration or the shame of meeting their sons in here instead of in church. . . . We have failed those who sit in our pews and suffer in silence because they cannot share the pain of an incarcerated son, daughter, spouse, dad, mom. They feel forgotten. . . . Paul's letter to the church at Philippi was written in such a place. . . . Tonight, my cellmate read Philippians 4 with me again. I am not forgotten, but one last time, before I leave this place, allow me to feel the pain of the forgotten. Lord, help me not to forget.[25]

Transforming policing practices and public policy, alongside efforts to rebuild trust at the community level and to empower Black and brown youth, must be part of our focus. As long as Black and brown people are treated as a menace and presumed guilty, our nation will fail our constitutional standard of treating everyone as equal under the law and our higher moral standard of viewing them as being made in God's image.

The beatitude of imago dei also requires ensuring that privilege, in addition to punishment, is not tied to race, ethnicity, gender, or sexual orientation and gender identity. In 1967, Dr. King gave a speech at the Hungry Club Forum in Atlanta, in which he said,

> For well now twelve years, the struggle was basically a struggle to end legal segregation. In a sense it was a struggle for decency. . . . It is now a struggle for genuine equality on all levels, and this will be a much more difficult struggle. You see, the gains in the first period, or the first era of struggle, were obtained from the power structure at bargain rates; it didn't cost the nation anything to integrate lunch counters. It didn't cost the nation anything to integrate hotels and motels. It didn't cost the nation a penny to guarantee the right to vote. Now we are in a period where it will cost the nation billions of dollars to get rid of poverty, to get rid of slums, to make quality integrated education a reality. This is where we are now.[26]

Unfortunately, the word *privilege* has become fraught. Most people naturally resist the notion that they enjoy privilege because of their skin color, gender, or sexual orientation. But at its most fundamental level, privilege signifies that each of us enjoys greater opportunities or advantages by virtue of the various combinations of our identities. All of us enjoy some privilege because of at least one facet of our identity and background. In my case, as an able-bodied, heterosexual, cisgender man, I enjoy privileges compared to women and people who are differently abled, as well as in comparison to my lesbian, gay, bisexual, and transgender brothers and sisters. Due to our nation's history, many of the most insidious and entrenched privileges continue to be tied to race and skin color.

It is often hard to conceive of what racial privilege looks like and what practical forms it takes. As a former track athlete, I especially appreciate the analogy of trying to compete in a four-hundred-meter race in which your competitors are given a significant head start based on historical advantages they have enjoyed over their lifetime. To make the race even more unfair, your competitors get to run in the innermost lane while you are stuck running a much longer distance in the outer lane due to the impact of present-day biases and barriers. Imagine how much faster and harder you would have to run just to keep up with the other runners, let alone overtake them.

Another illuminating metaphor compares America to a fish tank in which, due to historical disadvantages and current barriers, white fish constantly swim with the invisible force of the current propelling them forward while fish of color constantly have to work harder to swim the same speed because they are working against that same current. The challenge is that the white fish aren't even aware that current exists and are often blind to the ways the current has also helped their forefathers and foremothers, passing down benefits and advantages from one generation to the next.

Recall the adage that if you "give a person a fish, they will eat for a day, but if you teach a person to fish, they will eat for a lifetime." What this leaves out is what happens when you teach a person to fish but—because of past oppression and exclusion—their pond has been polluted and—due to enduring discrimination and injustices—their fishing rod is inferior and their bait isn't as good. None of these metaphors perfectly describe our current reality, but they all make the important point that injustices from the past show up in the present and the playing field continues to be tilted, leading to unjust outcomes that are self-perpetuating and often devastating to Black and brown communities.

It is easy to place the ugly injustices of our past in a time capsule, ignoring and denying the ways in which they continue to show up in the present. Far too many Americans are either blind to or in denial about the degree to which white Americans have benefited from both advantages and favoritism conferred upon them by government policies that were denied to non-white Americans. These forms of white affirmative action are not just tied to the much more distant legacy of slavery but to much more recent policies such as the Homestead Act, the GI Bill, redlining, and more. As Nikole Hannah-Jones, creator of the 1619 Project, argues in her powerful article "What Is Owed": "While unchecked discrimination still plays a significant role in shunting opportunities for black Americans, it is white Americans' centuries-long economic head start that most effectively maintains racial caste today."[27] Political scientist Ira Katznelson unpacks this further in his book *When Affirmative*

Action Was White, writing: "At the very moment a wide array of public policies was providing most white Americans with valuable tools to advance their social welfare—ensure their old age, get good jobs, acquire economic security, build assets and gain middle-class status—most black Americans were left behind or left out. . . . The federal government . . . functioned as a commanding instrument of white privilege." For example, Katznelson continues, "As part of the New Deal programs, the federal government created redlining maps, marking neighborhoods where black people lived in red ink to denote that they were uninsurable. As a result, 98 percent of the loans the Federal Housing Administration insured from 1934 to 1962 went to white Americans, locking nearly all black Americans out of the government program credited with building the modern (white) middle class."[28]

Hannah-Jones captures just how powerful an instrument intergenerational wealth has been in shaping American life:

Wealth, not income, is the means to security in America. Wealth—assets and investments minus debt—is what enables you to buy homes in safer neighborhoods with better amenities and better-funded schools. It is what enables you to send your children to college without saddling them with tens of thousands of dollars of debt and what provides you money to put a down payment on a house. It is what prevents family emergencies or unexpected job losses from turning into catastrophes that leave you homeless and destitute. It is what ensures what every parent wants—that your children will have fewer struggles than you did. Wealth is security and peace of mind. It's not incidental that wealthier people are healthier and live longer. Wealth is, as a recent Yale study states, "the most consequential index of economic well-being" for most Americans. But wealth is not something people create solely by themselves; it is accumulated across generations.[29]

Recent statistics paint a stark and unnerving picture of just how entrenched and deep-seated racial inequity and privilege remain. A 2019 Yale University study called "The Misperception of Racial Economic Inequality"[30] found that Americans believe that Black households hold

$90 in wealth for every $100 held by white households. Tragically, the actual amount is $10 for every $100 held by whites, and at current rates of progress this gap will take more than a century to reverse. According to research conducted between 2004 and 2016 by scholars at Duke and Northwestern, significantly before COVID-19 exacerbated these trends, the average Black family with children held just one cent of wealth for every dollar that the average white family with children held. To make matters worse, education, thought to be the great equalizer in our society, doesn't pay off for Black Americans the same way it does for other groups. For example, "Black college graduates are about as likely to be unemployed as white Americans with a high school diploma, and black Americans with a college education hold less wealth than white Americans who have not even completed high school."[31] Privilege is also often ingrained into our nation's racialized geography. Today Black Americans remain the most segregated group of people in America and are five times as likely to live in high-poverty neighborhoods as white Americans.

Remaking America into a nation in which privilege isn't tied to race can often feel like an impossible task. But we can set proximate goals aimed at setting our nation on the right trajectory. A basic principle that enjoys broad support is that every child should be able to achieve their full, God-given potential and that a child's life chances should not be determined by their zip code. Framing the principle of equality through the lens of a child makes it seem more achievable and easier to grasp. Giving children a good start in life is also essential; increasing scientific evidence shows just how determinative the first five years of life can be. Most of a child's brain is already developed by the age of two, and by age five a child's cognitive ability is basically set. Based on current realities, the world is baking inequality into the lives of a generation of children.

In the international arena, a great deal of attention has been paid to the alarming reality of childhood stunting due to malnutrition, which is sabotaging the future of millions of children around the world and compromising their physical growth. Yet it is only in the last few decades that development practitioners have noted the role of trauma and lack of stimulation in stunting cognitive and brain development in these formative years. The pernicious combination of malnutrition, trauma (due to exposure to abuse or violence), and lack of early education or brain stimulation is sabotaging the future of more than 150 million children around the world. The dire and often permanent consequences of factors in early childhood are also handicapping children in the US who often suffer from malnutrition, grow up in abusive homes or unsafe environments, or experience neglect at an early age. Since Black and brown children are disproportionately likely to live in poverty and experience trauma, they are more likely to have their potential sabotaged. To add insult to injury, discrimination and barriers associated with implicit bias and systemic racism further impede their progress and sabotage their future.

Black Panther has become one of my family's favorite films. In the movie, vibranium is the rare metal that powers the development of the nation of Wakanda, lending its people superhuman strength and intelligence.[32] Being Black and brown in America requires something akin to what I call "spiritual vibranium." In the face of historic and ongoing systemic barriers and injustices, it so often takes inner "vibranium" for young Black and brown people to succeed and thrive in this country. But it shouldn't take extraordinary grit, intelligence, and strength for Black and brown children to advance and thrive. Liberty and justice for all requires providing all our children the opportunity to realize their full potential.

Through the leadership of Dr. Jim Yong Kim, the first physician to lead the World Bank, the Bank took up the mantle of encouraging countries to invest in early childhood development, launching the Human Capital Project as a way of both incentivizing and pressuring governments to prioritize investments in education, health, and early childhood development. The same urgency needs to be applied to children suffering from poverty and neglect in the US. While many do not face the same degrees of extreme suffering as children abroad, there are millions who contend with destructive malnutrition, trauma, and neglect that will have debilitating lifelong consequences. Each child is made in God's image and deserves to realize their full potential. Building the Beloved Community requires greater investments in early childhood development, which could garner widespread support across the political and ideological spectrum and make a major down payment on our shared commitment to equality.

Advancing early childhood development is desperately needed for children in disadvantaged and marginalized communities across the

United States. One inspiring example of an effective venture is the LA Partnership for Early Childhood Investment, which is derived from the belief that the earliest years of life are the foundation of human development and that, as a society, our first responsibility is to protect the health and well-being of our youngest community members.[33] Kaci Patterson, one of the partnership's leaders, says, "In Los Angeles County, where more than 250,000 young children, birth to five, live in poverty, it means our moral responsibility is to create the systemic conditions where they can thrive." Patterson also believes this:

> Philanthropy is defined as *the love of humanity*. When we fund advocacy to resource early childhood education, we love humanity. When we support a full and accurate census count of every child in Los Angeles, regardless of citizenship status, we love humanity. When we resource the Home Visiting consortium to share data and make it easier for low-income families to access quality postpartum care, we love humanity. When we prioritize Black women as leaders and experts in creating solutions for Black infant and maternal health, we love humanity. When we convene candidates running for local office to discuss their early childhood policy priorities, we help ensure our government loves humanity.[34]

Since 2012, when the Baby Futures Fund was launched, the LA Partnership has marshaled over $8 million in grants to nonprofits working on early childhood development systems. Patterson believes that "Beloved Community requires more than simply a network of funders and government agencies; it involves a host of extended family members ranging from business and government to philanthropy, nonprofit organizations, and everyday parents, who together make up 'the village' where *our* children are *our* responsibility."[35]

Building the Beloved Community through a more radical commitment to imago dei also requires building a common language and shared understanding of why the present social and economic landscape looks the way it does in an environment that encourages candid dialogue free of recrimination and judgment. One example of how this is done is the Campaign for Equity: New Orleans (CENO), which was created when four business leaders came together to foster dialogue and action to make New Orleans "the most equitable city in America," as the campaign mission statement puts it. Led by a small group of entrepreneurs, CENO works to educate, connect, and mobilize leaders throughout the city to address areas of systemic racism and build a more equitable future.[36]

Shawn Barney, a real estate developer from New Orleans, co-created the organizing initiative to help transform a city whose geography has been dramatically shaped by race and racism. Barney realized that to move a racial equity agenda forward, the city's nontraditional leaders, especially those in the business community, needed to be much more informed and engaged. In particular, white business leaders needed to better understand how racism hurts them as well as their Black brothers and sisters.

The Campaign for Equity process requires personal reflection and "the courage to look critically at the systems in which we work, live, and lead." The group seeks to develop "a shared language to describe with specificity how systemic racism impacts every facet of life in New Orleans." In one example, the group's curriculum teaches how affirmative action started for whites in New Orleans in the seventeenth century with the introduction of slavery and continued in numerous forms through the twentieth century with Federal Housing Administration loans, the Homestead Act, and other measures. To bring the understanding home, the training asks participants to imagine the game of Monopoly, where whites are playing the game with full access to capital and credit from 1703 to 1964. Meanwhile, people of color don't gain access until 1964, and once they are in the game, the same rules apply for everyone, even though white players have already accumulated properties and wealth.[37]

CENO's training looks at New Orleans via converging histories, identities, and the interplay of systems—education, health, housing, criminal justice. Fostering an environment for candid, respectful conversation that expects discomfort and understands that disagreements may go unresolved, CENO seeks to build the capacity to make New Orleans better.

CENO emphasizes that racial inequity is a matter of life or death. Through disparities in health care and criminal justice, or the accumulated effect of poverty and stress, racism is killing Black families. "When a part of the New Orleans population is held back, it impacts all of us,"

Barney explains. "An equitable city is a prosperous city." For example, a recent Altarum Institute study estimates that Metro New Orleans stands to realize a $43 billion gain in economic output by 2050 by closing the racial equity gap.[38] CENO is currently active in five campaigns, focused on education, the environment, fair public contracts, health, and exonerating people with marijuana convictions. As of 2020, CENO trained 1,500 leaders and emerging professionals throughout New Orleans, addressing areas of systemic racism and building a more equitable future for the city. Making New Orleans more equitable will lead to making New Orleans more competitive economically. Barney says the Campaign for Equity is in the process of expanding to challenge other major cities in a virtuous race toward greater equity.

If we truly internalized, believed, and acted upon the belief that all people are made in the image and likeness of God, we would be intolerant of any ways in which punishment and privilege are tied to the color of a person's skin, their gender, or other aspects of their identity. The imago dei belief, put into practice, provides the moral foundation on which the Beloved Community is built.

Believing and living out imago dei requires us to ask, "How much are you willing to sacrifice for full freedom and justice?" In other words, how much are you willing to do so that imago dei can be seen and affirmed in everyone? Because this is essential to truly building the Beloved Community.

Chapter Ten

RADICAL WELCOME

*You know, and it gets into this whole issue of border security,
you know, who's gonna say that the borders are secure? We've got
the House and the Senate debating this issue. And it's, it's really
astonishing that in a country founded by immigrants, 'immigrant' has somehow become a bad word. So, the debate rages on
and we continue. —Lin-Manuel Miranda*

*We must learn to live together as brothers [and sisters] or perish
together as fools. —Martin Luther King Jr.*

AT ONE OF THE BUSIER BORDERS IN THE WORLD, IN JANUARY 2020 OUR GROUP OF
Christian leaders representing a broad cross section of the church stood
and prayed together, witnessing the stark contrast between the stunning
beauty of the sun setting over the Pacific Ocean and the sheer ugliness
of the border wall that divides Tijuana from San Diego. The wall has
become increasingly militarized, separating both cities and peoples, even
as Tijuana and San Diego function and exist as one dynamic and highly
fluid city of nearly six million. Each day prior to the COVID pandemic,
120,000 people crossed the border for work, tourism, and to visit relatives
because their families and lives stretch beyond borders.

On the two sides of this border wall, which juts out far into the ocean,
stand what are commonly referred to as the "twin towers." On the US
side stands a watchtower, a military structure that enforces the exclusion
and criminalization of immigrants. On the Mexican side stands a light-
house, a structure that provides refuge and welcome. The Mexican side
is a coastal beach strip filled with restaurants and a public park. The US

side is a remote and desolate strip of barbed wire with a lone Immigration and Customs Enforcement (ICE) patrol car to mark the existence of life. We were guided by a group of bilingual and bicultural millennial faith leaders who called themselves *puentes*, Spanish for "bridge." "People on the border," one of them said, "carry the border in their bones and in their souls. The border is within them, with all of its beauty and all of its ugliness."

The Faith Table, an informal group of Christian faith-based organization and denominational leaders, gathers for an annual retreat each year. Past retreats have taken place in Ferguson, Missouri, after the killing of Michael Brown; in Montgomery, Alabama, prior to the launch of the National Memorial for Peace and Justice; and in New Mexico with Father Richard Rohr and the Center for Action and Contemplation. The Faith Table retreat at the southern border took place during the liturgical season of Epiphany. In the Catholic Church and other Christian traditions, Epiphany honors the visit of the three kings who traveled from foreign lands to find Jesus, the one who was foretold as their messiah. But Herod was furious upon realizing he had been outwitted by the magi, so he ordered the killing of every infant in Bethlehem under the age of two, forcing Mary and Joseph to seek refuge in Egypt. In this liturgical season, it is a Mexican tradition for families to bake or purchase a *rosca de reyes* (or "king cake," as it's called elsewhere), a bread wreath decorated with candied fruits that represent the jewels on the crowns of the kings. Inside the wreath there is an inch-long baby Jesus. In celebrations with family and friends, whoever finds the baby Jesus in the wreath becomes the *padrino*, or godparent, and takes on the responsibility of caring for the baby Jesus until another celebration takes place in February, after which the manger scene is taken down. This tradition is a powerful way to remember Mary, Joseph, and Jesus—forced to flee their homeland due to persecution and violence and finding safe haven in Egypt. Yes, the very beginning of the Christian story has migration and asylum at its essence.

During that Epiphany gathering, we also spent time with Iglesia Bautista Camino de Salvación and Iglesia de Todas las Naciones, churches in Tijuana that embody the very ethic of radical welcome and hospitality. Both churches responded generously and courageously to the influx of immigrants from Central America seeking asylum in the United States.

Both decided to convert their churches into shelters and waystations of support and love. Their response to those in need has transformed their ministries. Former meeting and Bible study rooms are now filled with bunk beds. Sanctuaries are now weekday spaces for trauma care and social support and play areas for children. Both churches understood that following Jesus means providing care and services to migrants seeking asylum. They take seriously the command of Jesus in Matthew 25 as a command to care for migrants, and by doing so they care for Jesus himself. In those churches we witnessed radical welcome as love in action.

America is a land of immigrants, some colonized or brought by force, others arriving out of desperation, and many more coming in search of greater economic opportunity and personal freedom. America is a land of Indigenous peoples, forcibly displaced and tragically killed to make way for European conquest and expansion. This is America. Immigration, displacement, and a search for refuge have served as defining issues throughout our nation's history. And they continue to remain among the principal wedge issues in our politics.

Walls of separation represent powerful symbols of the dividing line around how we understand our nation and its sometimes hostile, sometimes welcoming relationship with immigrants, as the Trump border wall revealed. In contrast is the symbol of the Statue of Liberty, which for generations has served as a powerful reminder of America's welcome of people escaping persecution and peril. Both symbols—the outstretched light and the wall—embody the often-contradictory nature of America's treatment of immigrants. In our best moments, America has been a refuge for the persecuted and downtrodden, believing that our strength derives from our compassion and commitment to radical welcome. This is encapsulated in the inscription on the Statue of Liberty, by Emma Lazarus: "Give me your tired, your poor, your huddled masses yearning to breathe free." But in our nation's worst moments, we have demonized and dehumanized immigrants, imposing draconian policies and often racist restrictions barring their entry.

Radical welcome, the outstretched light, is a commitment rooted in an injunction found throughout the Hebrew Bible to welcome the migrant, often referred to as the stranger, and echoed in the gospel teachings of Jesus. This beatitude of radical welcome forms a critical aspect of realizing the Beloved Community. For Christians, the commitment to biblical justice and discipleship calls us to engage in deeper moral analysis as we identify and redress the root causes of the border crisis and immigration. At its roots, the crisis is a direct product of the protracted failure of Congress to negotiate in good faith and pass comprehensive, humane, and just reforms to fix our severely broken immigration system. In the absence of legislative reforms, Trump and others exploited this issue, stoking the fears of his base and scapegoating immigrants for our nation's ills. Immigration remains such a wedge issue because Republicans and Democrats have almost diametrically opposed perceptions of the problem and proposed solutions. According to the Public Religion Research Institute (PRRI) / the *Atlantic* Pluralism Survey, nearly nine in ten Republicans "strongly favor" or "favor" restrictive immigration policies. Among Democrats, the vast majority (68 percent) oppose those same measures.[1]

The poisonous rhetoric and lies that have been promulgated against immigrants cannot be counteracted simply with data or facts—we need the assertion of moral truths. From a Christian perspective, we must name the act of dehumanizing and denigrating immigrants as sinful. As civil rights leader Rev. Jim Lawson reminds us, "No human being in the sight of God is illegal. The fight for the civil rights of workers who come here from all over the world is the same as the Freedom Rides of 1961 and the continuing struggle for civil and human rights for all."[2]

Four of the Ten Commandments govern our relationship with God, while the other six govern our relationship with each other. When we take responsibility of caring for each other, we're called into a commitment to that radical welcome that will make us a stronger, safer, and better nation. This requires moving beyond polemical debates on immigration. It requires addressing people's instinctual need for safety and security. It requires responsibility and understanding that radical welcome in a modern age does not mean a completely open and porous border. Nor does it withhold consequences for those who enter the country illegally or overstay their visas. But it does start with communicating how immigrants are an essential part of who we are as a nation and who we have always been. It starts with living out our civic and religious values in which welcoming immigrants and loving and caring for our neighbor are central.

Radical welcome means that even when immigrants arrive illegally, they are treated humanely, as those who also carry the image of God. Radical welcome requires a more holistic view of the border crisis, understanding why families are willing to risk their lives to take the treacherous journey from Central America and other parts of the world to reach our border. It requires understanding that crossing a border—as the *rosca de reyes* Epiphany cake reminds us—is about fleeing difficult and often life-threatening circumstances with no possessions except a hope that the border will offer safety and welcome.

The lack of radical welcome sabotages the building of the Beloved Community. Instead, we've often seen a set of policies that manufacture even greater crises, forcing migrants seeking asylum to wait in Mexico and go through a counterproductive procedure called metering, which limits the number of daily applications processed. Without radical welcome, we witness onerous waiting times for court appearances and thus an increasing backlog of asylum cases. We have seen unconscionable conditions in detention centers, with inhumane treatment, including the dividing of families. The Trump administration reduced the number of people admitted through our refugee program to a shameful eighteen thousand people a year, the lowest in decades. Yet Lazarus's poetic words still sound out to asylum seekers looking for a refuge from persecution and violence.

We have an obligation to expose the lies that are used to justify and perpetuate such destructive systems. We must expose the lie that illegal border crossings account for most undocumented workers, when the larger numbers come from visa holders overstaying their limits, coming through legal channels and then staying.[3] We must expose the lie that crime and violence come from our borders, when we know that undocumented immigrants commit far fewer crimes on average than do American citizens.[4] Those committed to radical welcome would reveal that US imperialism toward Central America—including US interventions and propping up of brutal governments in countries such as Guatemala and El Salvador—has contributed to the growing numbers of migrants seeking asylum,[5] and point to the cutback of millions of dollars in international assistance to Central American countries, exacerbating the conditions of an already impoverished region.[6] Most important, a community of radical welcome knows that, according to both US government and independent studies, instead of being a burden or a threat, refugees and immigrants continue to be a positive force for America's shared prosperity.

The immigration system is a complex and convoluted one, and solutions are rarely simple or clear. One major exception was President Trump's heinous family separation policy, which rightfully elicited a resounding moral outcry as the administration used children as pawns to deter people from illegally crossing the border. A moment of moral clarity came when then attorney general Jeff Sessions misappropriated Romans 13 as he sought to defend this indefensible policy. A tsunami of public pressure forced the administration to partially reverse course.

Another immigration issue that carries moral clarity involves policies around the so-called Dreamers, undocumented immigrants who were brought to America at young ages. While the Obama administration granted these young people a renewable two-year period of deferred action from deportation, the Trump administration sought to reverse this policy, ultimately getting overridden by the Supreme Court. Congressional legislation that grants these young people permanent legal status leading to full citizenship is an overdue solution that the vast majority of Americans already support.[7]

Organizing and advocacy around immigration are exactly what the organization Mateo 25 / Matthew 25 is doing in Southern California.[8] Through a partnership with the Latino Center of Fuller Theological Seminary, Mateo 25 offers a professional certificate on the Church's Response to the Immigration Crisis. According to Mateo 25's founder, Rev. Alexia Salvatierra, the Beloved Community is best understood through the biblical metaphor of the body of Christ and the cultural metaphor of *familia*. She references 1 Corinthians 12:24, where Paul instructs the church to consider itself through the metaphor of the body, giving more honor to the parts of the body that have lacked honor. Paul makes clear that every part of the body—each person in their individual role—is essential to the whole. In the advocacy work it does, Mateo 25 appeals not only to political frameworks but also to how the body of Christ is meant to function. According to Salvatierra, "When you have a mutual concern and care for another, particularly for the asylum seeker, it surprises the world and demonstrates Christ's love in the world."[9]

Mateo 25 builds deep bonds of relationship and solidarity between Hispanic evangelical congregations and predominantly white evangelical congregations. Through an intensive cohort program, Hispanic pastors and church leaders are equipped to respond to the immigration crisis and then join learning circles. At the center of the Mateo 25 program are *puentes*, people who serve as "bridges." Salvatierra says, "These young bilingual/bicultural puentes, with one foot in both the Spanish- and English-speaking church worlds, are essential to the work. In other contexts, puentes—whether multiracial, white, or Hispanic—have often been on the margins of the church, but in the work of Mateo 25 their leadership is indispensable. Their dual identity serves as a major part of their calling and vocation."

A few years ago, many young people and families from Central America came to the United States seeking asylum, fleeing life-and-death situations in their home countries. People in both Spanish- and English-speaking congregations came alongside these families in "circles" organized by Mateo 25, a mode of response that changes the dynamic for the people being supported. These are not patronizing relationships or a power dynamic of being "helped" by those in power. Instead, the immigrant families and the church leaders confront the situation together, leading all parts of the body to mutual transformation. As those transformational relationships of solidarity develop, the work of building the Beloved Community begins in the unlikely center of a severely broken immigration system. And the Beloved Community grows to protect those who seek refuge, increasing in commitment not only to welcome but to build true community through direct advocacy and sometimes in nonviolent moral resistance against dehumanizing and unjust immigration policies.

A year before my pilgrimage to the border, I joined a group of Christian leaders in a nonviolent direct action in front of the White House to resist the immoral and inhumane family separation policy. On the day before the protest, I reflected on the reasons I felt it was necessary to engage in civil disobedience. In an article for *Sojourners*, I wrote,

I'm engaging in another nonviolent direct action today because the president's executive order, the zero-tolerance policy, which is still in effect, is an unjust policy that degrades human personality by detaining families indefinitely. I'm engaging in nonviolent direct action, because as a father of five- and seven-year-old sons, I can only imagine the agony of being separated from sons without any knowledge of their whereabouts and safety. The administration's family separation and zero-tolerance policy has already caused untold abuse and trauma that has no place in US policy. I'm engaging in nonviolent direct action, because as an American who cherishes our country's commitment to due process, to deny asylum seekers this opportunity is not only unconstitutional, it is morally unconscionable. I'm engaging in nonviolent direct action, because as an ordained minister I refuse to allow politicians to misuse and abuse scripture to justify deeply unjust policies.[10]

We all may not be called to engage in civil disobedience, but in an age in which fear has been weaponized and immigrants have been politicized, we are all called to a deeper commitment to radical welcome. Damage to our nation's immigration system, including our legal system, has been deep and often covert. As Catherine Rampell explains,

Without ever signing a single immigration law or completing his famous wall, Trump has cut the flow of foreigners by executive fiat. This fiscal year, the United States is on track to admit half the number of legal immigrants it did in 2016. This would bring levels of legal immigration down to what they were in 1987—when the US population was about a quarter smaller, substantially younger, and less in need of working-age immigrants than it is today. If this milestone has gone mostly unremarked, it's by design. It has been achieved through backdoor, boring-sounding, bureaucratic decisions. Small-bore and esoteric though many of them are, collectively they have crippled the legal immigration system and choked the flow of newcomers into the United States. Through hundreds of administrative changes, the machinery of the US immigration system has become even slower, more cruel, and more absurd than it was before.[11]

Applying radical welcome to our broken system requires prioritizing several key policy reforms that, if framed through the lens of America's best civic and religious values such as loving our neighbors and shared prosperity, would garner broad bipartisan support. One would be keeping families and communities together and thriving by providing permanent pathways for citizenship. The good news is that a June 2020 Pew Center survey found that a majority of both parties, 57 percent of Republicans and 89 percent of Democrats, support a path to citizenship for undocumented people.[12] Radical welcome requires ending the harsh criminalization of immigrants, mandatory detention, and cruel and unnecessary practices that harm immigrant people and expand the racialized prison system. Radical welcome rejects the false choice between immigration and national security and embraces humane and effective ways to secure our border through measures such as enhanced surveillance and cross-border cooperation. Radical welcome means reevaluating the rules that are making asylum practically impossible to attain in the US and dramatically increasing refugee resettlement quotas so they at least match historical precedents and even better far exceed them. Finally, discriminatory policies such as the Muslim ban, which were rooted in anti-Blackness and anti-Muslim sentiment, must be permanently abandoned.[13] Fortunately, some of these needed policy changes, including an end to the Muslim travel ban, were made by the Biden administration within its first few months in office by Executive Order. But instead of governing by Executive Orders, which can easily be changed by any new administration, what is overdue and needed most is congressional legislation that offers comprehensive, humane, just, effective, and more permanent fixes to the currently broken system.

To those who want to be a part of building the Beloved Community, the question begins with affirming the dignity of the whole body—which for Christians is akin to protecting Jesus, who crossed over a border to safety. Will we embrace a border wall or the Statue of Liberty as the symbol that defines our nation's moral posture toward immigration? Which symbol fulfills our deepest religious and civic values? Will we follow the clarion call from our sacred traditions to welcome the immigrant? Will our nation be again known for having an open door to the world's most persecuted and oppressed people?

The Beloved Community calls us to radical welcome—radical in the courage it requires and the moral imagination it inspires, and for the act of our becoming like the puentes who so inspired me on the border, who commit themselves to building bridges to the Beloved Community.

Chapter Eleven

UBUNTU INTERDEPENDENCE

In a real sense all life is interrelated. All [people] are caught in an inescapable network of mutuality, tied in a single garment of destiny. Whatever affects one directly, affects all indirectly. I can never be what I ought to be until you are what you ought to be, and you can never be what you ought to be until I am what I ought to be. . . . This is the interrelated structure of reality.
—Martin Luther King Jr.

When I liberate others, I liberate myself. —Fannie Lou Hamer

History will judge societies and governments—and their institutions—not by how big they are or how well they serve the rich and the powerful, but by how effectively they respond to the needs of the poor and the helpless. —César Chávez

WHEN I STUDIED ABROAD IN SOUTH AFRICA IN 1996, I LEARNED MUCH ABOUT THE power of our interdependence and mutuality. There I encountered and experienced the southern-African philosophy of *ubuntu*. Through Nelson Mandela's moral leadership and embodiment of ubuntu, the nation was led through transformational change. Like Dr. King, Mandela refused to hate his enemies, including those who kept him imprisoned for twenty-seven years, as he envisioned a future South Africa that included Black, white, and all people together.

Archbishop Desmond Tutu summarized ubuntu in what became a marker of both a movement and a philosophy: "I am because we are." Mpyana Fulgence Nyengele, author of *Cultivating Ubuntu*, offers this definition: "Ubuntu is the substance and core being of a person and speaks particularly about the fact that we cannot be fully formed as human beings in isolation."[1] Rather, as Stephen Lewis, Matthew Wesley Williams, and Dori Baker share in *Another Way*, Nyengele explains that "it is only through our communal participation and interaction with other people that we begin to develop trust, compassion, caring, humility, kindness, and forgiveness, which are all qualities of what it means to be human and humane toward others. Similar to the fruit of the spirit, *ubuntu* is possible because ntu or Spirit 'orients persons toward life-giving choices, actions and behaviors.' . . . Therefore, '*ubuntu* promotes and enhances the abundance of human life in community and beyond.'"[2]

I think of ubuntu as an expanded, vivid expression of the Golden Rule: We are called to do unto others as we would have them do unto us. Or, as King so often put it, we are to be our brothers' and sisters' keeper.

Interdependence is not often considered a cornerstone of the American ethos, but it lies at the heart of what binds us together, in both a moral and a practical sense. It constitutes an essential beatitude of building the Beloved Community. A greater understanding of how our lives are inextricably linked opens up new possibilities for developing empathy toward others and helps us counteract the atomized, overly individualistic excesses of American culture. Ubuntu also provides a needed lens to understand the ways in which all parts of the globe have become increasingly interdependent. Both our security and our prosperity are increasingly tied to the rest of the world. Global crises such as climate change and the COVID-19 pandemic require shared global leadership and cooperation.

The Beloved Community requires deepening our sense of interdependence. It involves a deeper appreciation that we are in this together socially, politically, and economically. Ubuntu interdependence forms the basis of expressions of solidarity and helps individuals and communities move beyond naked self-interest and hyper-individualism. Properly understood and practiced, ubuntu interdependence provides a compelling rationale behind many public-policy commitments that are central to promoting the common good, such as a strong and effective social safety net, universal access to good health care, strengthening families so they can thrive, and ensuring that every child has access to a quality education.

This kind of ubuntu interdependence provides a social and moral framework. It offers an organizational and governmental policy framework for fighting poverty and expanding economic justice and opportunity for all Americans, including advancing a greater commitment to the triple bottom line of generating benefit for shareholders, employees, and the broader society within the private sector.

South Africa provided the term *ubuntu*, but many other cultures and communities, such as Eastern Christianity and Asian culture, can teach us about the meaning and centrality of interdependent communities. According to Dr. Grace Ji-Sun Kim, "Asian culture is communal. The community and family are more important than the individual. In the communal setting in Korea, one never talks about 'my school' or 'my church'; it is always 'our school' or 'our church,' where they use the Korean word *ouri*. Likewise, one will say 'our husband' or 'our sister' to express the communal culture of society. This communal culture is also connected to *jeong*, a term that refers to the breaking down of the personal in order to build on the connectedness of people."[3] Author and activist Kathy Khang echoed this sentiment as she shared with me, "There's a strong sense of kinship, often tied to an understanding of jeong, which is difficult to put into words but speaks to an immediate sense of connection and mutual understanding, of being seen." When Khang considers this in light of the Beloved Community, she imagines "that everyone is your auntie or uncle. In other words, everyone is looking out for you and is in your business, for better or for worse."[4]

Cultures from across Latin America also share a deep sense of communal interdependence. Rev. Alexia Salvatierra speaks to how collective images are natural in Latin American culture based on the belief that just relationships naturally flow from our taking seriously that we are a family. In this notion of *la familia* is found a deep mutual understanding and commitment to each other, because "a family at its best is a Beloved Community."[5] Rev. Gabriel Salguero echoes this sentiment, describing la familia as "a radical social construct that shapes how we organize life."[6]

The Christian tradition is filled with references, stories, and metaphors that speak to this dynamic interdependence. Paul's metaphor comparing the community of the church to the human body captures the essence of our interdependence. When Paul wrote his letter to the church at Corinth, he understood that its members ministered within a bustling city much like many of our cities today. Corinth was a commercial center of six hundred thousand people. From the dawn of Greek civilization, it was a strategic maritime port, a crossing of shipping lanes, and a meeting point between East and West. Corinth also earned a reputation for vice, as a place for hedonistic pleasure and ostentatious wealth. Behind this wealth were pervasive and severe poverty and a culture that often neglected the poor. And Corinthian society was so riddled with competitive individualism and disregard for the poor that this sensibility spilled over into the church, where feuding groups were built around the personalities and teachings of rival leading figures from different house churches. Instead of creating unity out of their diversity, the Corinthian church experienced division and rancor. Sadly, we see similar polarization today in many of our faith communities and our nation.

What Paul wrote about the human body—the connectedness of bones and sinews, its fragility and remarkable ability to support the whole—is truly a miracle, one that I've come to appreciate more fully in my middle age. I have experienced lower back problems over the past several years. It started when I threw out my back trying to prevent my son from being hit by a car as we came out of church. It took me three long years of dealing with frequent agonizing pain before I finally relented and signed up for physical therapy. Physical therapy gave me a profound appreciation for the true interdependence of the human body. I learned that to heal my lower back, I had to gain greater flexibility and strength in the muscles that connect to my back, from my hamstrings to my glutes and particularly my core. What is true for healing my back is also true for healing our ailing country.

Paul's metaphor comparing the church to the functioning of the body is an image that applies to the health of our communities, our nation, and our world. The lesson of the body—interdependence—ties together three realizations and commitments:

- to protect the weakest, most vulnerable members of our society;
- to demonstrate an equal concern for one another; and
- to recognize that our security, our prosperity, and even our wholeness is tied to that of others.

"Those parts of the body that seem to be weaker are indispensable," Paul comments, adding that "its parts should have equal concern for each other." Finally, Paul reminds us that "if one part suffers, every part suffers with it; if one part is honored, every part rejoices with it" (1 Corinthians 12:22, 25–26).

After three years of physical therapy, I became overconfident and lazy. I stopped doing the very exercises that had helped so much and ended up reinjuring my back. The lesson I learned from my back is true for our society. If we stop protecting the most vulnerable among us and showing concern for one another, we will get stuck in a cycle of reinjuring ourselves and others. We will also be more susceptible to a politics that appeals to hate and fear and will retreat into partisan or ideological camps. As a result, embracing ubuntu interdependence is critical for restoring health to our democracy and building the Beloved Community.

There are many threats to our interdependence, including global climate change, which poses a signature challenge to living together on an interdependent planet. Poverty in all its forms and degrees assaults human dignity and represents a great test of our interdependence because, as Mahatma Gandhi said, "poverty is the greatest form of violence." Dr. King understood that fighting poverty represented the next chapter, the next frontier, of the civil rights struggle. In his final book, *Where Do We Go from Here: Chaos or Community?* King wrote, "The time has come for us to civilize ourselves by the total, direct, and immediate abolition of poverty." King's words offer a searing and prophetic diagnosis of poverty and are as true and relevant today as when they were written more than fifty years ago. The sobering truth is that not nearly enough has changed in the intervening years. King wrote, "We have proceeded from a premise that poverty is a consequence of multiple evils: lack of education, restricting job opportunities; poor housing which stultified home life and suppressed initiative; fragile family relationships which distorted personality development. The logic of this approach suggested that each of these could be attacked one by one. . . . At no time has a total, coordinated, and fully adequate program been conceived. As a consequence, fragmentary and spasmodic reforms have failed to reach down to the profoundest needs of the poor."[7]

Fifty years ago, King understood that solutions to poverty will require a comprehensive approach that addresses root causes. King later concluded that a guaranteed income represented the single most effective policy solution, writing: "I am now convinced that the simplest approach will prove to be the most effective—the solution to poverty is to abolish it directly by a now widely discussed measure: the guaranteed income."[8] Some may wrongly dismiss this as socialist, unrealistic, or utopian, but the proposal is worthy of serious moral and practical consideration and analysis.

I've seen similar proposals ignite the imagination of national governments and credible global organizations, including the World Bank, where I worked leading the Faith Initiative for four years. There, I was exposed to a range of evidence-based policy solutions that the Bank recommended to many low- and middle-income countries. One such policy was Conditional Cash Transfers (CCTs), which come in different forms, most famously through the Bolsa Familia program in Brazil and the Oportunidades program in Mexico (now known as Prospera). While far from perfect, initially both programs were successful in lifting hundreds of millions of families out of the quicksand of extreme poverty, in part by tying government financial support to very low-income families for spending the money on nutrition and education—which serve as two of the most critical ways to climb the ladder out of generational poverty. The welfare system in the US provides a much more limited version of support, and due to the backlash against welfare in the 1990s, this support has been diminished over time to the point that its impact and coverage are far too limited.

Chile and Turkey have also implemented Conditional Cash Transfers that focus more narrowly on extremely poor and socially excluded people. In Bangladesh and Cambodia, CCTs have been used to reduce gender disparities in education. Based on these and other experiences, the World Bank has made the case that CCTs can result in substantial reductions in poverty, especially when the transfer has been generous, well targeted, and structured in a way that does not discourage recipients from taking other actions to escape poverty, such as entrepreneurship, job skills training, and more. Because CCTs provide a steady stream of income, they have helped buffer poor households from the worst effects of unemployment, catastrophic illness, and other sudden shocks. And making cash transfers to women, as virtually all CCTs do, increases their economic agency.[9]

The American Rescue Plan, signed into law in March 2021, contains a critical expansion of the child tax credit, which constitutes one of the most sweeping and hopeful anti-poverty measures in decades in the US. In concert with other faith-based and anti-poverty organizations, Sojourners served as a major champion of this provision, recognizing that it is one of the most effective ways to combat child poverty. This fully refundable and nearly universal credit, which provides direct cash payments to parents with children, is forecasted to essentially cut child poverty in half.[10] It is now critical to build the political will to make this credit a permanent policy commitment as an indispensable way of ensuring that every American child can realize their full potential free from the grip of poverty, which represents a fundamental expression of ubuntu interdependence.

Direct cash transfers have also gained traction in the philanthropic world, uniting people across ideological and political divides. One hopeful example is the #GiveTogetherNow campaign in response to the COVID-19 crisis. Anticipating the economic fallout for families because of the pandemic, Stand Together partnered with the Family Independence Initiative to launch the campaign. As the pandemic mounted, lives and livelihoods were in jeopardy as millions of families faced mounting expenses without a sufficient safety net. To help these families, the groups launched a national movement for community relief. The campaign "was founded on the simple idea that the best way to make a difference for families was to address their needs directly with $500 cash payments, no strings attached. . . . #GiveTogetherNow raised $100 million in less than five months, providing financial lifelines to nearly 200,000 families nationwide. The scale of the campaign sets an innovative example for emergency relief, illustrating how creative thinking and strategic partnerships can get aid where it's needed, when it's needed. Fueled by the participation of thousands of individuals, it also showcases the power of unity in times of struggle."[11] The campaign was rooted in a shared belief in personal agency: that people experiencing financial hardship know best what they need most—whether it's paying for rent, childcare, or food.

The campaign tapped into the Family Independence Initiative's nearly twenty years of experience in direct cash transfers and a network of more than 250 nonprofits spanning the country, all with their fingers on the pulse of their communities. Donors were encouraged to give either through a cash donation or through acts of kindness—for example, something as simple as a phone call to an elderly neighbor who lives alone, or delivering a bag of groceries for someone else—with the recognition that people need community and relationships as much as cash to overcome this pandemic. The platform UpTogether provided the technical foundation for #GiveTogetherNow, enabling direct transfers to eligible families' bank accounts to get them cash quickly. Lauren McCann, former vice president at Stand Together and one of the architects who helped amplify the initiative on the national stage, captured the spirit of this effort. "People living in poverty are often the most resourceful, creative, and resilient people in our country," McCann told me. "When we see people through their strengths and [don't] define them by their circumstances, we realize the best way we can help people living in poverty is by trusting and believing in them. #GiveTogetherNow empowered hundreds of thousands of families to give and to receive with the flexibility to do what they knew was best for their family. It demonstrated the power of community when we come together and trust one another."[12]

The fiftieth anniversary of Dr. King's Poor People's Campaign provided a critical moment for our nation to pause and conduct a moral MRI of our efforts in combating poverty. Despite some progress, poverty remains deeply entrenched and pervasive. Roughly 13 percent of Americans are perpetually sinking in the quicksand of poverty. Events such as the coronavirus pandemic have only raised those numbers. Poverty disproportionately impacts people of color and women, the result of sexist and racist systems. And poverty continues to be deeply intergenerational, where burdens and disadvantages are passed on across generations. Poverty is both urban and rural, and now has become increasingly suburban as well. About 40 million Americans live in poverty, 18.5 million live in "extreme poverty," and more than 5 million live in what the United Nations calls "absolute poverty."[13]

According to a 2018 UN investigation, America already has the highest rates of youth poverty, infant mortality, incarceration, income inequality, and obesity among industrialized nations. The report goes on to explain that "for almost five decades the overall policy response has been neglectful at best, but the policies pursued over the past year seem deliberately designed to remove basic protections from the poorest, punish those who are not in employment, and make even basic health care into a privilege to be earned rather than a right of citizenship."[14]

The response to poverty by too many people has been what I call a mentality of "You will always have the poor with you." The root causes of poverty are often ignored, misunderstood, or oversimplified. People living in poverty are often invisible, marginalized, and, at worst, scapegoated for their struggles. As Jim Wallis points out in his *New York Times* bestselling book *God's Politics*, those words of Jesus in John 12:8— "You always have the poor with you"—often have been misappropriated to imply that the poor will be a permanent fixture in our public life. This mentality has justified a great deal of complacency around the imperative to combat and ultimately bring an end to the worst forms of poverty. But these words come from a moment when Jesus rebukes Judas—the treasurer for the band of disciples—for his hypocritical criticism of Mary's pouring expensive perfume as a blessing on Jesus's feet. Judas cynically suggests that the money could have been used for the poor. And Jesus replies with a kind of rabbinic response about there being a season for everything, including a time to bless. A more careful and contextual interpretation of Jesus's response reveals that what Jesus implies is that if we are his disciples, "we will always be among the poor." Jesus is really pointing out the disciples' continuing proximity to people living in poverty. This is because the Gospels make clear that as a poor Palestinian Jew, Jesus spent a disproportionate amount of his life and ministry with and among the poor.[15]

One major reason we are still losing the war against poverty is because we aren't communicating a compelling enough narrative centered in ubuntu interdependence. While many other countries have focused on the best solutions for ending extreme poverty by 2030, ever since the Sustainable

Development Goals were agreed to in 2015, America has been mired in a debate about the extent to which poverty even exists or is a major problem.

In the context of our national politics, the people trapped in poverty have also been trapped in a debate, which often pits a conservative emphasis on personal responsibility, market solutions, and the need for strong families against the liberal emphasis on strengthening the social safety net and rectifying structural and systemic injustices. Meanwhile, these debates rarely fully name the root causes of poverty or the best and holistic policy prescriptions to reduce it.

To break out of the denial, complacency, and ideological stalemate that so often cripples our nation's response to poverty, we need a new approach centered on three core commitments:

- encouraging greater proximity with people living in poverty;
- building consensus and momentum around evidence-based, comprehensive policies that can often transcend the left/right divide; and
- reframing and correcting the narrative around poverty to ignite greater empathy and moral urgency.

It is much easier to scapegoat people caught in poverty when you have very little real contact or relationship with them. The transformational power of authentic relationships is critical in the fight against poverty because relationships humanize the people most impacted and inevitably challenge many of our assumptions and prejudices about people trapped in or close to poverty. I have had many relationships with people trapped in poverty—through my work, through volunteering in my fraternity, Alpha Phi Alpha, Inc., and through church—even as I realize that my deeper encounters with poverty are often still too infrequent. I admire the work of the Christian Community Development Association, whose members make an incarnational commitment to relocate to live in and among communities struggling with poverty. While not everyone will feel called to relocate their families, all of us can accept the challenge to build authentic relationships with people trapped in poverty in ways that are mutually transformational.

No party or ideology has a monopoly on the solutions to ending poverty in America. With some exceptions, neither Republicans nor Democrats have prioritized a comprehensive agenda to combat let alone try to end poverty. In 2016, then Speaker of the House Paul Ryan put forward a Republican anti-poverty agenda called "A Better Way" that proposed creating stricter work requirements, conducting ongoing evaluations to assess whether federally funded programs are working, and expanding the Earned Income Tax Credit (EITC).[16] While some of these policy prescriptions, such as expanding the EITC, are helpful, others such as tightening already robust work requirements tied to welfare are misguided and unnecessary. The Republican-controlled Congress in recent years pushed through several policies that exacerbated poverty, including granting states the ability to impose work requirements on Medicaid and stripping or undermining key provisions in the Affordable Care Act.

On the Democratic side, anti-poverty agendas from the Progressive Caucus[17] and party leaders have emphasized the need to raise and index the federal minimum wage to $15 an hour and guarantee universal access to quality health care, and have proposed ideas such as a federal jobs guarantee,[18] free tuition for public colleges and universities, dramatic expansion of the Child Tax Credit,[19] and a targeted jobs program[20] for marginalized young people. Many of these proposals will require identifying and generating significant revenue and building greater political will.

These and other policy proposals could form the basis of a more comprehensive approach to ending poverty, particularly those that are evidence-based and bridge some of the left/right divides. But to build support for and enact these and other policies in a way that helps those in financial, educational, and essential-food need, we need to move beyond platitudes and offer a bold vision whose component parts work together to actually *solve* poverty, even as we know there is no magic bullet or panacea for combating poverty.

A comprehensive approach to poverty must include the following:

- It must address the breakdown of families[21] by ameliorating the economic pressures that accelerate this breakdown.

- It requires addressing the changing nature of work due to automation and technology.
- It requires dramatically increasing affordable housing and rental assistance and increasing investment in blighted and underserved communities and neighborhoods.
- It requires transforming our education system so that the quality of a child's education isn't tied to their zip code.
- It requires increasing access to jobs, partly by pursuing a federal jobs program that builds up infrastructure, increases investments in low-income communities, and strengthens job-training programs.
- It requires raising and indexing the minimum wage to become a living wage and strengthening both the EITC and the Child Tax Credit to ensure that people who work full time are not living below the poverty line due to poverty wages and to prevent children from having to grow up in the quicksand of poverty.
- It requires increasing access to quality health care for every American so that good health becomes a shared public good and health crises don't throw families into poverty.
- It requires increasing access and opportunities for people living with disabilities.
- It requires reforming our immigration system so that we can bring undocumented immigrants out of the shadows of our economy, providing a pathway to earned citizenship.
- It requires ending mass incarceration, in part by dismantling racial bias and injustice in our criminal justice system.
- It requires a more just tax system that more fairly and effectively taxes the wealthy, corporations, and Wall Street, including by closing tax loopholes and strengthening tax enforcement.
- It requires all these commitments—and more.[22]

Even amid our political impasse and polarization, there are a series of policy solutions to combat poverty that would garner a great deal of bipartisan support and represent low-hanging fruit. These include expanding EITC benefits to single adults, permanently making the Child Tax Credit fully refundable, setting up savings accounts for every child born into a low-income family, expanding access to childcare, and revamping job-training programs. Yet even the most thoughtful and comprehensive policy agendas will fail to gain traction as long as poverty remains a third-rail issue in our politics and a marginal matter in our public consciousness. What is missing in order to support and enable millions to lift themselves out of poverty is the moral imperative that prioritizes overcoming poverty and an economics centered in ubuntu interdependence.

These polices and priorities would also have positive spillover effects on other issues, including abortion, another issue I care deeply about that has too often been overly polarized in our politics. As someone who embraces a consistent ethic of life, I don't believe in criminalizing abortion as an effective or moral solution and have worked to forge common ground between the pro-life and pro-choice movements by identifying and advocating around policies that have been proven to dramatically decrease the number of unwanted pregnancies in the country. These include ensuring access to affordable health care, family planning, and contraception,[23] increasing access to childcare, combating domestic abuse and sexual violence, and increasing economic support and opportunities for women, among others. While this common-ground approach will not resolve the divide over legal restrictions and the right to choose, it would enable significant progress to be made to protect life at every stage and would demonstrate that the country is far less divided around the issue of abortion than is often believed.

Nick Hanauer is a leading critic of modern economic policy that so often produces poverty, and an advocate of what I call an ubuntu economics. A billionaire entrepreneur, Hanauer has founded, co-founded, or funded more than thirty companies across a range of industries. In arguably the most unexpected and most compelling TED Talk I've seen, titled "The Dirty Secret of Capitalism—and a New Way Forward," Hanauer says, "Over the last thirty years in the US, the top 1 percent got $21 trillion richer while the bottom 50 percent has grown $900 billion poorer."[24] He explains that rising inequality and growing political instability are the direct result of decades of bad economic theory and calls for the dismantling of the mantra that "greed is good"—an idea he describes as not only morally corrosive but also scientifically wrong.

He calls for a new theory of economics, one that better harnesses reciprocity and cooperation—and, I would add, also harnesses the power of our interdependence.

In making a case for his new economics, Hanauer argues that

- economic growth is created primarily by people, and not simply by capital;
- reciprocity promotes the public good, not simply self-interest; and
- cooperation, not purely competition, produces our prosperity.

"An economics that is neither just nor inclusive," Hanauer says, "cannot sustain the level of social cooperation needed for a healthy economy. New economics would treat economies as gardens that need to be tended rather than as jungles, because unconstrained by good government regulation, markets inevitably create more problems than they solve—think of the climate change crisis and the 2008 financial crash, both hallmarks of economics-faced-inward, inevitably spinning out of control into great harm." When we understand that this new economics creates economic growth and that greed and "being rapacious does not make you a capitalist, it makes you a sociopath," as Hanauer puts it, we begin to see that a new economics must be built in light of interconnection. At points Hanauer sounds like an Old Testament prophet, forewarning that "capitalism left to its own devices inexorably leads to inequality, concentration, and collapse."[25] Some of these ideas seem to be gaining currency in some pockets of corporate America. While it is too early to determine how much change it will lead to, an August 2019 statement by the Business Roundtable is a hopeful sign. Signed by 181 corporate CEOs, the statement commits them to leading their companies for the benefit of all stakeholders: customers, employees, suppliers, communities, and shareholders.[26]

One of the most unheralded success stories in the Trump years was the degree to which a broad coalition of Christian leaders, in concert with others, managed to maintain bipartisan congressional support for foreign assistance and many programs that benefit low-income Americans, despite repeated attempts by the administration to make draconian cuts to these vital, life-saving programs. The Circle of Protection is an inspiring example of Christian leaders putting the spirit of ubuntu interdependence into practice. The Circle was started in 2014 by a diverse cross section of Christian leaders during the height of a budget crisis, and the group continues to provide evidence of what is possible when people of faith from very different political perspectives put principles over politics and unite around the core biblical mandate to protect and care for the most vulnerable. Circle members range from the US Conference of Catholic Bishops and the National Association of Evangelicals to the National Council of Churches and the Friends Committee on National Legislation. Members disagree on many other issues, but working together has built deep and durable bonds of trust rooted in a shared commitment to protect and uplift people trapped in poverty.

The Circle's first major policy victory was convincing the Obama administration and then Speaker of the House John Boehner to protect programs that benefit low-income Americans, including food stamps, from being cut in a major budget deal. The Circle's success is due in part to having such clear and compelling shared moral principles, recognizing that federal budgets are moral documents. The Circle emphasizes that budgets determine what we prioritize and value, and that people of faith are called to defend programs that are effective in uplifting people trapped in poverty. Despite numerous attempts by the Trump administration to slash spending on anti-poverty and social safety-net programs, bipartisan congressional support remained resilient enough to defy and overturn the administration's wishes. The strong moral argument of faith leaders was instrumental in building and maintaining this bipartisan congressional leadership. The coalition also played an instrumental role in advocating and building bipartisan support behind many key provisions of the COVID-19 relief and stimulus bills, that helped protect and uplift low-income and vulnerable Americans: for example, expanding food stamp benefits, making the Child Tax Credit fully refundable, and extending unemployment insurance.

The modern-day Poor People's Campaign, co-chaired by Rev. Dr. William Barber II and Rev. Dr. Liz Theoharis, provides another hopeful glimpse of ubuntu interdependence. On a sweltering summer day in

2019, I stood proudly on the National Mall with thousands of faith, community, and civic leaders who were active in the campaign, a national call for moral revival. We stood facing the Lincoln Memorial on the same ground where a diverse cross section of Americans had gathered more than fifty years before during the original Poor People's Campaign launched and led by Martin Luther King Jr. shortly before his assassination. King had announced the campaign at a staff retreat for the Southern Christian Leadership Conference in November 1967. Seeking a "middle ground between riots on the one hand and timid supplications for justice on the other," King planned for an initial group of two thousand poor people to descend on Washington, DC, to meet with government officials to "demand jobs, unemployment insurance, a fair minimum wage, and education for poor adults and children designed to improve their self-image and self-esteem."[27] In summer 1968, civil rights leaders constructed Resurrection City, a tent city on the mall, to galvanize moral and political will to combat poverty. In the months before his death, King had invited not just Blacks and whites but also people of Mexican descent, Native Americans, and Puerto Ricans to join this march and demonstration. King envisioned that, together, this early rainbow coalition of Americans would dramatize the plight of poverty by bringing "waves of the nation's poor and disinherited to Washington, D.C., . . . to demand redress of their grievances by the United States government and to secure at least jobs or income for all."[28] After King's murder, Ralph Abernathy took the lead, but while the valiant effort persisted for six weeks, torrential rainfall and other challenges led to its demise, and the campaign failed to generate the greater and lasting impact the leaders had hoped for. While King and other civil rights leaders understood the need to focus the movement's attention on poverty and economic justice, the disappointing outcome portended the future failures of the war on poverty as the nation became increasingly consumed with race riots following King's assassination and deep divisions around the Vietnam War.

The modern Poor People's Campaign, which Sojourners joined as a national partner, has learned from and seeks to build upon the original campaign. The modern campaign is anchored in a commitment to change the narrative about poverty in America. The campaign's stated goal is to bring people together "to confront the interlocking evils of systemic racism, poverty, ecological devastation, militarism and the war economy, and the distorted moral narrative of religious nationalism. We understand that as a nation we are at a critical juncture—that we need a movement that will shift the moral narrative, impact policies and elections at every level of government, and build lasting power for poor and impacted people."[29] In the months leading up to the rally on the National Mall, people living in poverty and others from forty states engaged in a season of direct action, leading to the most expansive wave of nonviolent civil disobedience in the twenty-first-century United States.

Jonathan Wilson-Hartgrove, who serves on the national steering committee of the Poor People's Campaign, explains that "the working theory of change behind the campaign is that the poor and marginalized in this country, though they have often been pitted against each other because of systemic racism, have a lot more in common than what divides them." Wilson-Hartgrove told me that in his view, "the Beloved Community is a fusion coalition, connecting people across division. . . . It's an imagination for how people who have different histories and traditions that make it a challenge to be together can still imagine and celebrate being together. It must include justice and equality but also joy and celebrating the gifts that different people bring."[30] The campaign pursues an intersectional and comprehensive approach to fighting poverty, codified in a policy agenda that demands "voting rights, guaranteed incomes, work with dignity, living wages, health care, clean air and water, and peace in this violent world."[31]

You don't need to agree with every one of their policy prescriptions to be inspired by the ways in which the campaign is reframing and bringing greater moral urgency to the fight against poverty. With organizing committees in forty-six states and working together with nineteen national faith denominations and more than two hundred national partner organizations, the campaign offers a hopeful glimpse into what building the Beloved Community will require for the more than 140 million poor and low-income people living in the United States, or 43 percent of the country's population.

Ubuntu interdependence teaches us that our nation's health is inextricably linked to the thriving of all people. In particular, it teaches us that when the most vulnerable thrive, we all thrive. When one part of America suffers, all parts suffer with it. When one part rejoices, all parts rejoice with it.

Chapter Twelve

PRIORITIZING NONVIOLENCE

In the guilt and confusion confronting our society, violence only adds to the chaos. It deepens the brutality of the oppressor and increases the bitterness of the oppressed. Violence is the antithesis of creativity and wholeness. It destroys community and makes brotherhood impossible. —Martin Luther King Jr.

Until the philosophy which hold one race superior / And another inferior / Is finally and permanently / Discredited and abandoned / Everywhere is war . . . until that day, the dream of lasting peace, world citizenship / Rule of international morality / Will remain in but a fleeting illusion to be pursued, but never attained / Now everywhere is war / War. —Bob Marley

Blessed are the peacemakers, for they will be called children of God. —Jesus, Matthew 5:9

VIOLENCE TEARS AT THE VERY FABRIC OF THE BELOVED COMMUNITY, MARRING AND derailing its realization. Violence begets violence. Communities that are victims of violence internalize both trauma and oppression, forces that sabotage human flourishing and deny human dignity. Violence is often hidden and self-harming. Martin Luther King Jr. understood that violence has a cascading effect, externally and internally, on future generations. He responded with a commitment to nonviolence that formed the basis of how he and other civil rights leaders understood the Beloved Community. His commitment to nonviolence included his methods of resisting injustice; a philosophy of nonviolence was his ethical foundation.

It also included a commitment to dismantle what King referred to as "the giant triplets of racism, materialism, and militarism."

Peace both in the U.S. and around the world is impossible without the interdependent (ubuntu) work of healing and the presence of justice. The commitment to nonviolence is not simply about avoiding or resolving conflict. As we've seen in the lives of Representative John Lewis and so many others, getting in the way of injustice often requires being willing to directly confront violence.

In 2019 the Carnegie Endowment for International Peace and Princeton University convened fifty scholars, practitioners, funders, and elected and government officials to discuss political violence in America. The conclusions were both illuminating and sobering:

> America's history of political violence spans our civil war, decades of lynchings, and the assassinations of a president, presidential candidate, and national community leaders in the 1960s and 1970s. . . . while most polarized countries are divided along just one or two dimensions, America has three fissures—ideological, ethnic, and religious—that overlap and augment one another. . . . 20 percent of Republicans and 15 percent of Democrats believe that members of the other party "lack the traits to be considered fully human—they behave like animals." The FBI found hate crimes spiked 17 percent in 2017, with a 37 percent increase in anti-Semitic incidents. Based on such risk factors, the 2018 Fragile States Index ranked America among the top five "most worsened countries" for political stability, alongside Yemen and Venezuela. Moreover, the US represents just one front in what is now a global movement—violent white supremacists from New Zealand to Canada are interacting online, reading each other's manifestos, and inspiring one another.[1]

These and other trends and forces fueled the January 6, 2021, insurrection, an act of domestic terrorism that will remain a dark stain on our nation's democracy. These very real and dangerous fissures within American society could easily erupt again into even more overt violence.

Our nation has lacked the tools and imagination to move beyond our addiction to violence. Realizing the Beloved Community requires investment in harnessing the power of nonviolence as a form of resistance and transformation. In one of the beatitudes from the Sermon on the Mount Jesus says, "Blessed are the peacemakers." This isn't a hollow platitude or a utopian dream but an ethic to live by.

I vividly remember feeling paralyzed by grief when I heard the news of the massacre of nine members of the historic Mother Emanuel AME Church in Charleston, South Carolina, while they were engaged in Bible study and prayer on June 17, 2015. I heard the horrific news the next morning when I arrived at Sojourners' annual conference called the Summit. In the morning plenary session, three hundred participants looked shell-shocked at the heart-wrenching news. The organizers decided to pause the planned program and enter into a time of prayer and lament for the families of the people who were executed, for Charleston, and for our nation in our ongoing struggle to conquer the demons of hatred and white supremacy.

Four years later, I had the privilege of supporting a deeply moving film called *Emanuel*, by cowriting an official discussion guide designed to equip pastors and community leaders to foster dialogue around the themes of violence, forgiveness, repentance, and the costly demands of racial justice.[2] The documentary honors the lives and legacy of the Emanuel Nine by sharing their stories through the voices of their relatives. The film offers a courageous witness with the power to transform hearts and minds and to catalyze greater urgency for repairing the breach caused by hatred and violence in our country, which, King said, wounds and imprisons both the victim and the perpetrator.

In the aftermath of the massacre, the shooter, Dylann Roof, admitted that he was trying to incite a race war. He was often referred to by police and the media as the killer but almost never as a domestic terrorist. This distinction matters because the rising threat of domestic terrorism is so often underplayed or ignored by political leaders. And yet the Anti-Defamation League reported that, in the United States, "right-wing extremists collectively have been responsible for more than 70 percent of the 427 extremist-related killings over the past 10 years, far outnumbering those committed by left-wing extremists or domestic Islamist extremists—even with the sharp rise of Islamist-extremist killings in the past five years."[3] The white-power killer in New Zealand—a twenty-eight-year-old white Australian man who fatally shot fifty Muslims while they were worshipping—cited the Emanuel shooter as an inspiration.

From Oklahoma City to Charleston, Charlottesville to Pittsburgh, New Zealand to Norway and elsewhere in Europe, white nationalism and white supremacy represent a growing movement that we can't afford to ignore. This movement was emboldened by Trump's rhetoric during his four years in office. He repeatedly refused to condemn white supremacists, arguing that there were "fine people on both sides" in the 2017 Unite the Right rally in Charlottesville, and told the white supremacist group the Proud Boys to "stand back and stand by" during a 2020 presidential debate. He initially praised protesters, which included many white supremacist groups, who attempted a coup on January 6, seeking to disrupt and overturn the certification of the election results. This resurgent white supremacist movement is fueled by hatred and unified by a fear that white people's power and superiority is being taken away by the growth of more diverse and inclusive communities, including the changing racial demographics of the US—in which, the Census Bureau estimates, white people will no longer be a majority by the year 2045.

Dylann Roof showed no visible remorse at a court hearing soon after the massacre. In an unusual move, the judge asked whether family members of the victim wanted to address him. In that poignant moment, many family members were moved to publicly forgive him, even praying that he would come to know Christ's love and salvific mercy. This radical act of grace reverberated around the globe, offering a powerful, Christlike witness that helped to defuse tensions and the risk of violence in the aftermath of the massacre. But the courageous willingness to forgive shouldn't serve as a replacement or sedative for the demands for necessary systemic change and justice for perpetrators of hate and violence.

I believe in the power of forgiveness as a force for nonviolence and building the Beloved Community. I can only imagine the spiritual fortitude and courage it would take to forgive the seemingly unforgivable. Jesus instructed his followers, "Love your enemies . . . bless those who curse you, pray for those who abuse you" (Luke 6:27–28). And when Peter asks Jesus, "Lord, how many times shall I forgive my brother or sister who sins against me? Up to seven times?" Jesus answers, "I tell you, not seven times, but seventy-seven times" (Matthew 18:21–22). Forgiveness lies at the very heart of the Lord's Prayer, in which we ask that God "forgive us our trespasses as we forgive those who trespass against us." This is a tall order but one that can release us from pain and resentment, breaking the vicious cycle of vengeance and retribution that often begets greater enmity and more violence. King also warned against the destructive dangers of hate: "Returning hate for hate multiplies hate," he said, "adding deeper darkness to a night already devoid of stars. Darkness cannot drive out darkness; only light can do that. Hate cannot drive out hate; only love can do that."[4]

At the same time, we can't end at forgiveness. If we are to achieve real and lasting peace, we must also challenge and dismantle attitudes and structures of white supremacy and bigotry that so often degenerate into violence. Honoring the memory of the Emanuel Nine requires us to work on both interpersonal and systemic levels. The true meaning of repentance is important to understand in this context. Repentance is much more than saying sorry or feeling regret or sadness. True repentance means turning around and going in a new direction. As individuals and a society, this is what we need to do. We owe it to the Emanuel Nine and so many other victims of hatred and violence.[5]

There is arguably no more alarming and pervasive form of violence in American society than gun violence, with mass shootings having become a horrific fixture within American life. The shooting at Marjory Stoneman Douglas High School in Parkland, Florida, in 2018 killed seventeen people, making it one of the deadliest school shootings in modern American history.[6] Many hoped it would serve as a tipping point that would lead to real gun-policy reform. While the courageous and passionate activism of students from Parkland and around the country helped galvanize a shift in public opinion, these protests failed to break through the seemingly impenetrable congressional deadlock caused in large part by the GOP's steadfast refusal to take actions to control guns, often rooted in a misreading of the Second Amendment and cemented by the lobbying power of the National Rifle Association.

The Parkland shooting took place on Ash Wednesday, when many Christians remember their mortality as they begin the penitential season of Lent. Sadly, it was also Valentine's Day, when many Americans show appreciation to their loved ones. Rabbi Jonah Dov Pesner, director of the Religious Action Center of Reform Judaism, captured the moral indignation and exhaustion that so many religious leaders felt following the shooting, saying, "No other country in the world tolerates this level of deadly slaughter. Sandy Hook. Orlando. Las Vegas. Sutherland Springs. The many other attacks that have left families forever shattered by loss. And now Parkland. Until our elected officials stop issuing empty calls for thoughts and prayers and start protecting all Americans, we are left to wonder which community will be the next one added to this dreadful list."[7] Parkland served as a political awakening for a generation of young people, many of whom are refusing to accept the maddening status quo around guns and are expressing their outrage through their votes and activism.

Gun control is a stark example of how our politics—and especially the intransigence of most Republican lawmakers—is failing the nation, particularly given the overwhelming public support for long-overdue gun control reforms such as a ban on assault weapons and high-capacity magazines, and the requirement of stronger background checks. These and other reforms do not come at the expense of the right to bear arms, which would still enable Americans to responsibly own guns for hunting and other reasons. In addition to thoughts and prayers for the thousands of yearly victims of gun violence, from mass shootings to gun-involved suicide and other gun violence, it is time for significant reforms.

Violence also destroys the possibilities for Beloved Community in cities and communities across the country, from Chicago to my own Washington, DC. In one section of DC with a high incidence of homicides and economic duress, pastors are working together to build the Beloved Community. Rev. Delonte Gholston, who grew up in DC, has been leading a series of "peace walks" every other Friday night in DC's Ward 7. Gholston pastors a multiracial congregation in the neighborhood, fittingly called Peace Fellowship Church, which is part of Peace Walks DC, a coalition of more than forty congregations, gun violence survivors, and community organizers who in 2019 engaged in seven months of facilitated trainings, peace walks, intentional engagement, and deep listening in some of the communities most impacted by gun violence. Peace Walks were started after a triple homicide took place in this neighborhood and were inspired by an initiative involving clergy walking the streets at night in Oakland, which contributed to a 40 percent reduction in homicides.

When envisioning the Peace Walks, Rev. Gholston tapped into his experience as a student at Fuller Seminary, when he led "Trust Talks," a series of facilitated conversations around race and policing in downtown Los Angeles. As he witnessed names such as Trayvon Martin, Michael Brown, and Sandra Bland become hashtags, according to a profile by the Center for Religion and Civic Culture at the University of Southern California Gholston couldn't help wondering, "Am I next?"[8] The Trust Talks team invited participation from community activists, police officers, representatives of the city attorney's office, business owners, and those living downtown—whether in lofts high above the bustle of the city or in tents on the sidewalks. In the final Trust Talk, Gholston said, "We as clergy are here to be that bridge of healing," adding: "How can we restore the humanity to the people who have been traumatized over and over again by a system that seems to be fine with the erasure and demonization of Black lives?"

Gholston describes his work in DC mobilizing clergy and community leaders as an effort "to turn over tables of injustice and to build a new table of Beloved Community."[9] During the wave of protests against police violence and systemic racism after George Floyd's murder, Gholston mobilized a clergy response, collecting more than six hundred signatures from faith leaders on a letter asking the mayor and other District of Columbia officials to transfer 20 percent of the police budget into violence prevention programs.[10] The letter, titled "The Time is Now: Repent. Refund. Reimagine. Reinvest," powerfully reframes public safety through the lens of violence prevention and nonviolence:

Anytime someone invests their hard-earned money into a product, good, or service that is inherently defective, they do not ask for an upgrade, they do not ask for an exchange, they do not ask for a rain check, they ask for a full refund. Black people in America now have 401 years of receipts on bad policing practices in America, 401 years of rain checks, 401 years of exchanges, 401 years of upgrades, 401 years of substitutions. The time for the promise of an "upgrade" is over. The time for reform has passed. The money that is in police budgets belongs to the people and what we need now is a refund. Refund the money that belongs to our community and let us reprioritize and reinvest it in a vision that works for our communities and moves us toward real healing and freedom.

Gholston emphasizes the power of building agency, arguing, "If white people took responsibility for their power and agency and Black people took responsibility for theirs, we would see more Beloved Community being built, because ultimately peace is the presence of justice."[11]

Violence comes in many forms. One form that rarely receives due attention involves hate crimes, including those directed at the LGBTQ community, disproportionately harming people of color.[12] As multiple government and private agencies have documented, we've seen a rise in hate groups, hate speech, and hate-inspired violence,[13] increasingly directed at people who are lesbian, gay, bisexual, transgender, or queer. According to FBI data, of the 7,120 hate-crime incidents reported in 2018, more than 1,300—or nearly 19 percent—stemmed from anti-LGBTQ bias.[14] Reports of anti-trans violence are increasing at an even higher rate: between 2017 and 2018, the number of these reported incidents increased 34 percent. The lesbian, gay, bisexual, transgender, and queer community is estimated by Gallup to comprise 4.5 percent of the US population, yet according to the FBI, 18.5 percent of hate crime victims are LGBTQ. Building the Beloved Community requires humanizing and protecting those who have been most marginalized and dehumanized, including the LGBTQ community; this commitment is both a faith imperative and a civic virtue.

I have been inspired by the courageous and resourceful work of L. B. Prevette, whom I met through the Aspen Institute Civil Society Fellowship program. She was one of the youngest members of our cohort, yet I was immediately struck by her humble wisdom, disarming wit, and deep authenticity. As an openly lesbian woman, she has experienced both exclusion and abuse. Prevette is the daughter of a poultry farmer in tiny Union Grove in Wilkes County, North Carolina. As a teenager, Prevette was ready to leave the area. One night at a party, she was called a derogatory, homophobic name, assaulted, and left unconscious. "I love my community," she said. "There's nowhere more beautiful than the foothills. But I told my dad, 'I can't be here.'" She went away to college to escape the threat of violence. In her sophomore year, her dad died. She returned to Wilkes County to help take care of the farm.

Prevette refers to her community as her "intentional family." At St. Paul's Episcopal Church, she is part of Forward Wilkes, a community group that Megan Barnett started a few years back to make the community more vibrant and engaged. The organization supports LGBTQ youth who experience exclusion, marginalization, and violence in their very conservative county. They jokingly refer to themselves as the heathens on the hill. Prevette says the organization, founded in large part by queer women, offers church space and resources, enabling queer youth to feel safe and cared for. Some adults offer trauma therapy. Adults also support youth through their life milestones, as basic as getting over their first breakup. "This youth outreach and building intentional community took off," Prevette told me. "People were craving community connection. It's the same hole in our life that church and bowling leagues used to fill. People want to be engaged but don't know how to access it."[15]

Prevette is among a group of Wilkes County residents working to rewrite their county's narrative, from one that gained notoriety for its plummeting median income and number of meth labs to one with a rich cultural history, beautiful scenery, and goodhearted people.[16] Prevette explains, "Many of my neighbors are just people who are already walking the walk of Beloved Community. Coming from a farm community, you don't make it unless you have a system of sharing." Prevette's story underscores how peace is not simply the absence of conflict, but requires the presence of both justice and of community relationships that affirm and protect human dignity.

Prevette is part of a growing set of initiatives sewn together through the Weaver movement, which was launched by the Aspen Institute and inspired by *New York Times* columnist David Brooks. The Weaver movement, according to Brooks, is "repairing our country's social fabric, which is badly frayed by distrust, division, and exclusion." People across the country are working to "end loneliness and isolation and weave inclusive communities," writes Brooks, seeking to shift our culture "from hyperindividualism that is all about personal success, to relationalism that puts relationships at the center of our lives."[17] Across the country, Brooks and others found people serving their neighbors and healing communities: "It wasn't hard to find such people. They are everywhere."[18]

The project's "relationalist manifesto," a version of which appears in Brooks's book *The Second Mountain*, points to the "amazingly diverse" work of the Weavers, from working with gang members in Chicago and building gathering places in rural Montana to engaging with single moms and malnourished infants in North Carolina. All the work involves building connections and creating relationships. People engage in these efforts, according to the manifesto, "because they want to serve their town, unleash the promise in others, ease suffering, live good lives, and help create a world in which love is plentiful, not scarce." And the endeavors cross the country's traditional boundaries. "Whether it was red America or blue America," the report says, "we had [the] same sensation—there are common values here, common actions, common goals. The social fabric is being ripped apart by a thousand forces, but these Weavers are a coherent movement of people trying to knit it back together."[19] The inspiring stories of Rev. Gholston, Prevette, and so many others serve as powerful reminders that nonviolence is more than simply an ethic; it is also a way of life. It requires weaving new relationships out of fractured ones and building trust where it has been eroded.

Growing up, I was infatuated with the Student Nonviolent Coordinating Committee, often wishing I had been born a few generations earlier so I could have come of age as an active participant in this movement. I was mesmerized by the courage and passion of leaders such as Diane Nash, Ella Baker, Bob Moses, and John Lewis. SNCC's founding statement captures this notion of nonviolence as both an ethic and a way of life for building the Beloved Community: "We affirm the philosophical or religious ideal of nonviolence as the foundation of our purpose, the presupposition of our belief, and the manner of our action. Nonviolence, as it grows from the Judeo-Christian tradition, seeks a social order of justice permeated by love. Integration of human endeavor represents the crucial first step towards such a society. Through nonviolence, courage displaces fear. Love transcends hate. Acceptance dissipates prejudice; hope ends despair. Faith reconciles doubt. Peace dominates war. Mutual regards cancel enmity. Justice for all overthrows injustice. The redemptive community supersedes immoral social systems."[20]

The Beloved Community requires this kind of moral clarity and resolve, with a commitment to nonviolence at the center.

Chapter Thirteen

ENVIRONMENTAL STEWARDSHIP

Today, however, we have to realize that a true ecological approach always becomes a social approach; it must integrate questions of justice in debates on the environment, so as to hear both the cry of the earth and the cry of the poor. —Pope Francis

Climate change is the single biggest thing that humans have ever done on this planet. The one thing that needs to be bigger is our movement to stop it. —Bill McKibben

FINANCIAL STEWARDSHIP IS CENTRAL TO THE LIFE OF FAITH. IN THE CHRISTIAN TRA-dition, it is tied to the biblical command to tithe 10 percent of our earnings back to God; in Islam, *zakat* (almsgiving) is one of the Five Pillars. From the vantage point of faith, everything we have already belongs to God. We are simply stewards, or caretakers, of what God has created and given. My church introduces our time of giving by emphasizing that giving is not about obligation but is sowing back to the church what God has blessed us with. There are no attempts to induce a sense of guilt or shame.

In a broader sense, stewardship is the belief that God gave human beings a special responsibility to cultivate creation, guard it, and use it wisely. With the increasing impacts and growing threat of climate change as well as other environmental destruction, a greater embrace of stewardship of the earth has become both a faith imperative and a personal and political priority that is fundamental to building the Beloved Community.

The air we breathe, the water we drink, the plants and animals that sustain life, and the earth itself are all essential to our livelihood and well-being.

In recent years we've seen horrific and uncontrollable wildfires on the West Coast, record flooding in the Midwest, a battery of hurricanes hitting the Gulf Coast—just some of the sobering reminders that the impacts of climate change are becoming much more real and dire. Climate scientists have reached a consensus that based on current global emissions, our world has less than a decade to dramatically reverse course before we cause irreparable harm to our planet. Predictions like that cause me to lose sleep at night, particularly when I think about the world that my two sons, let alone our possible future grandchildren, will inherit. Our world's addiction to carbon and overconsumption is causing profound consequences right now. While sound, evidence-based policy solutions exist, we have lacked the needed transformation of the hearts and minds of communities and nations to break us out of the thick fog of denial and delay. If we remain on our current trajectory, that world will be tragically different from the one we have known throughout history.

Yet these alarming developments are not inevitable, nor are we powerless to change course. Preventing the worst consequences and putting the planet on a zero-carbon trajectory require a revolution of social and political will. The good news is that unlike carbon, social and political will are renewable resources.[1]

Pope Francis's encyclical *Laudato Si': On Care for Our Common Home*, which came out in 2015, offers a moral clarion call and a blueprint on caring for people trapped in poverty and for the earth.[2] Before the encyclical was released, I attended an interreligious conference hosted by the Pontifical Academy of Science at the Vatican. Cardinal Peter Turkson, one of the primary shapers of the encyclical and then president of the Pontifical Council for Justice and Peace, gave us a preview of the contents, followed by a robust discussion of how the pope's forthcoming message would resonate across many religious traditions. *Laudato Si'* is the first papal encyclical addressed to the entire world, not simply to the Catholic faithful. It is also one of the most political of the encyclicals, outlining specific policy prescriptions and solutions to the crises of climate change and environmental destruction as both moral and existential threats.

Without a healthy planet there can be no healthy communities; environmental stewardship is central to building the Beloved Community. From a religious and spiritual perspective, this requires that we shift from the "dominion" narrative that has long wrongly justified human rule over the earth to a narrative of shared and responsible stewardship, where we serve as co-caretakers of the earth's fragile resources and incredible beauty.

Far too many religious communities have been blinded by the false theology of dominion, which has long been used to justify subduing the earth—its creatures, elements, and land—based on a narrow reading of Genesis 1:28. It is often dangerous and misleading to base one's entire theology on a single verse. Christians have frequently fixated upon and misapplied the first of two creation directives in Genesis, with the result being a perverted theology. The first directive is one God gives Adam and Eve—to have dominion over all the animals—which has sometimes been mistakenly assumed to mean that humans are charged with controlling the Earth. This is contrasted with the second reference in Genesis to the human relationship to creation, in which God gives us a divine assignment to care for the earth. Genesis 2:15 says that "the Lord God took the man and put him in the Garden of Eden to work it and take care of it." The original Hebrew uses the two words *avad* and *shamar*, which mean "to serve" and "to protect." Thus, we are commanded to tend the earth and protect it.[3] Never did God give humanity unrestrained authority to misuse the earth. Scripture does not warrant wanton control; it calls for stewardship—to cultivate, guard, and care for the earth.

The larger scope of scripture teaches a liberating theology of stewardship and interdependence. The good news is that the destructive narrative of the past may be shifting. Research conducted by Sojourners shows that Christians, and evangelicals in particular, respond most positively to moral and theological arguments such as "We have a moral duty to take care of creation and preserve it for future generations" and "We have an obligation to care for the 'least of these'—including those who suffer most from food scarcity, droughts, flooding, and increased diseases caused by climate change." It is good news that this argument is so persuasive; the bad news is that this biblical imperative to care for the planet is not being preached or taught nearly enough in pulpits, Sunday schools, or Bible study groups.

Some conservative groups have even claimed that the extremes of floods, wildfires, and massive storms are some kind of wrath of God. Climate change is not caused by the wrath of God. Rather, it's a clear result of our greed, selfishness, myopic vision, and misguided policy priorities. A clear-eyed look at how our earth has been affected by climate change—with its effects often exacerbated by inequalities and injustices—gives us the impetus to reorder our economy and framework for living on the earth in ways that are far more equitable, regenerative, and sustainable.

In a sermon he called "I Can't Breathe," my pastor, Rev. Howard-John Wesley of Alfred Street Baptist Church outside of DC, made the case that we are on the brink of ecological destruction as the result of our bad stewardship of the planet. Pastor Wesley preached that almost one hundred thousand species go extinct every year. We are burning the earth out, creating environments in which creatures can no longer live. Americans constitute 5 percent of the world's population but burn 25 percent of the world's fossil fuels, Wesley explained from the pulpit. The average American consumes three hundred pounds of plastic a year. Because of these and other trends of conspicuous consumption, we are in the midst of an ecological crisis. We have treated the earth as though it only exists for our benefit and pleasure. As he preached, Wesley lifted up the tragic last words of Eric Garner, the Black man asphyxiated by New York police using a reckless chokehold. Quoting Garner's words, which were later spoken as well by George Floyd, Wesley preached, "Our planet is yelling out, 'I can't breathe.'" Every tsunami, Wesley said, should remind us of the words "I can't breathe." Through hurricanes such as Katrina and Harvey, we hear the call "I can't breathe." Many from our Black communities have cried, "I can't breathe." The planet is hollering, "I can't breathe."[4]

Communities and nations that contribute the least to rising greenhouse gases bear the greatest burden of climate disaster. Added to the tragedy is the fact that so many parts of the Christian church are saying so little about it.

The beatitude of environmental stewardship also requires an understanding of environmental racism and a commitment to advancing environmental justice. In the US, African Americans have greater exposure to toxins than do white people for thirteen out of fourteen air pollutants.[5] Hispanics have higher exposure for ten out of fourteen. These factors present multiple health challenges to these communities, including cardiovascular disease, asthma and other respiratory diseases, cancer, and premature death. More than 50 percent of people who live within two miles of a toxic waste facility are people of color. Even as people of color grow closer to becoming the majority of the US population, one may wonder why environmental justice issues have not yet become national priorities. In the wake of natural disasters profoundly exacerbated by climate change, Black and brown communities are most at risk physically, financially, mentally, and socially and face further marginalization during the disaster recovery process.[6]

A report from the NAACP and the Clean Air Task Force showed that African Americans are 75 percent more likely than other Americans to live in so-called fence-line communities, areas situated near facilities that produce hazardous waste.[7] To make matters worse, "though Black communities bear disproportionate hardships of the environmental crisis, they historically have been left out of the environmental movement. . . . white people made up 85 percent of the staffs and 80 percent of the boards of the 2,057 environmental nonprofits."[8] As Linda Villarosa writes in the *New York Times Magazine*, "The first stirrings of the Black-led environmental-justice movement began in the late 1970s as a convergence of a growing interest in environmental issues and the civil rights and Black-power movements. Alarmed and angry community members began raising concerns about the placement of facilities that contaminate air, water, and soil—including incinerators, oil refineries, smelters, sewage-treatment plants, landfills and chemical plants—near communities of color."[9] Environmental stewardship requires further bridging the divides between the climate change and the environmental justice movement, which will require the still predominantly white environmental movement to more strongly embrace the battle against environmental racism.

The threat of climate change has become a common theme in films, as though Hollywood sought to shock us into a sense of urgency, from the over-the-top *The Day after Tomorrow* to the much more thoughtful *Interstellar* and *Mad Max: Fury Road*, going all the way back to one of my favorite films, *Blade Runner*. Other movies with climate-change themes include *Alita, Iron Man II*, and the dystopian film trilogy, *The Hunger Games*. Daniel Craig's James Bond even drives an electric car! While film and TV can help paint a picture of what may seem unimaginable today, our best teacher is the real-life climate events taking place before our very eyes: the floods that swept the Midwest, the horrific wildfires in California and Australia, the hurricanes that have devastated Puerto Rico and other places. The challenge is to offer science-based explanations of these events in the context of our changing planet, rather than seeing them as isolated and freakish anomalies.

While commitments like new automobile mileage efficiency standards are a critical and hopeful step, we can't "efficiency" our way out of the climate crisis. In the 1970s, the proposed solution to the energy crisis was to impose new efficiency standards on cars and appliances. But we now face a trajectory in which even cutting our carbon use by half in the next ten-plus years will not prevent the 1.5-degree Celsius rise that scientists indicate as being catastrophic. We need to bring to bear the same degree of urgency in addressing the climate crisis as we did in the 1940s regarding World War II.[10]

This colossal challenge requires new stories that galvanize a greater sense of urgency and capture the moral imagination around what is possible if we act together boldly. One such story is that of Max Edkins. A few years ago, I attended a moving memorial service for Edkins, a friend and colleague from my time working at the World Bank Group. Edkins was a climate leader who helped lead the World Bank's Connect4Climate initiative. Edkins, a beloved father, filmmaker, and scientist, lost his life in the 2019 crash of Ethiopian Airlines Flight 302, which killed the 157 people on board. Edkins was an indefatigable advocate and change maker who combined deep knowledge of environmental science with a charming personality and natural communication skills. He understood that people's hearts and minds will not be won over with facts and figures alone—instead, the climate crisis needs to be felt and understood through the lens of real people's struggles and triumphs. Telling the stories of people's connection to our glorious but fragile planet has the power to transform the hearts and minds of listeners, Edkins believed. And he was determined to give the microphone to the people living in places where the impacts of climate change are already the costliest.

In 2011, Edkins won a short-film competition sponsored by Connect 4Climate with his *The World Has Malaria*.[11] In a clever and disarming way, the film explains the cause and impacts of climate change through a one-minute dialogue between Maasai farmers in Tanzania. In recent years, the Maasai have experienced more frequent extreme droughts that have killed their cattle, a critical source of their livelihoods. In the video a man uses a soccer ball to explain how the burning of fossil fuels, primarily in the Global North, is putting more and more carbon dioxide into the blanket that protects the earth, causing warming and, ultimately, climate change. A Tanzanian farmer responds with a straightforward but compelling metaphor that helps him make sense of what is happening: "So now the planet is like someone who is suffering from malaria," he says. His assessment is fitting. Until you contract it, it's easy to be complacent about the threat of malaria. Its signs and symptoms (including fever and chills) often don't show up until weeks after being bitten by an infected mosquito. But the delay in the body's response can be deadly.

The malaria metaphor relates to public action about climate change, where the lack of early response will also be deadly. Environmental action morphed from a bipartisan issue in the 1970s and '80s into a highly partisan and polarized issue from 1992 to the present. The lobbying influence and disinformation campaigns of the big oil and coal industries played a key role in making it so partisan and forestalling action. When an issue about our existential future and the health of our planet became a partisan campaign complete with disinformation and outright lies, the threat became more difficult to overcome. It should never have become such a partisan or politicized cause, but this trend can and must be reversed.

I understand the difficult challenge of rallying public sentiment on climate change. For too long, while I believed the overwhelming science about the threat of climate change, my sense of urgency was stunted by an all-too-common notion that it was not a pressing or dire threat to human dignity and the sacredness of life. Instead, in the 1990s and early 2000s, as I was finishing my education and starting my career, I was preoccupied with addressing what felt like more immediate threats: the crisis of AIDS, extreme poverty, human trafficking, and the utterly preventable suffering and deaths of millions of children due to malnutrition and disease.

In all my work for human dignity, I failed to realize the degree to which climate change is directly related to every life and justice issue I care about. I now see, beyond the shadow of a doubt, that combatting climate change is about protecting the sanctity of life now and for future generations.

One of my favorite faith-based projects that the World Bank directly funded through a concessional loan to the government of Nigeria was through the Nigerian Interfaith Action Association (NIFAA). NIFAA worked tirelessly to overcome the scourge of malaria in Northern Nigeria by equipping and mobilizing pastors and imams to educate and persuade their communities to use insecticide-treated bed nets. Previous efforts to combat malaria in Northern Nigeria had largely failed due to distrust between the government and communities and the difficulties associated with changing people's behavior. Bishop Sunday Onuoha, founder of NIFAA, often comments that mosquitos engage in interfaith work because they bite Christians as much as they bite Muslims. NIFAA turned to the moral authority of Christian and Muslim leaders in these communities. As respected leaders, they voiced their concerns, convincing people that the threat of malaria was real and that by using insecticide-treated bed nets they could protect themselves and their families. The approach was wildly successful, and bed-net use quadrupled in places where the program was active. In a similar vein, respected faith leaders are positioned to speak to communities about the climate crisis in support of change that supports life—they can persuade those in their traditions and houses of worship to take the threat of climate change seriously. In the process they will help transform climate spectators and denialists into climate champions who, in caring for the earth, care for those whose thriving is so closely related to the air they breathe, the water they drink, and the food they eat.

We know how to prevent climate change and help cure a planet suffering from an increasing case of "malaria." The Beloved Community requires investing in the things that support abundant life and enable all people to thrive. This calls for personal changes, but also for community, national, and global change. We must embrace political and policy cures, including placing a price on carbon, dramatically increasing investments and incentives that accelerate a desperately needed shift to renewable energy, reducing our overconsumption and waste, incentivizing and requiring greater energy efficiency and the rapid phasing out of fossil fuel use in automobiles, buildings, and factories, and much more.

Yes, the world has a worsening case of malaria. But the most pertinent and pressing question now is: Are we willing to make the sacrifices and commitments—are we willing to use our personal resources and our positions of influence—to become the cure? Are we willing to become true stewards of the earth?

The beatitude of environmental stewardship involves personal decisions and commitments as well as systemic and policy change, and these are often mutually reinforcing. For example, Interfaith Power and Light has ignited a movement of people of faith across the country who are doing their part to prevent global warming in their own homes and places of worship through the Cool Congregations program, while saving thousands of dollars and tons of carbon from entering the atmosphere.[12] The Environmental Protection Agency's Energy Star program estimates that if America's 370,000 congregations cut energy use just 20 percent, it would save nearly $630 million per year that could be applied to missions. These energy savings would be the equivalent of eliminating emissions from 480,000 cars or planting 60,000 trees every year.

A commitment to stewardship is embraced across the world's faith traditions, as evidenced by the inspiring work of GreenFaith to build a worldwide, multifaith climate and environmental movement. Its theory of change is this:

Our religions teach us to care for the earth and each other; we seek to live by these values. Right now, however, the world is deeply out of balance and we are frightened and concerned. The most vulnerable among us are suffering while ineffective or authoritarian governments, polluting and extractive industries, and extremist cultural and religious forces place our planet at great risk. But we know that we have an opportunity now for bold transformation, to build a life connected to each other and the Earth. . . . The climate emergency we face is enormous. The forces working against us—the fossil fuel industry, corrupt or inadequate administrations, the culture of consumerism, simple inertia—are powerful. But our community is responding. We're pressing governments to commit to a global recovery from COVID-19 that invests in a just transition to 100 percent renewable energy, healthy food, clean water and air for everyone—and millions of green jobs to remake the world. We're organizing religious groups to divest from fossil fuels, industrial agriculture, and the banks that finance the planet's destruction and invest in climate solutions, especially those providing clean energy to the millions living without electricity. We're striving to lead by example, adopting climate-friendly consumption habits at home and at our places of prayer and worship.[13]

The model of GreenFaith shows how environmental stewardship increasingly involves this dual commitment to personal and systemic action and change—local as well as global. As we explored earlier, it also requires a lens of and a commitment to environmental justice. Rev. Mariama White-Hammond's activism and organizing in Boston show how these can and must be integrated. Rev. White-Hammond was a convert to the environmental movement after many years of racial justice activism, including leading Project HipHop. A 2005 service trip to New Orleans in the wake of Hurricane Katrina served as a catalyst, as she began making connections between environmental concerns and racial and economic justice while helping residents apply for federal aid after they lost their homes, possessions, and sometimes even loved ones when their families lacked resources to evacuate.[14] Michael Blanding wrote about her in *Boston* magazine: "White-Hammond has worked pulpits and podiums across the city to bridge Boston's racial divide, with a powerful—if somewhat blunt—unifying message: If the environment goes to hell, we're all screwed, so we better start working together. If it's a familiar idea, White-Hammond's goal adds a novel, local twist: By reaching out to Boston's white liberals about environmentalism—an issue that's comfortable, uncontroversial, and often overwhelmingly pale—she hopes she can also get them to become more fervent advocates for racial justice."[15]

White-Hammond combined a commitment to local issues with broader policy change when she united a Black congregation, a white mainline church, and a synagogue to secure solar panels to green their congregations and provide surplus energy to their community. She asked me, "Why would we drill into the ground when God gave us an energy source in the sky? We could get there if all our congregations worked together rather than doing it on their own."[16] After realizing that solar subsidies were going almost exclusively to affluent communities with resources and connections, the group lobbied the state house to push for solar power for low-income communities to cut pollution and lobbied for jobs for working-class residents as part of the push to close coal plants and create wind farms in poor communities such as New Bedford.

According to White-Hammond, Beloved Community was one of the frames she used to help young people understand the civil rights movement in deeper ways than "we get to sit next to white people." The Beloved Community starts from the notion, she said, that "a loving God would never put us in a situation where there wasn't enough for us all." She believes that "rejecting scarcity is critical for the work of imagination, otherwise you can't imagine and get stuck in 'Who deserves what?'" Environmental stewardship that builds the Beloved Community requires breaking out of a scarcity way of thinking and embracing a mindset of both abundance and racial justice.

Our personal actions may seem tiny and insignificant on their own, but when multiplied, they make a major impact. This includes living within our fair share of the world's resources and environmental limits. This relates to the food we eat and the food we throw away; it calls for traveling in more eco-friendly ways, making our homes more energy efficient, and reducing our overconsumption of unnecessary stuff.

Our daily stewardship decisions are important. Even more important is how we use our voices and power as citizens, consumers, and voters. We must transform the politics of denial, delay, and incrementalism into a politics of urgent, audacious, and transformational action.

In testimony delivered before the House Select Committee on the Climate Crisis, Melody Zhang, Sojourners' climate justice coordinator, offered a poignant and passionate entreaty:

As a Christian, I believe God calls us to a total and radical reimagination and transformation of our relationship with others and the earth. We yearn for a vision of complete reconciliation for all of God's created order. As political leaders, especially those of you grounded in faith and values, I implore you to respond faithfully and with full force to love God and neighbor by enacting just, compassionate, and transformative climate policies that rise to the challenge of the climate crisis. We don't have a lot of time. Congress, I invite you to dream beyond deeply rooted partisanship into co-creating a world of wholeness together.[17]

Living into this new reality will require sacrifice and the long view of environmental and intergenerational justice. Our future does not have to be characterized by pain and havoc. The supposed sacrifice, however, is also one of the benefits. As we adjust our lives to create positive changes to our climate, we will be changed for the better—including our economies, our way of life, and how we care for our neighbors, our community, and our planet. As we build the Beloved Community to steward the planet and better the world, the Beloved Community builds us.

Chapter Fourteen

DIGNITY FOR ALL

Remember, we are not fighting for the freedom of the Negro alone, but for the freedom of the human spirit, a larger freedom that encompasses all [humankind]. —Ella Baker

I have the audacity to believe that peoples everywhere can have three meals a day for their bodies, education and culture for their minds, and dignity, equality, and freedom for their spirits. I believe that what self-centered men have torn down, other-centered men (people) can build up. —Martin Luther King Jr.

"A WORLD OF DIGNITY FOR ALL"—THAT'S HOW WORLD LEADERS FRAMED THEIR NEW and ambitious vision when they launched the Sustainable Development Goals (SDGs).[1] Most Americans have likely never heard of these goals, even though just prior to their announcement, the pope came out with his encyclical *Laudato Si'*, a letter calling us to "care for our common home," a world where dignity is the foundation—a dignity the pope describes as inalienable, unique, infinite, equal, intrinsic, and God-given.[2]

The SDGs have their origin in the Millennium Development Goals (MDGs) agreed upon by the United Nations in 2000, which helped galvanize global leadership to cut extreme poverty in half in fifteen years, a goal that was achieved before its target date largely due to remarkable progress in China and India. After the MDGs expired in 2015, they were replaced by the SDGs, which represent a more integrated and comprehensive global agenda centered on seventeen goals and 169 targets that apply to every country in the world, not only to low- and middle-income countries. They combine a commitment to end extreme poverty by the year 2030—especially in countries across sub-Sahara Africa and fragile, conflict-affected states where progress has been so uneven—with commitments to protect the environment, address climate change, combat inequality, promote peace, and improve governance.

Rooted in the principle of dignity for all, these new goals also include the sacred obligation to leave no one behind, echoing the biblical mandate to care for and prioritize the welfare of the widow, orphan, stranger, and people living in poverty.

It is striking that the world's leaders at the time chose the word *dignity*, which has deep religious roots. "As we embark on this great collective journey," their 2030 agenda for sustainable development declares, "we pledge that no one will be left behind. Recognizing that the dignity of the human person is fundamental . . . we will endeavour to reach the furthest behind first."[3] Unfortunately, the goals experienced major setbacks with the devastating impact of the COVID-19 pandemic, as well as indifference and seeming hostility toward sustainable development on the part of the Trump administration and other leaders.

Across other parts of the world, the goals have served as a galvanizing force to catalyze greater progress around sustainable development. The goals provide a policy framework to help create a world in which the Beloved Community is made more real, with a vision that includes zero hunger, good health and well-being, quality education, gender equality, clean water and sanitation, affordable clean energy, reduced inequality, sustainable cities and communities, responsible consumption and production, climate action, protecting life below and above water, and peace and justice, among others. In the United States, despite federal disregard for these goals over the course of the Trump administration, many cities—including Orlando, New York, and Los Angeles—have used the SDG blueprint to promote inclusive growth and shared prosperity.

Arguably the most well-known passage in scripture is John 3:16— "For God so loved the world that he gave his only begotten Son." Sadly, the American church is far too often nationalistic in its lived theology, as though these eternal words apply only to our own country rather than to all of humanity—as if Jesus had proclaimed, "For God so loved *the United States* that he gave his only begotten Son." But God's love applies equally to all nations, enveloping the entire world in the promise of new life in all its fullness. And the COVID-19 crisis showed us how, in an increasingly interconnected world, our well-being in our own nation is inextricably linked to the health of the rest of the world.

Global crises have the power either to bring the world closer together in response to a common threat or to drive us further apart by bringing out our most nativist and provincial impulses. Since the United States tragically became the global epicenter of the pandemic, with the highest absolute number of both infections and deaths in its first year, it is understandable that we initially focused most of our time, attention, and resources on addressing the domestic impact of the virus. But the best of American values and the mandates of our faith traditions call on us to show equal concern for and solidarity with our brothers and sisters around the world.

Dr. Paul Farmer, co-founder of Partners in Health, refers to deaths caused by malaria, malnutrition, and tuberculosis as "stupid deaths."[4] I agree with his provocative language because these deaths are so utterly preventable in our modern age and are so often the consequence of extreme poverty and apathy. Over the course of my career, from my advocacy with college students through Global Justice, the organization I co-founded, and later leading advocacy efforts at World Vision US, one of the world's largest relief and development organizations, I have tried to build greater political will to end these stupid deaths because even modest investments, compared to our overall national budget, make a profound difference in people's lives and livelihoods around the world. These investments project the best of America's values and help us build a safer, healthier, and more prosperous world.

Unfortunately, human rights and international development assistance rarely, if ever, make headlines in national politics. But living as we do in an increasingly interconnected and interdependent world and from the perspective of faith, they should. They factor into our discernment both as people of faith and as Americans because our moral obligations and concerns cannot be confined to our borders. Around the world, extreme poverty, the alarming erosion of human rights, the elusive prospects for sustainable peace in the Middle East, the unconscionable scale of human trafficking and modern-day slavery, religious persecution, and ongoing war and conflict should matter deeply to all of us.

The COVID-19 pandemic has been particularly devastating to the world's efforts to combat extreme poverty, hunger, malnutrition, and child mortality. According to the World Bank, COVID-19 dealt an unprecedented setback to the worldwide effort to end extreme poverty, raise median incomes, and create shared prosperity. The World Bank's poverty projections suggest that an additional 110 to 150 million people are at risk of falling into extreme poverty compared to in 2019. This means that the pandemic and global recession may push 1.4 percent of the world's population into extreme poverty. In the first nine months of the outbreak, more than 1.6 billion children in developing countries were out of school, representing a potential loss of as much as $10 trillion in lifetime earnings for these students. Making matters worse, gender-based violence increased, and estimates suggest a potential increase of up to 45 percent in child mortality because of health-service shortfalls and reductions in access to food. I have spent my career advocating for greater global leadership to end the dehumanizing impacts of extreme poverty; these trends are heartbreaking.

A global pandemic requires a global response. The ONE campaign, a global effort to end extreme poverty, emphasizes that we must include efforts to support the most vulnerable and the equitable global distribution of vaccines and treatments for viruses, including the novel coronavirus. Bold leadership is needed to end AIDS worldwide by 2030. International cooperation to fight preventable disease—through organizations such as the World Health Organization and the Global Alliance for Vaccines and Immunization—is essential. As COVID-19 has cost millions of lives and driven a global financial crisis, it is imperative that US leaders pressure the Group of 20, the International Monetary Fund, and other multinational bodies to increase debt relief and cancellation through the Catastrophe Containment and Relief Trust and other processes.

The fragile state of human rights and democracy has been exacerbated by the COVID-19 pandemic and the abdication of US leadership in protecting and upholding human rights during the four years of the Trump administration. A recent report from Freedom House found that "governments have responded by engaging in abuses of power, silencing their critics, and weakening or shuttering important institutions, often undermining the very systems of accountability needed to protect public health. The crisis of democratic governance, having begun long before the pandemic, is likely to continue after the health crisis recedes, as the laws and norms being put in place now will be difficult to reverse."[5]

Positive American leadership in the world is critical, but it must resist the temptations and dangers of American exceptionalism, militarism, and triumphalism. American global engagement must also recognize and resist the ways in which racism and white supremacy have often seeped into our nation's foreign policy, leading to the neglect, exploitation, and, at worst, domination of many nations. A US foreign policy that is overly militarized and fails to prioritize diplomacy and peacebuilding as central tools for preventing conflict and promoting peace also poses a threat to dignity for all. Aligning US global leadership with the goal of advancing dignity for all will require a robust overhaul of our ballooning military expenditures with the goal of finding substantial savings by eliminating waste and fraud, as well as refitting the military to the purpose of protecting our safety and promoting peace. The Biden administration's early reversal of the harmful Muslim travel ban and return to the Paris climate accord, alongside its commitment to dramatically increase the US refugee quota, rejoin the Iran nuclear deal, pledge four billion dollars to the 184-nation COVAX initiative aimed at making two billion doses of COVID-19 vaccinations available worldwide, and rebuild trust with our traditional allies—if fulfilled, all will contribute to rehabilitating US global engagement.[6]

Combating the cancer of corruption is also crucial to advancing dignity for all. Samantha Power, former US ambassador to the United Nations, argues persuasively:

The United States is the central hub of a global financial system that between 1999 and 2017 moved at least $2 trillion in funds connected to arms dealers, drug traffickers, money launderers, sanctions evaders, and corrupt officials. The real amount of illicit money coursing through the global economy is surely much greater (the $2 trillion includes only what banks themselves flagged), with the annual cost of corruption in 2019 perhaps reaching some $4 trillion—five percent of global GDP. The World Bank estimates that each year, individuals and businesses pay $1 trillion in bribes alone. For the good of people at home and abroad, the Biden administration can take the lead in driving changes that reduce corruption, money laundering, and global tax evasion—practices that finance autocratic leaders and parties, exacerbate income inequality, and violate individual rights.[7]

People of faith and conscience must hold the Biden and future administrations accountable to serve as a bold champion of human rights and emboldened leadership in the fight against global corruption.

Unlike the Millennium Development Goals, the Sustainable Development Goals apply to all countries in the world, from low- to high-income countries. This is in part because even within high-income countries such as the United States, there are populations and regions that experience poverty and deprivation similar to many of the lowest-income countries in the world. Far too often the historic and current injustices and struggles of the Indigenous population in the US are out of mind and sight.[8] Through years of intentional governmental policies that removed lands and resources, Native Americans have been separated from the wealth that was rightfully theirs. Native Americans have the highest poverty rate of all minority groups, with 25.4 percent trapped in poverty compared with 20.8 percent of Black Americans and 8.1 percent of white Americans, according to 2018 Census data cited by Poverty USA.[9]

Land and home are essential facets of dignity for all. Native Americans have been denied both more than any other community in the US. Joseph Kunkel, a citizen of the Northern Cheyenne Nation, is director of MASS Design Group's Sustainable Native Communities Design Lab. Recognizing that COVID-19 was exacerbating the inequalities facing Indigenous and tribal communities, Kunkel responded with an inspiring initiative to improve the quality and condition of Native housing. Kunkel "led teams to complete projects in New Mexico and Northern California in less than two months to build up to ten 400- to 600-square-foot units for elders in the 225-member Big Valley Rancheria community in Northern California and four 1,800-square-foot, four-bedroom houses for the Santa Clara Pueblo Housing Authority in New Mexico." The compressed timeline—from vetting prefab manufacturers in August to delivering move-in-ready residences by November 30—was necessary to help these communities access funds under the emergency Coronavirus Aid, Relief, and Economic Security assistance program, the CARES Act. Kunkel explained to *Metropolis* that "typically, FEMA responds with temporary homes that become permanent, . . . and this has led to further injustice, because the end users are forced to renovate the poorly constructed homes." Kunkel insists that federally funded emergency structures can be built better: "We're stuck in this mentality of constant low-balling. Instead, we can push the boundaries of what those federal funds can accomplish," rather than rushing a bare-bones solution, which is common in the midst of a crisis.[10]

"When I think about design and architecture," Kunkel told me, "I try to design for love and in ways that model Beloved Community." He also believes that "marginalized communities must have a voice in what their built environment looks like." While he has been working on delivering two thousand individual units, his goal is to scale up to provide the two hundred thousand units that are needed in Native communities across the country. At the current rate of federal subsidies meant to address the dire need for housing for the 574 federally recognized tribes in the US, this would take 117 years to accomplish, a time frame Kunkel is determined to condense. Kunkel believes that land is sacred and that planning and design must embrace the fact that "all systems are interconnected—our physical and natural environments—which is why this will take generational change."[11]

The contributions and advocacy of faith-inspired groups remain essential for generating the political will necessary to ensure progress toward the vision of *Laudato Si'* and the SDGs, a world far closer to dignity for all. But we must ensure that the SDGs don't join the graveyard of broken promises.

In 2015, Dr. Jim Yong Kim, then president of the World Bank Group, joined a roundtable—which was almost canceled by a major snowstorm up and down the East Coast—with more than thirty leaders of many of the largest faith-based organizations around the world, representing Baháʼí, Buddhist, Christian, Hindu, Jewish, Muslim, and Sikh communities. I had been working with a subset of the group to draft a statement on the shared commitment among the world's religions to combat poverty among the world's religions. I was convinced that the Sustainable Development Goals agenda, which was being debated and finalized that year, needed a more compelling narrative that could inspire and galvanize support from across the religious community. The draft statement was discussed at the roundtable and received strong support. Faith communities have been deeply engaged in development work for millennia, and many of the SDGs are already embedded in many religious traditions. For example, faith organizations have a long track record of caring for the most vulnerable, providing assistance in times of disaster, promoting stewardship of the environment, and advocating to protect human dignity. Religious communities were also well positioned to popularize the goals in ways that connect to people's core values and conscience.[12]

The statement our group drafted, titled *Ending Extreme Poverty: A Moral and Spiritual Imperative*, called for an end to the "scandal of extreme poverty."[13] Religious leaders pledged to use their "voices to compel and challenge others to join us in this urgent cause inspired by our deepest spiritual values," and added that they would commit to hold "all levels of leadership accountable—public and private, domestic and international." Dr. Kim commented: "Ending extreme poverty in the next fifteen years will require two things: gathering evidence on what works to reduce poverty and using it to implement critical initiatives. . . . Just as important, we need to build a movement to end poverty." The *Ending Extreme Poverty* statement generated trust and a spirit of collaboration between faith leaders and the World Bank, enabling the creation of an initiative designed around three pillars: strengthening the evidence base around the impact of faith organizations in helping to end extreme poverty; engaging in advocacy efforts to hold governments and other stakeholders accountable for the successful implementation of the Sustainable Development Goals; and enhancing collaboration between faith-inspired organizations and the World Bank, the United Nations, and national governments.

Achieving the SDGs will require more than technical fixes; changes in hearts and minds are also needed. Since the goals are not politically binding, they will only succeed if undergirded by a tidal wave of public pressure to hold governments accountable for promises made. While imperfect, the goals provide a visionary blueprint for building the Beloved Community. And when we commit to supporting leaders who advance dignity for all, at home and across the world, this contributes to building the Beloved Community.

Dignity for all is so much more than a platitude or a political statement; it is a moral compass to guide and evaluate our social and political priorities. The English word *dignity* comes from the Latin word *dignitas*, which means "worthiness." Dignity implies that each person is worthy of honor and respect for who they are, not just for what they can do. In other words, human dignity cannot be earned and cannot be taken away. As the Universal Declaration of Human Rights puts it, "Recognition of the inherent dignity . . . of all members of the human family is the foundation of freedom, justice, and peace in the world."[14] Every person and every sector of society has indispensable roles to play in achieving such a world. In the Beloved Community, every person's dignity is seen and matters, no matter where they are born or where they live. Isaiah 65, one of my favorite passages of scripture, provides a poignant glimpse of what a world honoring dignity for all looks like. The prophet proclaims the word of God:

> I'm creating new heavens and a new earth. All the earlier troubles, chaos, and pain are things of the past, to be forgotten. Look ahead with joy. . . . No more sounds of weeping in the city, no cries of anguish; No more babies dying in the cradle, or old people who don't enjoy a full lifetime; One-hundredth birthdays will be considered normal—anything less will seem like a cheat. They'll build houses and move in. They'll plant fields and eat what they grow. . . . For my people will be as long-lived as trees, my chosen ones will have satisfaction in their work. They won't work and have nothing come of it. . . . For they themselves are plantings blessed by God, with their children and grandchildren likewise God-blessed. (vv. 17–23)

Through the Sustainable Development Goals, global institutions such as the United Nations and the World Bank, as well as global leaders from nearly every country in the world, have embraced human dignity as a central value and priority. The question now is whether we will work together to turn these words into deeds to co-create a radically more just, healthy, and sustainable world, a world of Beloved Community.

Chapter Fifteen

REVITALIZING AND REINVENTING DEMOCRACY

The right to vote is precious, almost sacred. It is the most powerful nonviolent tool or instrument in a democratic society. We must use it. —Representative John Lewis

Cowardice asks the question, "Is it safe?" Expediency asks the question, "Is it politic?" Vanity asks the question, "Is it popular?" But conscience asks the question, "Is it right?" —Martin Luther King Jr.

THE ROAD TO A MORE PERFECT UNION HAS BEEN LONG AND UNEVEN. THERE IS NO path there without progress in becoming a more perfect democracy. And while our democracy will never be perfect, we must continually defend the rights, institutions, laws, and norms that safeguard our freedoms and advance the common good. Increasingly, politics has become less about policy differences and more about whether we will work to realize an inclusive, multiracial democracy for all. Our democratic system is under assault, jeopardizing hopes for building the Beloved Community.

America's democratic system is damaged, often undermined, frequently in question, but not beyond repair. A recent survey of independent experts for the Protect Democracy project indicated "substantial erosion" of American democracy, scoring the current threat to democracy at 52 out of 100 (with 100 being "complete democratic breakdown"). In the lead-up to the 2020 election, the *Washington Post*'s editorial board raised an alarm about the erosion of democratic norms, including "commitment to democratic values, constitutional checks and balances, faith in reason and science, concern for earth's health, respect for public service, belief in civility and honest debate, beacon to refugees in need, aspirations to equality and diversity and basic decency."[1] I would add one more item to the list: the erosion of faith in our democracy to carry out fair elections, due to harmful rhetoric and unsubstantiated claims of election fraud that undermine the entire process.

Building a healthy, resilient society requires restoring faith in government, which will in turn require the transformation of our broken politics. Instead of rewarding zero-sum and short-term thinking and politicians who exploit and stoke our deep-seated divisions, we need to support politicians who prioritize the common good over rapacious partisanship or cult-of-personality loyalty. Honor, integrity, empathy, and truthfulness matter for our politics, just as they matter for our lives in community. The allure of false populism and the inordinate influence of money in our politics pose real threats to our democracy—particularly because the rules around democratic processes are often rigged to protect certain interests and because "justice" is rarely blind.

Extreme polarization and the corruption of some of our nation's long-standing institutions have combined to make it harder than ever to enact the will of the people. For example, gerrymandered districts in many states so often favor the more extreme candidates and harm democracy. Since the Supreme Court's *Citizens United* decision in 2010, corporate money has poured into political campaigns at an unprecedented pace. And the rushed confirmation of Supreme Court Justice Amy Coney Barrett on October 26 through a purely partisan vote just days before the 2020 presidential election risked damaging the credibility of our judicial branch.

Politicians' use of violent rhetoric makes this polarization worse, and it is further exacerbated by social media. It can lead to derision, undermine public confidence, and treat democracy as a football in partisan debates. Partisanship now affects everything from marriage to business, and high levels of inequality, social distrust, and an unjust criminal justice system contribute to a greater likelihood of instability and violence.

On a chilly Election Day morning in 2020, I stood outside a community recreation center in north Philadelphia, encouraging voters in a predominantly Black neighborhood who were patiently waiting to cast their ballots. Many had been in line since five a.m., even though the polls didn't open until seven. I was serving as a "poll chaplain" that morning. I was deeply inspired to see so many people, young and old, determined to exercise what Representative John Lewis referred to as their "sacred right" and the "most powerful nonviolent tool in a democracy." I was moved to tears as an elderly Black woman told me about the deep pride she felt at having served as a poll worker in every election since she was fifteen years old. An initiative of Sojourners and the Skinner Leadership Institute called Lawyers and Collars / Turnout Sunday had trained and mobilized more than 2,000 clergy and other people of faith in thirty-six cities across nine states to serve as chaplains at vulnerable polling sites. Clergy worked alongside lawyers to provide a moral presence to prevent intimidation, suppression tactics, and even violence. After the election, we joined the Count Every Vote coalition to insist that every vote be counted and that our democratic process be protected, working to counteract unprecedented efforts by President Trump and his allies to invalidate absentee ballots and pressure GOP politicians to overturn the legitimate results.

I was not surprised after the election by how far Trump and his campaign went to try to discredit and overturn the outcome, in which Joseph Biden received over seven million more popular votes and won by seventy-four electoral votes. But I was surprised by the silence and capit-ulation of the vast majority of Republican members of Congress, sowing even more distrust and division in an already combustible situation. For-tunately, the judicial system provided a last defense, with more than fifty lawsuits thrown out or denied, all the way up to the Supreme Court, due to the campaign's inability to produce evidence to back its baseless claims of widespread election fraud. The big lie of a stolen election culminated in the atrocious siege of the Capitol on January 6, which led to President Trump's second impeachment by the House of Representatives on the charge of incitement of an insurrection.

After the 2020 election, Geoffrey Kabaservice, author of *Rule and Ruin: The Downfall of Moderation and the Destruction of the Republican Party, from Eisenhower to the Tea Party*, offered an important historical perspective and warning about the ongoing allure and impact of Trump-ism: "The tea party never really faded away. It mutated. It became the Trump movement, which is likely to dominate the Republican Party and have a major impact on politics for years to come. If the best guide to conservatism was once Arthur Schlesinger Jr.'s 'The Cycles of American History,' now it might be Leon Trotsky's 'The Permanent Revolution.' Conservatism's familiar pattern of advance, consolidation, retrenchment, and renewal has vanished. In its place is something that looks like #MAGA Forever."[2]

In the weeks after the election, Joe Scarborough, former Republican member of Congress and cohost of the *Morning Joe* TV program, also offered an insightful indictment of the GOP's current trajectory. Scarborough wrote, "For four years, Republicans averted their eyes as Trump broke the law, defied constitutional norms, trashed governing traditions, dehumanized political opponents, and further radicalized a party that had long ago become unmoored from conservative tradition—and yet that proved to be but a preview of worse things to come. Now, Republican leaders are either actively engaged in sedition against the United States or offering their silent support to a president furiously working to overturn an election. The leveling wind against liberalism has instead become a gale-force wind beating away at the foundations of American democracy."[3]

Time will tell how much lasting damage Trumpism will have done to our democratic system and body politic, but all of us—those who lean left, right, and everyone in between—must be an active part of healing public trust and revitalizing the norms and institutions that are necessary for civic health.

Free, fair, and safe elections are the lifeblood of a healthy and vibrant democracy. Sadly, the right to vote has been intentionally restricted ever since our nation's founding, when it was only granted to landowning white males. It must be continually protected and broadened until all adult citizens are truly free to exercise their right to the ballot box. Voter suppression disfigures our democracy and has propped up white supremacy from our nation's inception. The Florida recount of 2000, and the Supreme Court decision that ultimately decided the election, initiated a ramping-up of the Republican Party's baseless accusations of voter fraud, and they have intensified over the past twenty years. Many Republicans seem addicted to a strategy of depressing turnout and making it more difficult for certain communities, particularly people of color, to vote—a last-ditch way to win elections and hold on to power despite the nation's changing demographics. Republican operatives have admitted that this is their deliberate strategy. President Trump tweeted that voting by mail would hurt Republicans, which helps to explain why he relentlessly sought to cast doubt on mail voting and made baseless claims of widespread voter fraud in an election his own Department of Homeland Security declared "the most secure in American history."[4] According to the Brennan Center for Justice, in a seeming backlash to historic voter turnout in the 2020 election, by February 19, 2021, Republican leaders in thirty-three state legislatures had already proposed over 165 pieces of legislation that would further restrict the right to vote by limiting mail voting, imposing stricter voter ID requirements, slashing voter registration opportunities, and enabling aggressive voter roll purges.[5]

The big lie of widespread voter fraud distracted attention from the real fraud that has been orchestrated in states across the country through voter suppression tactics such as robocalls targeting Black and Latino voters with disinformation, spreading conspiracy theories, and seeking to depress turnout. It's purges that seek to remove people from voter rolls who haven't voted consistency or have changed their address. It's long lines and broken voting machines that just happen to be concentrated in communities of color. It's the threat of voter intimidation and even violence fomented by the rhetoric of President Trump and other politicians. "One person, one vote" is a mirage if we are silent about and don't actively resist these and other insidious tactics. Protecting every vote should be a nonpartisan cause and commitment. Protecting every voter is also a faith imperative.

Jim Crow is like a mutating gene that continues to show up in these covert and overt tactics to suppress the vote of minority populations—most acutely against the Black community. This is nothing new. The right to vote has been deeply contested since the founding of our nation. More stringent voter-ID laws and the purging of voting rosters simply represent contemporary versions of poll taxes and literacy tests. In the timeless words of Frederick Douglass, "There is no progress without struggle." The work must continue in the ongoing struggle for voting rights. Progress, this struggle proves, can be fragile and fleeting—and must be continually defended.[6]

Following the Supreme Court's decision in *Shelby County v. Holder* in 2013, states were free to adopt voting laws adversely impacting minority voters, including laws instituted to eliminate polling places, move them to less accessible locations, or reduce the hours they are open. Many states have put in place new laws to enact stricter voter-ID requirements and reduce early voting and Sunday voting, which are popular among minority voters in certain regions. The Brennan Center for Justice found that from 2010 to 2018, twenty-three states enacted more restrictive voter registration or hyper-partisan gerrymandering.[7]

The Lawyers and Collars / Turnout Sunday initiative I mentioned earlier, which Sojourners and the National African American Clergy Network partnered together around in the 2018 and 2020 elections, was rooted and motivated by our understanding and commitment to imago dei—embracing every person as made in the image of God—which confers upon every voter equal worth and dignity. Dr. Barbara Williams-Skinner, president of the Skinner Leadership Institute, which also led Lawyers and Collars / Turnout Sunday, says, "During the 2020 election, our network of over a thousand clergy wearing sacred collars and lawyers provided moral and legal protection at vulnerable voters' polling sites and secured their right to vote in free, fair, and safe elections. This multiracial and interfaith clergy network modeled Dr. King's Beloved Community by affirming the image of God in historically disenfranchised citizens, whose vote became acts of moral resistance to long-standing racially motivated voting barriers."[8] And so it becomes clear that protecting the right to vote affirms the divine image and inherent value of all God's children. In the theological context of imago dei, we see that nothing diminishes the rule of law and our precious democracy more than voter suppression and efforts to disenfranchise or squelch the voice of minority voters. The Beloved Community supports those who are most vulnerable and ensures that they have a voice in the decisions that affect their lives.

Particularly during election seasons, people of faith grapple with what the Bible has to say about the role of government. While our modern-day system of representative democracy was never fully practiced in biblical times, both the Old and New Testaments offer core principles and purposes for government that can be applied today. Dr. Ron Sider argues that scripture (in Romans 13) shows that governments are called to "restrain evil and punish evil-doers" and to be a "servant for your good."[9] Sider further explains that "fortunately, democratic societies implement the vision of limited government in numerous ways. These include the constitutional separation of powers (legislative, judicial, and administrative); the several, substantially independent spheres of national, regional, and local government; regular, free democratic elections; autonomous nongovernmental institutions; holding government officials accountable to the law; and freedom of speech, assembly, and dissent."[10]

Revitalizing and reinventing our democracy will require a series of both immediate and longer-term reforms, such as enacting automatic voter registration, allowing same-day and online registration, protecting against flawed voter purges, reinstating the Voting Rights Act, restoring voting rights to people with prior convictions, instituting nationwide early voting, and more effectively protecting against deceptive practices. Revitalizing our democracy also requires more comprehensive campaign finance reforms such as small-donor public financing of elections, improving federal disclosure law, and overhauling the Federal Election Commission. Moving forward, we must prioritize other key reforms, including redistricting reform, greater election security, robust ethics reform, finally making the District of Columbia a state with voting representatives ("no taxation without representation"), abolishing the Electoral College, and even temporarily or selectively suspending the filibuster, which in the current hyper-partisan political environment may be the only way to enact the majority of these essential democratic reforms.

Fortunately, many victories have been won at the state level to revitalize our democracy. For example, in the past few years, hundreds of pro-voter bills were introduced in forty-six states. Maine enacted automatic voter registration, New Mexico same-day registration, and New York small-donor public financing. Voting rights were restored or expanded for those with past criminal convictions in Kentucky, Colorado, Nevada, Illinois, Louisiana, and New Jersey. In 2019, the House passed H.R. 1, the "For the People Act of 2019." While Senator Mitch McConnell refused to take up the bill in the Senate, this watershed legislation contains key reforms to revitalize American democracy—

including automatic voter registration, small-donor public financing, redistricting reform, and a commitment to restore the Voting Rights Act. It would make voting easier and more accessible, lower barriers to running for office, and empower voters to choose their representatives, rather than let representatives choose their voters.[11] A report of the American Academy's Commission on the Practice of Democratic Citizenship called Our Common Purpose: Reinventing American Democracy for the 21st Century provides a timely, thoughtful, and more comprehensive set of recommendations to reinvent and revitalize our democracy.

Revitalizing democracy also requires embracing a greater commitment to truth and integrity in our public life. Jesus's iconic words "The truth will set you free" (John 8:32) offer a vital antidote to the deficit of integrity and truthfulness in our politics. Yes, the truth can be hard. It can be elusive and inconvenient, particularly in hyper-partisan and polarized times. And seeking and defending the truth often requires courage and sacrifice. It becomes nearly impossible to find common ground and advance the common good when there is no verifiable truth. Facts are like a referee that helps to keep the game of politics fair and constructive. Undermining the importance of truth, rejecting the very existence of facts, is one of the most tried-and-true tactics of autocratic and authoritarian leaders around the world.

For years, many church denominations and leaders eschewed political engagement, in part out of a fear of dividing their churches and a desire to stay above the messiness of politics. Meanwhile, many churches, particularly ones associated with the Religious Right, have engaged in politics in the wrong way, seeking to take over and ultimately becoming beholden to one political party. My organization, Sojourners, has long argued that the country doesn't need a Religious Left to replace the Religious Right. Instead, the church and other religious communities should serve as the state's conscience, seeking to work with and hold all sides accountable to our faith inspired values and priorities. This conscience is needed now. Churches and other houses of worship, at their best, are among the few places left where people are invited to come together across our partisan and political divides. The church should be a space in which we can engage in genuine prayer for our political leaders and real dialogue about how to best pursue the common good. The health of our democracy depends on it.

Nonparticipation in our democracy is a tacit approval of the status quo, and since our faith has such profound implications for every facet of our life, civic and political engagement is a vital way in which we live out our faith—in Christian terms, to exercise discipleship. Other churches have been reticent to engage in electoral politics, and are distrustful of the state, out of a belief that the church itself is meant to be the primary vehicle for delivering justice and righteousness. While the church is certainly indispensable in advancing justice, it is a misreading of scripture to place this responsibility solely on the church and to overly separate the role of the church from the broader society.

A groundbreaking recent study on spirituality in the United States, carried out by the Fetzer Institute, found a positive correlation between spirituality and pro-social behavior, including civic engagement and voting. With eight in ten Americans identifying themselves as spiritual, the study found that the "more strongly someone identifies as spiritual, the more likely they are to hold pro-social attitudes and take civic and community action."[12] As an advisor to the study, I wrote that the results offer hopeful seeds to heal and revitalize our democracy in the midst of such dangerous levels of polarization.

While many forces are undermining our democracy, our voices, our activism, and our votes represent both the antidote and a renewable resource for revitalizing democracy. These are essential to exercising our civic discipleship and upholding the biblical mandate to restrain evil and advance the common good. By revitalizing and reinventing our democracy, we can even the playing field and enable the Beloved Community to flourish.

"Who is my neighbor?" a man asked Jesus in the well-known parable of the good Samaritan (Luke 10:25–37). In this teaching, Jesus makes clear that our neighbors are not simply those who are like us but also those who are unlike us or who are seen as the "other." The significance of that question becomes clear as we begin to understand that a healthy democracy and the Beloved Community are built by those who love, advocate with, and support their neighbors. Politics matters because our neighbors matter. At the root of the word *politics* is the Greek word *polis*, which refers to "a small state run by citizens." I like this definition because revitalizing democracy will require the active engagement and participation of each of us, particularly those who historically have been shut out. Revitalizing our democracy is imperative because it provides the groundwork for building the Beloved Community.

EPILOGUE: WHERE DO WE GO FROM HERE?

In the work of fighting monsters, we must be careful not to become monstrous. —*Friedrich Nietzsche*

It is precisely the collision of immoral power with power-less morality which constitutes the major crisis of our times. —*Martin Luther King Jr.*

IN 1967, MARTIN LUTHER KING JR. WAS IN DESPERATE NEED OF RESPITE FROM THE unrelenting demands of leading a movement. He went to Jamaica to recover and to write what would be his final book, *Where Do We Go from Here: Chaos or Community?* Over a recent Christmas holiday, I made a similar pilgrimage to Jamaica, with my wife and her parents, who hail from there, for both restoration and writing. There is something about the Jamaican sun that breathes new life into dry bones.

King's question—Where do we go from here?—is a provocative and timely one. My contemporary remix of that question shaped the writing of this book: Where do we go from here: a politics of division or a politics of the Beloved Community?

Given the trauma inflicted by the noxious politics of recent years and the catastrophic harm caused by both COVID-19 and the virus of racism, our nation has the imperative to be remade, to be transformed. We have both the need and the opportunity for a "hard reset" as we co-create a new normal—what others have called a Third Reconstruction or a third founding of our nation. I've argued in this book that where we go from here depends on whether we are willing to reach a new, shared understanding of our history, which will require a greater commitment to truth-telling and debunking the internalized myths and lies that undergird the nation's self-understanding.

We have endured an era of Trumpism that started with the pernicious lie about the nation's first Black president's citizenship and led to the destructive falsehood that the 2020 election was rigged and stolen, inflicting ongoing damage to public trust and our democracy. But Trump did not invent the deep divisions in our nation; he was only a brilliant marketer in manipulating and exploiting long-standing grievances and divisions for his own benefit.

I have resisted the temptation to make this book primarily a response to Trumpism. This hasn't been easy, as his brand of politics has poisoned the public sphere. Instead, I've sought to replace the distorted narrative of making America great again with the redemptive narrative of the Beloved Community. This moral vision involves making the American creed of liberty and justice for all real for and inclusive of all people—constructing from the ashes of injustice and division a society in which neither punishment nor privilege is tied to race, ethnicity, gender, ableness, or sexual orientation and gender identity.

A hard reset, a Third Reconstruction, or a third founding is possible but certainly neither guaranteed nor inevitable. The dual pandemics of COVID-19 and systemic racism have been apocalyptic (a revelation, in the original Greek meaning of the word). COVID-19 has revealed deep, racialized cracks in our society that perpetuated inequality and led to disproportionate death and hardship. The senseless and brutal cycle of racialized police violence has shined a spotlight on the insidious lie that has haunted and corrupted our nation from its founding, that some lives are worth more than others and that Black lives, in particular, are less deserving of equal justice under the law. As our nation and world come through and get beyond the darkness of the COVID-19 pandemic, we can't and shouldn't go back to a broken old normal but instead must create together a new and radically more just "abnormal."

A more perfect union feels like a mirage to many, but I still believe it is within our grasp. Our constant striving for that union is bound up with our efforts to extend and guarantee liberty and justice for all. The project of building the Beloved Community will take us even deeper. And that deeper work of conversion, of repentance, of transformation will be necessary to vanquish our worst demons and overcome the temptations and dangers of toxic polarization, fake populism, destructive nationalism, and hyper-partisanship.

I started the book with a question my older son asked me the night after the 2016 election when we told him that Donald Trump had won. With the innocence of a five-year-old, he replied, "I don't understand how someone who has said and done such mean things can win." After seeing our speechless and anguished reaction, my son replied with a wisdom beyond his years, "It will be OK because you and Mommy will make it OK." Needless to say, I felt a heavy responsibility in that moment. In many respects, this book has been my attempt to offer a thoughtful and thorough answer to my son—but also to myself and, hopefully, to everyone who reads the book.

I've thought a lot about that night back in 2016 and how I failed miserably to give my son an answer that could do justice to the gravity of the moment, let alone to the profound depth of his question. At that time, I didn't have the words, and perhaps he was too young to fully understand what my heart wished to say in response. But four years later, during the next presidential election, I was more ready to answer. This time it was my younger son, Nathaniel, then seven, who was obsessed with the election. He asked me every day, "Daddy, who won?" As votes were counted and Trump continued to deny the results, he said, "This is madness. President Trump will never concede because he is just a sore loser." This time, I wasn't caught unprepared by my son's questions. I was ready to respond, whatever the outcome, by telling the truth in a spirit of tough love. I was ready to share my commitment to building the Beloved Community and my belief that my sons' generation and those that follow will reenvision what building the Beloved Community requires for their time.

Before we knew the outcome of the election, I wrote this letter to my sons, knowing that some parts would only be fully understood as they got older:

Sons, this country has been terribly divided since even before the Constitution was agreed upon and our nation was born. It was bitterly divided over the evil of slavery, the annihilation of the Native population, the subjugation of women, and so much more.

Division has been a defining feature of our politics. But so have struggle and hope.

What all of us 200-plus years later can agree on and still should embrace are the ideals that America was built on. Those ideals of equality, dignity, freedom, and inalienable rights are precious and worth fighting for. They are also based on and resonate with the very ideals and values of our faith.

But these ideals are not a given—they do not come easily or without a price. They must be continually fought for and expanded to include all people.

"We the people" in these yet-to-be-fully-united United States of America includes you, it includes me, your brother, mother, and everyone who is in this incredible country. Despite all of its flaws and wounds, we continue to believe in these ideals and that they can regularly be reborn and more fully realized. Our faith says that Christ can make all things new, and that applies to this nation as well. Our faith enlists us to be part of the vision and work of making all things new, of building the Beloved Community and forming a more perfect union.

Throughout this book you have seen glimpses of what the Beloved Community looks like and how it is already being realized in small and significant ways. I have shared many of my hopes and aspirations around what the Beloved Community means to me, drawing from the nation's deepest civic values and from my Christian faith, as well as briefly tapping into other religious and cultural traditions. But there is so much more to say about the Beloved Community—that definition and full story will never be fully complete without including your perspective and story as well. The beatitudes of the Beloved Community—imago dei, radical welcome, ubuntu interdependence, environmental stewardship, nonviolence, and dignity for all—provide a road map for getting there. And these beatitudes offer an antidote to the destructive forces of fear, hate, and hypocrisy that fuel the politics of division.

I've come to learn that the Beloved Community is less a destination and more of a journey of continual renewal and transformation. A major stumbling block in this journey is prematurely believing that we have somehow arrived. Replacing harmful narratives will be hard; embodying countercultural values and commitments will not be easy. Converting and transforming hearts and minds will take grace, patience, and determination. It will take a refusal to demonize those with whom we disagree and a commitment to love even our enemies.

Beloved Community does not start or end with our politics, but transforming our broken politics is an indispensable part of how we must co-create it. A shared moral vision of the Beloved Community will not be a panacea to cure our nation's ills, but it will help provide an essential treatment program. And while we may be hardwired for division and polarization, it is also engrained in us to yearn and strive for justice and community.

This journey of building the Beloved Community will be a hard one requiring sacrifice, vigilance, and courage, but it will not be defined purely around struggle. The pursuit of the Beloved Community will also be filled with great joy, and in it we will find deeper purpose, belonging, and meaning. That's why it is worth pursuing—because the fruits of human flourishing, right relationship, and thriving communities are unlocked and experienced in the very acts of building the Beloved Community. Paraphrasing the prophet Isaiah (58:9–12): After we feed the hungry and break the yoke of injustice, then our light will rise in the darkness and we will be called the repairers of the breach, restorers of streets to live in. In other words, doing the work of building the Beloved Community unlocks our own potential and is essential for our own thriving and wholeness.

Life is filled with and defined by choices. This is true for individuals, communities, and nations. Choices are contagious—particularly courageous ones. We face a collective choice that will define and shape the trajectory of our nation for subsequent generations. I'm asking that together we make the choice of Beloved Community. Let us choose continual rebirth, hoping and believing that our nation can also be reborn and remade if enough of us choose the journey of Beloved Community.

Beloved Community means being seen, heard, and valued. It is believing that every voice matters and embracing the principle "Nothing about us without us." Beloved Community is agape love, deep connection, and constant curiosity. Beloved Community is a deep embrace. It is the relentless pursuit of equity and justice. It is understanding that our own wholeness and flourishing is tied to the flourishing of others, particularly the most marginalized and most vulnerable in our midst. Beloved Community offers a sense of belonging and security, because it is a place where brotherly and sisterly love is operative. In Beloved Community, loneliness and nihilism are replaced by connection, sacred purpose, and respect for human dignity. And Beloved Community relentlessly announces to us all: Always remember that you are beloved and made for community.

The road to a radically more inclusive and just America and world has been and will continue to be a long and arduous one. We can take heart in the apostle Paul's words: "Let us not become weary in doing good, for at the proper time we will reap a harvest if we do not give up" (Galatians 6:9). I fervently believe that if we walk this road together—tapping into God's limitless grace and strength, knowing by faith that ultimately the race has already been won, and thus that nothing is impossible—the Beloved Community will prevail.

ACKNOWLEDGMENTS

The journey of writing this book reaffirmed that it truly takes a village . . . to write a book. I'm deeply grateful for the large and dedicated village that made this book possible, both in terms of giving me the grace and space to write it, as well as guidance, encouragement, and invaluable feedback along the way.

First and foremost I need to thank my wife Sharee, who became the anchor to keep me grounded and the glue that held our family together in the midst of this writing project, including in the middle of a pandemic. This book literally would not have been written without her selfless and loving support.

I want to dedicate this book to my two sons Joshua and Nathaniel. I wrote this book in the hope that they will inherit a nation and world that more closely resembles the beloved community and that this book will help their generation as well as subsequent ones better define and build the beloved community for themselves.

I owe a debt of gratitude to my brother Derek who helped edit the earliest beginnings of this book. I'm deeply grateful to my editor Lil, who believed in and guided this writing process from start to finish with the right mix of tough love and grace. I also want to thank the longtime editor of Sojourners magazine Jim Rice, who lent his copyediting brilliance to make the book even better.

I want to thank an array of family and dear friends who generously lent me hospitality and support so that I could get away and focus on writing. This includes my beloved parents Kit and Saundra, Tim Dixon, Rick Little, Louise and Steve Coggins and Anne and David Grizzle.

I'm also deeply grateful to my fellow inaugural class of Aspen Fellows in the Civil Society Program, many of whom show up in the book as glimpses of building the beloved community. Every one of them could easily have been featured as I continue to be inspired by their authentic leadership.

Finally, I want to thank my fellow staff at Sojourners and the larger village of friends who supported this project in so many subtle and significant ways along the way—from offering advice, being a sounding board, through prayer, and more. You all reinforce my conviction that the beloved community is not some distant ideal or abstract concept but really can be an experienced reality.

NOTES

Epigraph Notes (*in the order in which they appear*)

1. Embracing a Bigger Story of Us

Martin Luther King Jr., Christmas Sermon on Peace, 1967
Jill Lepore, This America

2. Why America Must Be Reborn

Martin Luther King Jr., Where Do We Go from Here: Chaos or Community?
John 3:3

3. E Pluribus Unum: Out of Many, One

Bob Marley, "One Love"
Martin Luther King Jr., Where Do We Go from Here: Chaos or Community?

4. Reimagining the Beloved Community

Coretta Scott King, My Life, My Love, My Legacy

5. Unmasking America's Myths

Jill Lepore, These Truths
Martin Luther King Jr., Strength to Love

6. Telling the Whole Truth to Set Us Free

John 8:31–32
James Baldwin, "The Creative Process"
Maya Angelou, "On the Pulse of Morning"
West African proverb

7. Overcoming Toxic Polarization

Romans 12:2
Dietrich Bonhoeffer, The Cost of Discipleship
Matthew 12:25

8. Redeeming Patriotism

Charles de Gaulle attributed to de Gaulle in a conversational setting
Beyoncé Knowles, 2017 Sports Illustrated Awards

9. Equality: The Imago Dei Imperative

Common, "Letter to the Free"
Martin Luther King Jr., *Where Do We Go from Here: Chaos or Community?*
Thomas Jefferson, The Declaration of Independence

10. Radical Welcome

Lin-Manuel Miranda, "Immigrants (We Get the Job Done)," from *The Hamilton Mixtape*
Martin Luther King Jr., speech in St. Louis, 1964

11. Ubuntu Interdependence

Martin Luther King Jr., Letter from a Birmingham Jail
Fannie Lou Hamer, "The Special Plight and Role of Black Women," speech delivered in 1971
César Chávez, as quoted in *Cesar Chavez: A Triumph of Spirit*

12. Prioritizing Nonviolence

Martin Luther King Jr., *Where Do We Go from Here: Chaos or Community?*
Bob Marley, "War"
Matthew 5:9

13. Environmental Stewardship

Pope Francis, Laudato Si': On Care for Our Common Home
Bill McKibben, "Celebrate Earth Day with Bill McKibben," Seattle University, 2016

14. Dignity for All

Ella Baker, Freedom Day speech in Hattiesburg, Mississippi
Martin Luther King Jr., 1963 Nobel Peace Prize acceptance speech

15. Revitalizing and Reinventing Democracy

Representative John Lewis, on Twitter, July 26, 2016
Martin Luther King Jr., "Remaining Awake Through a Great Revolution"

Epilogue: Where Do We Go from Here?

Friedrich Nietzsche, Beyond Good and Evil: Prelude to a Philosophy of the Future
Martin Luther King Jr., *Where Do We Go from Here: Chaos or Community?*

Chapter Notes

Foreword

1   John Lewis, afterword to *Mobilizing Hope: Faith-Inspired Activism for a Post-civil Rights Generation*, by Adam Russell Taylor (Downers Grove, IL: IVP, 2010), 225.

Prologue

1   William J. Barber II, "We Are Witnessing the Birth Pangs of a Third Reconstruction," ThinkProgress, December 15, 2016, https://archive.thinkprogress.org/rev-barber-moral-change-1ad2776df7c/.

2   Eddie S. Glaude Jr., *Begin Again: James Baldwin's America and Its Urgent Lessons for Our Own* (New York: Crown, 2020), xix.

3 Glaude, 115.

4 Shawn Barney, "Leading in a Time of Crisis: Equity Centered COVID-19 Recovery—The Hard Reset We Need," Aspen Institute, May 21, 2020, https://www.aspeninstitute.org/events/leading-in-a-time-of-crisis-equity-centered-covid-19-recovery-the-hard-reset-we-need/.

5 Amanda Gorman, "The Hill We Climb," CNN, January 20, 2021, https://www.cnn.com/2021/01/20/politics/amanda-gorman-inaugural-poem-transcript/index.html.

Introduction

1 "The Constitution of the United States," National Archives, last modified March 16, 2020, https://www.archives.gov/founding-docs/constitution.

2 "Declaration of Independence: A Transcription," National Archives, last modified July 24, 2020, https://www.archives.gov/founding-docs/declaration-transcript.

3 Jill Lepore, *This America: The Case for the Nation* (New York: Liveright, 2019), 3.

4 Kirk Cheyfitz, "Failing to Form a More Perfect Union: Our Fault," A More Perfect Story, January 28, 2018, https://amoreperfectstory.com/failing-to-form-a-more-perfect-union-our-fault/.

5 Glaude, *Begin Again*, 203.

6 Eddie S. Glaude Jr., in conversation with the author, 2020.

7 William Faulkner, *Requiem for a Nun* (New York: Vintage, 2012), 73.

8 Stephen Hawkins et al., *Hidden Tribes: A Study of America's Polarized Landscape* (New York: More in Common, 2018).

9 "The Beloved Community," King Center, n.d., https://thekingcenter.org/about-tkc/the-king-philosophy/.

10 Martin Luther King Jr., *Where Do We Go from Here: Chaos or Community?* (Boston: Beacon, 2010).

1. Embracing a Bigger Story of Us

1 Hawkins et al., *Hidden Tribes*, 137.

2 "Hidden Tribes Midterms Update," More in Common, 2020, https://hiddentribes.us/midterm-updates/.

3 Hawkins et al., *Hidden Tribes*, 5.

4 Rabbi Hillel, quoted in *Pirkei Avot* 1:14, trans. Dr. Joshua Kulp, https://tinyurl.com/yudwsu22.

5 Marshall Ganz, quoted in "The Story of Us," Voices across Borders, n.d., http://www.voicesacrossborders.com/story-of-us.html.

6 Ganz.

7 Ganz.

8 Shahram Heshmat, "What Is Confirmation Bias?," *Psychology Today*, April 23, 2015, https://www.psychologytoday.com/us/blog/science-choice/201504/what-is-confirmation-bias.

9 Stephen Heintz and Walter Isaacson, *U.S. in the World: Talking Global Issues with Americans* (New York: Rockefeller Brothers Fund, n.d.), https://tinyurl.com/avh435c.

10 "About," FrameWorks Institute, 2021, https://www.frameworksinstitute.org/about/.

11 Nat Kendall-Taylor and Sean Gibbons, "Framing for Social Change," Stanford Social Innovation Review, April 17, 2018, https://ssir.org/articles/entry/framing_for_social_change.

12 Robert P. Jones, "Trump Can't Reverse the Decline of White Christian America," *Atlantic*, July 4, 2017, https://www.theatlantic.com/politics/archive/2017/07/robert-jones-white-christian-america/532587/.

13 David L. Chappell, *A Stone of Hope: Prophetic Religion and the Death of Jim Crow* (Chapel Hill: University of North Carolina Press, 2004), 102.

14 Chappell, 2.

15 "A New Generation Expresses Its Skepticism and Frustration with Christianity," Barna, September 21, 2007, https://tinyurl.com/56mcm47s.

16 Veronica Selzler, Gillian Gonda, and Mohammed Mohammed, *What Does Spirituality Mean to Us? A Study of Spirituality in the United States* (Kalamazoo, MI: Fetzer Institute, 2020), 2, 4, https://tinyurl.com/yaeauj8j.

17 Selzler, Gonda, and Mohammed, 76.

18 Robin DiAngelo, *White Fragility: Why It's So Hard for White People to Talk about Racism* (Boston: Beacon, 2018), 2.

2. Why America Must Be Reborn

1   "Suicide and Self-Harm Injury," Centers for Disease Control and Prevention (CDC), March 1, 2021, https://www.cdc.gov/nchs/fastats/suicide.htm.

2   "Drug Overdose Deaths," CDC, March 19, 2020, https://www.cdc.gov/drugoverdose/data/statedeaths.html.

3   Caroline Ratcliffe, *Child Poverty and Adult Success* (Washington, DC: Urban Institute, 2015), https://tinyurl.com/twstcjzu.

4   Philip Bump, "FBI Director Wray Reconfirms the Threat Posed by Racist Extremists," *Washington Post*, March 2, 2021, https://tinyurl.com/ke5ukfvy.

5   Tami Abdollah and Trevor Hughes, "Hate Crimes against Asian Americans Are on the Rise. Here's What Activists, Lawmakers and Police Are Doing to Stop the Violence," *USA Today*, February 27, 2021, https://tinyurl.com/a9t6c8fp.

6   Peter Wagner and Wendy Sawyer, "States of Incarceration, the Global Context 2018," Prison Policy Initiative, June 2018, https://www.prisonpolicy.org/global/2018.html.

7   Jones, "Trump Can't Reverse the Decline."

8   Tom McCarthy, "Faith and Freedoms: Why Evangelicals Profess Unwavering Love for Trump," *Guardian*, July 7, 2019, https://www.theguardian.com/us-news/2019/jul/07/donald-trump-evangelical-supporters.

9   Jim Wallis, *Christ in Crisis: Why We Need to Reclaim Jesus* (New York: HarperOne, 2019), 10–11.

10 Martin Luther King Jr., "A Knock at Midnight" (sermon, June 5, 1963), Martin Luther King Jr. Research and Education Institute, Stanford University, https://kinginstitute.stanford.edu/king-papers/documents/knock-midnight.

3. E Pluribus Unum: Out of Many, One

1   Debra Redalia, "E Pluribus Unum—Of Many One," *Lifely* (blog), https://lifelyforlife.com/e-pluribus-unum-of-many-one.

2   National Advisory Commission on Civil Disorders, *The Kerner Report* (Princeton, NJ: Princeton University Press, 2016), 1.

3   Whitney Parnell, "Knowledge Is Dangerous to Institutionalized Power," *Sojourners*, October 6, 2020, https://sojo.net/articles/knowledge-dangerous-institutionalized-power.

4   Jim Wallis, *America's Original Sin: Racism, White Privilege, and the Bridge to a New America* (Grand Rapids, MI: Brazos, 2016).

5   Ian Hainline and Anna Bross, "Americans Deeply Divided by Party on Ideals of Religious and Ethnic Pluralism," Public Religion Research Institute (PRRI), February 21, 2019, https://tinyurl.com/rrx8me8w.

6   Hainline and Bross, "Americans Deeply Divided by Party on Ideals of Religious and Ethnic Pluralism."

7   Republicans are nearly twice as likely as Democrats to state a preference for a Western European majority in the country (13 percent vs. 7 percent). Additionally, over half (56 percent) of Republicans place themselves somewhere in the middle on this issue, compared to one-quarter (25 percent) of Democrats. Majorities of Black (52 percent) and Hispanic (51 percent) Americans mostly agree with the first statement, compared to slightly fewer white Americans (44 percent). Ian Hainline and Anna Bross, "Americans Deeply Divided by Party on Ideals of Religious and Ethnic Pluralism."

8   Najle and Jones, "American Democracy in Crisis."

9   "On This Day in 1962: Jamaica Accepts Motto 'Out of Many, One People,'" Travel Noire, April 3, 2019, https://tinyurl.com/yy453tnn.

10 Glaude, *Begin Again*, 7.

11 Ta-Nehisi Coates, *Between the World and Me* (New York: Spiegel & Grau, 2015), 149.

12   Mary Papenfuss, "Trump Uses Racist Terms 'Kung Flu' and 'Chinese Virus' to Describe COVID-19," HuffPost, June 22, 2020, https://www.huffpost.com/entry/trump-kellyanne-conway-corona virus_n_5eeebc5dc5b6aac5f3a46b45.

13   Russell Jeung, et al, "Stop AAPI Hate National Report," n.d., https://secureservercdn.net/104 .238.69.231/a1w.90d.myftpupload.com/wp-content/uploads/2021/03/210312-Stop-AAPI-Hate -National-Report-.pdf.

14   Ibram X. Kendi, *How to Be an Antiracist* (New York: One World, 2019), 46, 47.

15   DiAngelo, *White Fragility*, 9, 21.

16   Kendi, *How to Be an Antiracist*, 9.

17   Kendi, 11.

18   Isabel Wilkerson, *Caste: The Origins of Our Discontents* (New York: Random House, 2020), 16.

19   Wilkerson, 17–18.

20   Erna Kim Hackett, "Why I Stopped Talking about Racial Reconciliation and Started Talking about White Supremacy," *Inheritance*, March 25, 2020, https://tinyurl.com/m348rwa9.

21   "Diversity, Inclusion, Belonging, and Anti-racism at Harvard Kennedy School," Harvard Kennedy School, September 3, 2020, https://tinyurl.com/23un6w87.

22   PRRI, *American Values Survey 2013* (Washington, DC: PRRI, 2014), http://publicreligion.org/site/ wp-content/uploads/2014/08/AVS-Topline-FINAL.pdf.

23   Among Black Americans, 83 percent of people in their social networks are also Black, while 8 per-cent are white and 6 percent are some other race. Among Hispanic Americans, approximately two-thirds (64 percent) of the people who compose their core social networks are also Hispanic, while nearly one in five (19 percent) are white and 9 percent are some other race.

24   Interview with Whitney Parnell, March 2020.

25   Parnell interview.

26   Parnell interview.

27   Parnell interview.

28   Interview with Joseph Tomás McKellar, November 2020.

29   McKellar interview.

30   Penny Bender Sebring et al., *The Essential Supports for School Improvement* (Chicago: Consortium on Chicago School Research, University of Chicago, 2006), https://consortium.uchicago.edu/sites/ default/files/2018-10/EssentialSupports.pdf.

31   Sebring et al., *The Essential Supports for School Improvement*.

32   Robert Putnam, *Our Kids: The American Dream in Crisis* (New York: Simon & Schuster, 2015).

33   Interview with Laura Wilson Phelan, January 2020.

34   Megan Gallagher and Erica Greenberg, "Kindred Pilot Summary: Summary of Findings from Par-ent Surveys and Focus Groups," The Urban institute, January 2019, 7–9, https://kindredcommunities. org/wp-content/uploads/2019/02/2018-01-30_Kindred-Memo_finalized.pdf.

35   Phelan interview.

36   Ta-Nehisi Coates, "The Case for Reparations," *Atlantic*, June 2014, https://www.theatlantic.com/ magazine/archive/2014/06/the-case-for-reparations/361631/.

37   "General Sherman Enacts 'Forty Acres and a Mule,'" African American Registry, n.d., https:// aaregistry.org/story/general-sherman-enacts-forty-acres-and-a-mule/.

38   David A. Love, "The Case for Reparations: 40 Acres and a Mule Would Cost America at Least $6.4 Trillion Today," Atlanta Black Star, May 23, 2015, https://tinyurl.com/42sf8jps.

39   Kelly Brown Douglas, "A Christian Call for Reparations," *Sojourners*, July 2020, https://sojo.net/ magazine/july-2020/christian-call-case-slavery-reparations-kelly-brown-douglas.

40   "H. R. 40—Commission to Study and Develop Reparation Proposals for African-Americans Act," 116th Congress (2019–20), https://www.congress.gov/bill/116th-congress/house-bill/40/text.

41   Eduardo González and Kelebogile Zvobgo, "As America Seeks Racial Justice, It Can Learn From Abroad," Foreign Policy, March 14, 2021, https://foreignpolicy.com/2021/03/14/racial -justice-truth-reconciliation-commissions-international/.

42   Urging the Establishment of a United States Commission on Truth, Racial Healing, and Transfor-mation, H.Con.Res. 100, 116th Cong. (2019–20), https://www.congress.gov/bill/116th-congress/ house-concurrent-resolution/100/text.

4. Reimagining the Beloved Community

1   Fred Smith, "To Serve the Present Age, Our Calling to Fulfill Shalomalization: To Create the Beloved Community," Oxford Institute of Methodist Theological Studies, n.d., https://oimts.files .wordpress.com/2013/04/2007-6-smith.pdf.

2   "Beloved Community."

3   Martin Luther King Jr., "Facing the Challenge of a New Age" (address delivered December 3, 1956), Martin Luther King Jr. Research and Education Institute, Stanford University, https://tinyurl.com/ 59etnzej.

4   Martin Luther King Jr., "I Have a Dream" (speech delivered August 28, 1963), Martin Luther King Jr. Research and Education Institute, Stanford University.

5   "Beloved Community."

6   Charles Marsh, *The Beloved Community: How Faith Shapes Social Justice from the Civil Rights Movement to Today* (New York: Basic, 2005), 118.

7   Isabella Mercado, "The Black Lives Matter Movement: An Origin Story," Underground Railroad Education Center, n.d., https://undergroundrailroadhistory.org/the-black-lives-matter-movement -an-origin-story/.

8   Richard H. Sander, Yana A. Kucheva, and Jonathan M. Zasloff, *Moving toward Integration: The Past and Future of Fair Housing* (Cambridge, MA: Harvard University Press, 2018).

9   "Segregation in America," Economist, April 4, 2018, https://www.economist.com/graphic -detail/2018/04/04/segregation-in-america.

10   Elizabeth Kneebone and Natalie Holmes, "U.S. Concentrated Poverty in the Wake of the Great Recession," Brookings, March 31, 2016, https://www.brookings.edu/research/u-s-concentrated -poverty-in-the-wake-of-the-great-recession/.

11   Daniel Cox, Juhem Navarro-Rivera, and Robert P. Jones, "Race, Religion, and Political Affiliation of Americans' Core Social Networks," Public Religion Research Institute (PRRI), August 3, 2016, https://www.prri.org/research/poll-race-religion-politics-americans-social-networks/.

12   Cox, Navarro-Rivera, and Jones.

13   Eddie S. Glaude Jr., *Democracy in Black: How Race Still Enslaves the American Soul* (New York: Crown, 2016), 31.

14   Bill George, *Discover Your True North: Becoming an Authentic Leader* (Hoboken, NJ: John Wiley & Sons, 2015).

15   Stephen Lewis, Matthew Wesley Williams, and Dori Baker, *Another Way: Living and Leading Change on Purpose* (St. Louis, MO: Chalice, 2020).

16   Interview with Stephen Lewis, March 2020.

17   Grace Ji-Sun Kim, "They'll Know We Are Christians by Our 'Jeong': Five Asian Concepts That Can Deepen Our Understanding of the Holy Spirit," *Sojourners*, February 2019, https://sojo.net/ magazine/february-2019/they-ll-know-we-are-christians-our-jeong.

18   Interview with Kathy Khang, March 2020.

19   *Ending Extreme Poverty: A Moral and Spiritual Imperative* (New York: Bahá'í International Community Representative Offices, 2021), https://www.bic.org/sites/default/files/pdf/moral_imperative _final_english.pdf.

20   Interview with Rabbi Jonah Pesner, March 2020.

21   Islamic Relief Worldwide (IRW), "An Islamic Perspective on Human Development," Policy, Research and Publications, 4, https://www.islamic-relief.org/publications/.

22   IRW, 5.

23   Interview with Dr. Eboo Patel.

24   Interview with Dr. Mohamed Elsanousi, March 2020.

25   "Kimberlé Crenshaw on Intersectionality, More Than Two Decades Later," Columbia Law School, June 8, 2017, https://tinyurl.com/3eacz9by.

5. Unmasking America's Myths

1 Richard T. Hughes, *Myths America Lives By: White Supremacy and the Stories That Give Us Meaning*, 2nd ed. (Urbana: University of Illinois Press, 2018).

2 Hughes, 10.

3 Hughes, 2.

4 Hughes, 32.

5 "John Winthrop's Sermon aboard the *Arbella*, 1630," Landmark Events, April 23, 2018, https://landmarkevents.org/john-winthrop-sermon-aboard-the-arbella-1630/.

6 Hughes, *Myths America Lives By*, 42.

7 Hughes, 52.

8 Hughes, 83, 86.

9 Jonathan Edwards, The Works of Jonathan Edwards vol. 1 (Avon: The Bath Press, 1834), 382, https://www.ccel.org/ccel/edwards/works1/works1.ix.iii.ii.html.

10 Hughes, *Myths America Lives By*, 88.

11 Katherine Stewart, *The Power Worshippers: Inside the Dangerous Rise of Religious Nationalism* (New York: Bloomsbury, 2020), cover, 2.

12 Glaude, *Begin Again*, 9.

13 Hughes, *Myths America Lives By*, 204, 205, 204.

14 Hughes, 205, 210, 225, 186.

15 Hughes, 3.

6. Telling the Whole Truth to Set Us Free

1 "Declaration of Independence."

2 Parts of this chapter are adapted or excerpted from Adam Russell Taylor, "And the Whole Truth Will Set You Free," *Sojourners*, February 21, 2019, https://sojo.net/articles/and-whole-truth-will-set-you-free.

3 Bryan Stevenson, *Just Mercy: A Story of Justice and Redemption* (New York: Random House, 2014).

4 Matthew Shaer, "A New Memorial Remembers the Thousands of African-Americans Who Were Lynched," *Smithsonian*, April 2018, https://tinyurl.com/4y66ud5u.

5 "The National Memorial for Peace and Justice," Equal Justice Initiative, n.d., https://museumandmemorial.eji.org/memorial.

6 Birmingham Civil Rights Institute (website), https://www.bcri.org, Accessed March 4, 2021.

7 "The 1619 Project," *New York Times Magazine*, August 14, 2019, https://www.nytimes.com/interactive/2019/08/14/magazine/1619-america-slavery.html.

8 Jill Lepore, *These Truths: A History of the United States* (New York: W. W. Norton, 2018).

9 David Treuer, *The Heartbeat of Wounded Knee: Native America from 1890 to the Present* (New York: Riverhead, 2019).

10 Steve McQueen, dir., *12 Years a Slave* (Los Angeles: Plan B Entertainment; Los Angeles: New Regency Pictures, 2013).

11 The Fourteenth Amendment, adopted in 1868, established birthright citizenship: "All persons born or naturalized in the United States, and subject to the jurisdiction thereof, are citizens of the United States and of the State wherein they reside." It guaranteed citizens equal rights: "No state shall make or enforce any law which shall abridge the privileges or immunities of citizens to the United States." And it provided protections to noncitizens: "Nor shall any state deprive any person of life, liberty, or property, without due process of law; nor deny to any person within its jurisdiction the equal protection of the laws" (Lepore, *These Truths*, 63).

12 History.com editors, "Compromise of 1877," History, November 27, 2019, https://www.history.com/topics/us-presidents/compromise-of-1877.

13 Angie Maxwell, "What We Get Wrong about the Southern Strategy," *Washington Post*, July 26, 2019, https://www.washingtonpost.com/outlook/2019/07/26/what-we-get-wrong-about-southern-strategy/.

14 Maxwell.

15   Michelle Alexander, "The Injustice of This Moment Is Not an 'Aberration,'" *New York Times*, January 17, 2020, https://www.nytimes.com/2020/01/17/opinion/sunday/michelle-alexander-new-jim-crow.html.

16   Randall Balmer, "The Real Origins of the Religious Right," *Politico Magazine*, May 27, 2014, https://www.politico.com/magazine/story/2014/05/religious-right-real-origins-107133.

17   Bonnie Eisenberg and Mary Ruthsdotter, "History of the Women's Rights Movement," National Women's History Alliance, 1998, https://nationalwomenshistoryalliance.org/history-of-the-womens-rights-movement/.

18   Eisenberg and Ruthsdotter.

19   Alex Cohen and Wilfred U. Codrington III, "The Equal Rights Amendment Explained," Brennan Center for Justice, January 23, 2020, https://www.brennancenter.org/our-work/research-reports/equal-rights-amendment-explained.

20   Eisenberg and Ruthsdotter, "Women's Rights Movement."

21   Lepore, *This America*, 41.

22   "Chinese Exclusion Act," History, last modified September 13, 2019, https://www.history.com/topics/immigration/chinese-exclusion-act-1882.

23   Lepore, *This America*, 88.

24   Lyndon Baines Johnson, "State of the Union 1964" (address delivered January 8, 1964), American History: From Revolution to Reconstruction and Beyond, n.d., http://www.let.rug.nl/usa/presidents/lyndon-baines-johnson/state-of-the-union-1964.php.

25   Sandy Ovalle, "'Threats of Annihilation Live in Our Bones': The Enduring Resilience of Latinx Communities," *Sojourners*, August 8, 2019, https://tinyurl.com/23rum6xh.

26   Ovalle.

7. Overcoming Toxic Polarization

1   Adam Russell Taylor, "For Heaven's Sake, 'Wear a Damn Mask,'" *Sojourners*, June 30, 2020, https://sojo.net/articles/heaven-s-sake-wear-damn-mask.

2   Ruth Igielnik, "Most Americans say they regularly wore a mask in stores in the mast month; fewer see others doing it," Pew Research Center. June 23, 2020. https://www.pewresearch.org/fact-tank/2020/06/23/most-americans-say-they-regularly-wore-a-mask-in-stores-in-the-past-month-fewer-see-others-doing-it.

3   "We Are More in Common," More in Common, 2020, https://www.moreincommon.com/.

4   Jeffrey Goldberg, "A Nation Coming Apart: The Meaning of the American Idea in 2019," *Atlantic*, December 2019, https://www.theatlantic.com/magazine/archive/2019/12/a-nation-coming-apart/600730/.

5   Public Religion Research Institute (PRRI) staff, "Dueling Realities: Amid Multiple Crises, Trump and Biden Supporters See Different Priorities and Futures for the Nation," PRRI, October 19, 2020, https://tinyurl.com/dz6rezc7.

6   Davey Alba and Jack Nicas, "As Local News Dies, a Pay-for-Play Network Rises in Its Place," *New York Times*, October 20, 2020, https://www.nytimes.com/2020/10/18/technology/timpone-local-news-metric-media.html.

7   "The Social Dilemma," Exposure Labs, n.d., https://www.thesocialdilemma.com/.

8   "Partisan Antipathy: More Intense, More Personal," Pew Research Center, October 10, 2019, https://www.people-press.org/2019/10/10/partisan-antipathy-more-intense-more-personal/.

9   Hainline and Bross, "Americans Deeply Divided."

10   The American Values Survey 2019 revealed that polarization related to "facts" and values also carried out around party lines with issues. None of the top three critical issues for Democrats overlap with the top three critical issues for Republicans. Democrats are most likely to regard health care (77 percent), climate change (72 percent), and foreign interference in presidential elections (63 percent) as the most critical issues. By contrast, Republicans' top three critical issues are terrorism (63 percent), immigration (60 percent), and crime (50 percent). PRRI, "Fractured Nation, Widening Partisan Polarization and Key Issues in 2020 Presidential Elections," October 20, 2019, https://www.prri.org/wp-content/uploads/2019/10/PRRI_Oct_AVS-web.pdf.

11 Rachel Kleinfeld, "The U.S. Shows All the Signs of a Country Spiraling toward Political Violence," *Washington Post*, September 11, 2020, https://tinyurl.com/6nemrhn2.

12 "The Perception Gap," More in Common, 2019, https://perceptiongap.us/.

13 Nichole Argo Ben Itzhak et al., *Building U.S. Resilience to Political Violence* (Washington, DC: Over Zero and New America, 2019), 4, 7, https://d1y8sb8igg2f8e.cloudfront.net/documents/2019 _OverZero_vPages_5.pdf.

The report continues,

> Recent research reveals the U.S. Congress is more factionalized than at any other time since the post–Civil War Reconstruction period 150 years ago. A second factor, inextricably intertwined with elite factionalization, is increasing polarization within American society. In addition to intensifying, our polarization has changed in nature. Whereas once political divisions stemmed from disagreements over a particular issue or policy, they now stem from how people feel about those on the other side of the political spectrum, known as identity-based or affective polarization. This has occurred alongside a process of social sorting: Our personal identities have grown in alignment with our political ones. With this, we are no longer merely competing for political victories, but also for the victories of our racial, religious, ethnic, and gender identities—leading to an ever-heightened need for victory. . . . As Americans increasingly connect political differences to core identities rather than issues, the space for deliberation, dialogue, and compromise recedes. With this, the use of absolutist, moralistic rhetoric rises (with opposing groups mirroring one another's use of moralistic language), and intergroup hostility, partisan animus, and intolerance grow. Indeed, as of 2018, 24 percent of Republicans and 17 percent of Democrats believed it is occasionally acceptable to send threatening messages to public officials, and 9 percent of both Democrats and Republicans agreed that violence would be acceptable if their opponents won the 2020 election. Polarization fuels the segmenting of our media into self-selected media bubbles—and then is further compounded as citizens no longer hear the same presentation of facts. Rhetoric can be particularly powerful when its audience has limited (or no) alternative sources of information. While today's media environment enables access to a wide variety of information sources, studies suggest that individuals are instead likely to draw key beliefs from sources that reinforce polarized views. For example, in a landscape where political positions are tied to group identity, exposure to information that challenges existing beliefs (and identity) may backfire, leading individuals to reject such information and cling to their existing beliefs more strongly [than] before.

14 Summarized from Rachel Kleinfeld's remarks at the Depolarization Summit, November 19, 2020, and subsequent correspondence with Kleinfeld, November 2020.

15 Interview with Andrew Hanauer, January 27, 2020.

16 Martin Luther King Jr., *Strength to Love* (Minneapolis, MN: Fortress, 2010), 48.

17 "Metaperception," AlleyDog.com, n.d., https://www.alleydog.com/glossary/definition.php?term =Metaperception.

18 "Study Finds Intractable Conflicts Stem from Misunderstanding of Motivation," ScienceDaily, November 4, 2014, https://www.sciencedaily.com/releases/2014/11/141104083946.htm.

19 Martin Hanselmann and Carmen Tanner, "Taboos and Conflicts in Decision Making: Sacred Values, Decision Difficulty, and Emotions," *Judgment and Decision Making* 3, no. 1 (January 2008): 51–63, http://journal.sjdm.org/bb5/bb5.html#:~:text=A%20sacred%20value%20has%20been,853.

20 Kendra Cherry, "Why the Halo Effect Influences How We Perceive Others," Very Well Mind, July 19, 2020, https://www.verywellmind.com/what-is-the-halo-effect-2795906.

21 Hanauer interview.

22 Mona Charen, "Arthur Brooks's *Love Your Enemies*: A Call for Civic Healing," *National Review*, June 6, 2019, https://tinyurl.com/2mscrz28.

23 Hanauer interview.

24 Stephen Hawkins and Taran Raghuram, *American Fabric: Identity and Belonging* (New York: More in Common, 2020), https://www.moreincommon.com/our-work/publications/.

25 Interview with Mike Berkowitz, November 2020.

26 Joel Rainey, Aaron Alexander, and Lauren Holtzblatt, "Opinion: Conversations about Our Broken System Aren't Enough," *Washington Post*, April 27, 2018, https://tinyurl.com/2tr7ecpb.

27 Richard Rohr, "The Dualistic Mind," Center for Action and Contemplation, January 29, 2017, https://cac.org/the-dualistic-mind-2017-01-29/.

28 Ryan Thomas Neace, "Father Richard Rohr on Racism, Non-dual Thinking, and Jesus Christ," Huff-Post, February 4, 2015, https://www.huffpost.com/entry/father-richard-rohr-on-ra_b_6606206.

29 Martin Luther King Jr., "Draft of Chapter II, 'Transformed Nonconformist'" (sermon, 1962–63?), Martin Luther King Jr. Research and Education Institute, Stanford University, https://tinyurl.com/3js9d65j.

8. Redeeming Patriotism

1 *The Undefeated Presents: Hamilton In-Depth with Kelley Carter*, DisneyPlus, July 3, 2020, https://www.disneyplus.com/movies/the-undefeated-presents-hamilton-in-depth/1hW3q3zFfabD.

2 "Fact Check: Trump's Address to the Republican Convention, Annotated," NPR, August 27, 2020, https://tinyurl.com/e7we677u.

3 Lepore, *This America*, 127.

4 Lepore, 129.

5 David F. Wright, "313 The Edict of Milan," *Christianity Today*, n.d., https://www.christianitytoday.com/history/issues/issue-28/313-edict-of-milan.html.

6 Howard Thurman, *Jesus and the Disinherited* (New York: Abingdon-Cokesbury, 1949).

7 René Girard, "Scapegoat," in *I See Satan Fall like Lightning* (Maryknoll, NY: Orbis, 2001), 154–60; excerpt at Girardian Lectionary, http://girardianlectionary.net/res/iss_12-scapegoat.htm.

8 Theodore R. Johnson, "The Challenge of Black Patriotism," *New York Times Magazine*, November 18, 2020, https://www.nytimes.com/2020/11/18/magazine/black-voters-election-patriotism.html.

9 Hawkins and Raghuram, *American Fabric*.

10 Johnson, "Challenge of Black Patriotism."

11 "Joint Statement from Elections Infrastructure Government Coordinating Council & the Election Infrastructure Sector Coordinating Executive Committees," Cybersecurity & Infrastructure Security Agency (CISA), November 12, 2020, https://tinyurl.com/26sx3vj5.

9. Equality: The Imago Dei Imperative

1 Hainline and Bross, "Americans Deeply Divided."

2 PRRI Staff, "Summer Unrest over Racial Injustice Moves the Country, but Not Republicans or White Evangelicals," PRRI, August 21, 2020, https://www.prri.org/research/racial-justice-2020-george-floyd/.

3 "Christians Struggled with Relational Health Prior to the Crisis—So What Has Changed?," Barna, September 23, 2020, https://www.barna.com/research/christians-relational-health/.

4 Deborah Hardoon, "An Economy for the 99%," Oxfam International, January 16, 2017, https://www.oxfam.org/en/research/economy-99.

5 Taylor Telford, "Income Inequality in America Is the Highest It's Been since Census Bureau Started Tracking It, Data Shows," *Washington Post*, September 26, 2019, https://tinyurl.com/xbp66bm7.

6 Lewis, Williams, and Baker, *Another Way*, 42.

7 Lepore, *These Truths*, xiv.

8 "Criminal Justice Reform," Equal Justice Initiative, n.d., https://eji.org/criminal-justice-reform/.

9 Emily Bazelon, "The Message Is Clear: Policing in America Is Broken and Must Change. But How?," *New York Times Magazine*, June 13, 2020, https://www.nytimes.com/interactive/2020/06/13/magazine/police-reform.html.

10 Megan Lasher, "Read the Full Transcript of Jesse Williams' Powerful Speech on Race at the BET Awards," *Time*, June 27, 2016, https://time.com/4383516/jesse-williams-bet-speech-transcript/.

11 Kendi, *How to Be an Antiracist*, 42, 41.

12 Glaude, *Begin Again*, 7.

13   Christopher Ingraham, "The U.S. Has More Jails Than Colleges. Here's a Map of Where Those Prisoners Live," *Washington Post*, January 6, 2015, https://tinyurl.com/85hdytpa.

14   "Criminal Justice Facts," Sentencing Project, n.d., https://www.sentencingproject.org/criminal -justice-facts/.

15   John Gramlich, "The Gap between the Number of Blacks and Whites in Prison Is Shrinking," Pew Research Center, April 30, 2019, https://tinyurl.com/j28km4xs.

16   "Bryan Stevenson," Equal Justice Initiative, 2021, https://eji.org/bryan-stevenson/.

17   Marlon Peterson (website), https://www.marlonpeterson.com, Accessed March 4, 2021.

18   Interview with Marlon Peterson, December 2020.

19   Dietrich Bonhoeffer, *The Cost of Discipleship* (New York: Touchstone, 1995), 45.

20   Harmeet Kaur, "About 93% of Racial Justice Protests in the US Have Been Peaceful, a New Report Finds," CNN, September 4, 2020, https://www.cnn.com/2020/09/04/us/blm-protests-peaceful -report-trnd/index.html.

21   Richard Chumney, "Lynchburg Police Hold First Listening Session in Wake of Protests against Inequality in Law Enforcement," *News & Advance*, July 1, 2020, https://tinyurl.com/3f3xcbs3.

22   Interview with Ryan Zuidema, November 2020.

23   "The Boston TenPoint Coalition (BTPC)," Boston TenPoint Coalition, 2021, https://btpc.org.

24   *President's Task Force on 21st Century Policing* (Washington, DC: COPS US Department of Justice, 2015), https://cops.usdoj.gov/pdf/taskforce/taskforce_finalreport.pdf.

25   Harold Dean Trulear, "A Reflection on Incarceration: I Am Not Forgotten," Christians for Social Action, January 8, 2020, https://www.evangelicalsforsocialaction.org/compassion-and-justice/i-am -not-forgotten/.

26   Martin Luther King Jr., "Martin Luther King, Jr. Speech: 'The Three Evils'" (address delivered May 10, 1967), published in the *Atlantic*, February 2018, https://tinyurl.com/2rssbf76.

27   Nikole Hannah-Jones, "What Is Owed," *New York Times Magazine*, June 30, 2020, https://www .nytimes.com/interactive/2020/06/24/magazine/reparations-slavery.html.

28   Ira Katznelson, *When Affirmative Action Was White: An Untold History of Racial Inequality in Twentieth-Century America* (New York: W. W. Norton, 2006).

29   Hannah-Jones, "What Is Owed."

30   Michael W. Kraus et al., "The Misperception of Racial Economic Inequality," Association for Psychological Science, 2019, https://spcl.yale.edu/sites/default/files/files/Kraus_etal2019PoPS.pdf.

31   Christine Percheski and Christina Gibson-Davis, "A Penny on the Dollar: Racial Inequalities in Wealth among Households with Children," SAGE Journals, June 1, 2020, https://journals.sagepub .com/doi/full/10.1177/2378023120916616.

32   Ryan Coogler, dir., *Black Panther* (Burbank, CA: Marvel Studios; Burbank, CA: Walt Disney Pictures, 2018).

33   "The LA Partnership for Early Childhood Investment," LA Partnership for Early Childhood Investment, 2021, https://investinkidsla.org/who-we-are/.

34   Interview with Kaci Patterson, November 2020.

35   Patterson interview.

36   "Campaign for Equity New Orleans," Campaign for Equity New Orleans, 2021, https://www .campaignforequity.com.

37   Interview with Shawn Barney, November 2019.

38   Robyn Rosenthal and Rebecca Noricks, "New Studies by W. K. Kellogg Foundation and Altarum Make the Business Case for Racial Equity in New Orleans and Mississippi," W. K. Kellogg Foundation, June 19, 2018, https://tinyurl.com/vvt6m2eb.

10. Radical Welcome

1   Hainline and Bross, "Americans Deeply Divided."

2   Daniel Lee, "'A Totally Moral Man': The Life of Nonviolent Organizer Rev. James Lawson," James Lawson Institute, June 26, 2017, https://tinyurl.com/yxvpruzh.

3   Cataline Gonella, "Visa Overstays Outnumber Illegal Border Crossings, Trend Expected to Continue," NBC News, March 7, 2017, https://tinyurl.com/kzkffxpv.

4 Michael T. Light, Jingying He, and Jason P. Robey, "Comparing Crime Rates between Undocumented Immigrants, Legal Immigrants, and Native-Born US Citizens in Texas," Proceedings of the National Academy of Sciences, December 22, 2020, https://www.pnas.org/content/117/51/32340.

5 Christopher Ingraham, "Two Charts Demolish the Notion That Immigrants Here Illegally Commit More Crime," *Washington Post*, June 19, 2018, https://tinyurl.com/4rnv8et4.

6 "Opinion: The Right Way to Respond to the Migrant Influx," *Washington Post*, June 25, 2018, https://tinyurl.com/yndevnnv.

7 Jens Manuel Krogstad, "Americans Broadly Support Legal Status for Immigrants Brought to U.S. Illegally as Children," Pew Research Center, June 17, 2020, https://tinyurl.com/r7fmkj4.

8 "DACA Stories," Matthew 25 Social, n.d., https://www.matthew25socal.org/english-home.

9 Interview with Rev. Alexia Salvatierra, March 2020.

10 Adam Russell Taylor, "At What Cost to Our Soul?," *Sojourners*, June 26, 2018, https://sojo.net/articles/what-cost-our-soul.

11 Catherine Rampell, "Trump Didn't Build His Border Wall with Steel. He Built It Out of Paper," *Washington Post*, October 29, 2020, https://tinyurl.com/cyjaxftb.

12 Krogstad, "Americans Broadly Support."

13 Sandy Ovalle, "Who Gets a Vote in God's Beloved Community," *Sojourners*, October 15, 2020, https://sojo.net/articles/who-gets-vote-gods-beloved-community.

11. Ubuntu Interdependence

1 M. Fulgence Nyengele, "Cultivating Ubuntu: An African Post-colonial Pastoral Theological Engagement with Positive Psychology," *Journal of Pastoral Theology* 24, no. 2 (Winter 2004): 4–18.

2 Lewis, Williams, and Baker, *Another Way*, 59–60.

3 Kim, "Christians by Our 'Jeong.'"

4 Khang interview.

5 Salvatierra interview.

6 Interview with Rev. Gabriel Salguero, October 2020.

7 King, *Where Do We Go from Here*, 615.

8 King, 615.

9 Ariel Fiszbein et al., "Conditional Cash Transfers Reducing Present and Future Poverty," World Bank Policy Research Report, International Bank for Reconstruction and Development, 2009, https://tinyurl.com/4znmumtd.

10 Megan Leonhardt, "The Expanded $3,000 Child Tax Credit Would Help 10 Million Kids Living in Poverty. Democrats Aim to Make It a Permanent Increase," CNBC, March 4, 2021, https://tinyurl.com/3b25mncv.

11 "#GiveTogetherNow Campaign Raises $100 Million for Families Impacted by COVID-19," Stand Together, 2020, https://tinyurl.com/4bvysckc.

12 Interview with Lauren McCann, October 2020.

13 Parts of this chapter are adapted and excerpted from Adam Russell Taylor, "No, We Didn't 'Win' the War on Poverty. But Here's How We Can," *Sojourners*, August 2, 2018, https://sojo.net/articles/no-we-didnt-win-war-poverty-heres-how-we-can.

14 "Report of the Special Rapporteur on extreme poverty and human rights on his mission to the United States of America," United Nations General Assembly, May 4, 2018, http://undocs.org/A/HRC/38/33/ADD.1.

15 Jim Wallis, *God's Politics: Why the Right Gets It Wrong and the Left Doesn't Get It* (New York: HarperSanFrancisco, 2005), 209–11.

16 "A Better Way," Office of Speaker of the House Paul Ryan, June 2016, https://web.archive.org/web/20161227220830/https://abetterway.speaker.gov/_assets/pdf/ABetterWay-Poverty-Snapshot.pdf, Accessed March 4, 2021.

17 "The Progressive Promise," Congressional Progressive Caucus, n.d., https://progressives.house.gov/the-progressive-promise/.

18   Jeff Stein, "Bernie Sanders to Announce Plan to Guarantee Every American a Job," *Washington Post*, April 23, 2018, https://tinyurl.com/ytadfkep.

19   Jordan Weissmann, "Democrats Have a Bill That Would Halve the Child Poverty Rate. It Likely Costs Less Than Trump's Tax Cut," Slate, October 26, 2017, https://tinyurl.com/22ccy5rc.

20   "Making the Rich Pay Their Fair Share in Taxes," Friends of Bernie Sanders, n.d., https://berniesanders.com/issues/tax-increases-for-the-rich/.

21   Isabel V. Sawhill, "How Marriage and Divorce Impact Economic Opportunity," Brookings, May 6, 2014, https://www.brookings.edu/opinions/how-marriage-and-divorce-impact-economic-opportunity/.

22   Taylor, "No, We Didn't 'Win.'"

23   Joerg Dreweke, "New Clarity for the U.S. Abortion Debate: A Steep Drop in Unintended Pregnancy Is Driving Recent Abortion Declines," Guttmacher Policy Review, March 18, 2016, https://tinyurl.com/pp85r2tm.

24   Nick Hanauer, "The Dirty Secret of Capitalism—and a New Way Forward," TEDSummit 2019, https://tinyurl.com/y9hwh48d.

25   Hanauer.

26   "Business Roundtable Redefines the Purpose of a Corporation to Promote 'an Economy That Serves All Americans,'" Business Roundtable, August 19, 2019, https://tinyurl.com/y5w5d66x.

27   "Poor People's Campaign" (event, 1968), Martin Luther King Jr. Research and Education Institute, Stanford University, https://kinginstitute.stanford.edu/encyclopedia/poor-peoples-campaign.

28   Gordon Keith Mantler, "Black, Brown and Poor: Martin Luther King Jr., the Poor People's Campaign and Its Legacies" (PhD diss., Duke University, 2008), https://tinyurl.com/4m3jwd3s.

29   "About the Poor People's Campaign: A National Call for Moral Revival," Poor People's Campaign, n.d., https://www.poorpeoplescampaign.org/about/.

30   Interview with Jonathan Wilson-Hartgrove, October 2020.

31   "A Moral Policy Agenda to Heal and Transform America: The Poor People's Jubilee Platform," Poor People's Campaign, July 2020, https://www.poorpeoplescampaign.org/about/jubilee-platform/.

12. Prioritizing Nonviolence

1   Rachel Kleinfeld, "Should America Be Worried about Political Violence? And What Can We Do to Prevent It?" (workshop summary), Carnegie Endowment for International Peace, September 16, 2019, https://tinyurl.com/m923b9xa.

2   *Emanuel: Discussion Guide in Partnership with Sojourners*, Sojourners, n.d., https://sojo.net/sites/default/files/emanueldiscussionguide23.pdf.

3   Jonathan Greenblatt, "Right-Wing Extremist Violence Is Our Biggest Threat. The Numbers Don't Lie," Anti-Defamation League, January 24, 2019, https://tinyurl.com/yr6ed8mh.

4   King, *Strength to Love*, 47.

5   This content was adapted from Adam Russell Taylor, "How a New Documentary Honors the Emanuel Nine," *Sojourners*, June 18, 2019, https://sojo.net/articles/how-new-documentary-honors-emanuel-nine.

6   Julie Turkewitz, Patricia Mazzei, and Audra D. S. Burch, "Suspect Confessed to Police That He Began Shooting Students 'in the Hallways,'" *New York Times*, February 15, 2018, https://tinyurl.com/267nepn6.

7   Emily McFarlan Miller, "Religious Leaders Call for Prayer and Action following Florida School Shooting," *Sojourners*, February 16, 2018, https://tinyurl.com/2vxzy5pf.

8   "Working toward the *Shalom* of God: A Profile of Delonte Gholston," Center for Religion and Civic Culture, n.d., https://crcc.usc.edu/pilgrimage/delonte/.

9   Interview with Rev. Delonte Gholston, March 2020.

10   Adelle M. Banks, "'Racialized Policing' Program Takes Faith Leaders from Grief to Action," Religion News Service, June 22, 2020, https://tinyurl.com/tmd3k4c.

11   Gholston interview.

12   Staff, "People of Color Are Far More Likely to Be Victims of Anti-LGBT Crimes," *Pacific Standard*, June 14, 2017, https://psmag.com/news/people-of-color-are-far-more-likely-to-be-victims-of-anti-lgbt-crimes.

13 Ben Itzhak et al., *Building U.S. Resilience*, 3–5.

14 Criminal Justice Information Services Division, "2018 Hate Crime Statistics," FBI: UCR, 2018, https://ucr.fbi.gov/hate-crime/2018/tables/table-1.xls.

15 Interview and conversation with L. B. Prevette, March 2020.

16 Lisa O'Donnell, "Wilkes Weavers: Young Woman Gains National Recognition for Building Community and Building Up Wilkes County," *Winston-Salem Journal*, June 1, 2019, https://tinyurl.com/k6fy9htc.

17 "Weave: The Social Fabric Project," Aspen Institute, 2021, https://www.aspeninstitute.org/programs/weave-the-social-fabric-initiative/.

18 "The Relationalist Manifesto," Weave: The Social Fabric Project, February 13, 2019, https://www.aspeninstitute.org/blog-posts/the-relationalist-manifesto/.

19 "Relationalist Manifesto."

20 "Student Nonviolent Coordinating Committee Founding Statement," Southwide Youth Leadership Conference, Shaw University, Raleigh, NC, April 15–17, 1960, https://www.crmvet.org/docs/sncc1.htm.

13. Environmental Stewardship

1 Parts of this chapter are adapted and excerpted from Adam Russell Taylor, "Why We Must Become Climate Warriors," *Sojourners*, May 16, 2019, https://sojo.net/articles/why-we-must-become-climate-warriors.

2 Pope Francis, *Laudato Si': On Care for Our Common Home* (Vatican City: Libreria Editrice Vaticana, 2015).

3 Melody Zhang, "It's Time for Policies That Rise to the Challenge of the Climate Crisis," *Sojourners*, April 4, 2019, https://sojo.net/articles/its-time-policies-rise-challenge-climate-crisis.

4 Howard-John Wesley, "I Can't Breathe" (sermon), Alfred Street Baptist Church, Alexandria, VA, August 11, 2019, https://www.youtube.com/watch?v=fc0KaXUhwK8.

5 Jasmine Bell, "5 Things to Know about Communities of Color and Environmental Justice," Center for American Progress, April 25, 2016, https://tinyurl.com/5cfse7v8.

6 Melody Zhang, "True Climate Justice Is Impossible without Racial and Economic Justice," *Sojourners*, July 29, 2019, https://sojo.net/articles/true-climate-justice-impossible-without-racial-and-economic-justice.

7 Lesley Fleischman and Marcus Franklin, *Fumes across the Fence-Line: The Health Impacts of Air Pollution from Oil & Gas Facilities on African American Communities* (Baltimore, MD: NAACP; Boston, MA: Clean Air Task Force, 2017), https://tinyurl.com/yey8h6vx.

8 Linda Villarosa, "Pollution Is Killing Black Americans. This Community Fought Back," *New York Times Magazine*, July 28, 2020, https://www.nytimes.com/2020/07/28/magazine/pollution-philadelphia-black-americans.html.

9 Villarosa, "Pollution is Killing Black Americans."

10 Bill McKibben, "A World at War: We're under Attack from Climate Change—and Our Only Hope Is to Mobilize like We Did in WWII," *New Republic*, August 15, 2016, https://newrepublic.com/article/135684/declare-war-climate-change-mobilize-wwii.

11 Max Thabiso Edkins, "The World Has Malaria" (YouTube video), Connect4Climate, December 22, 2011, https://www.youtube.com/watch?v=1btpuEwBBVs.

12 "Programs," Interfaith Power & Light, n.d., https://www.interfaithpowerandlight.org/programs/.

13 "About," GreenFaith, n.d., https://greenfaith.org/about/.

14 Shannon Larson, "As Warming Risks Rise, Boston Pastor Sees Need to Spur 'Climate Justice,'" Thomson Reuters Foundation, June 8, 2020, https://news.trust.org/item/20200608152903-nzmle/.

15 Michael Blanding, "How Reverend Mariama White-Hammond Is Bridging Boston's Racial Divide," *Boston Magazine*, August 20, 2017, https://www.bostonmagazine.com/news/2017/08/20/mariama-white-hammond/.

16 Interview with Rev. Mariama White-Hammond, September 2020.

17 Zhang, "Policies That Rise."

14. Dignity for All

1   *Transforming Our World: The 2030 Agenda for Sustainable Development (A/RES/70/1)* (New York: United Nations, n.d.), https://tinyurl.com/ry89vuzd.

2   Pope Francis, *Laudato Si'*.

3   *Transforming Our World*, 6–7.

4   Paul Farmer, "How We Can Save Millions of Lives," *Washington Post*, November 17, 2011, https://tinyurl.com/2uncv6mw.

5   Adam Russell Taylor, "When One Part Suffers, the U.S. Looks Away," *Sojourners*, October 8, 2020, https://sojo.net/articles/when-one-part-suffers-us-looks-away.

6   Taylor.

7   Samantha Power, "The Can-Do Power: America's Advantage and Biden's Chance," *Foreign Affairs*, January/February 2021, https://www.foreignaffairs.com/articles/united-states/2020-11-20/samantha-power-can-do-power.

8   Dedrick Asante Muhammad, Rogelio Tec, and Kathy Ramirez, "Racial Wealth Snapshot: American Indians / Native Americans," National Community Reinvestment Coalition, November 18, 2019, https://ncrc.org/racial-wealth-snapshot-american-indians-native-americans/.

9   "The Population of Poverty USA," PovertyUSA.org, accessed March 5, 2021, https://www.povertyusa.org/facts.

10 Kelly Beamon, "Joseph Kunkel Is Fast-Tracking Quality Housing for Indigenous People," *Metropolis*, October 12, 2020, https://tinyurl.com/52xd39by.

11 Interview with Joseph Kunkel, November 2020.

12 Adam Russell Taylor, "Meeting the Moral Imperative to End Extreme Poverty," World Bank Blogs, October 2, 2015, https://blogs.worldbank.org/voices/meeting-moral-imperative-end-extreme-poverty.

13 *Ending Extreme Poverty: A Moral and Spiritual Imperative* (New York: Bahá'í International Community Representative Offices, 2021), https://www.wvi.org/faith2endpoverty#:~:text=The%20pledge%2C%20Ending%20Extreme%20Poverty%3A%20A%20Moral%20and,and%20responsibility%20of%20faith%20communities%20in%20ending%20poverty.

14 "Universal Declaration of Human Rights," United Nations, n.d., https://www.un.org/en/universal-declaration-human-rights/.

15. Revitalizing and Reinventing Democracy

1   Editorial Board, "A Second Trump Term Might Injure the Democratic Experiment beyond Recovery," *Washington Post*, August 21, 2020, https://tinyurl.com/7rs6zdb7.

2   Geoffrey Kabaservice, "The Forever Grievance: Conservatives Have Traded Periodic Revolts for a Permanent Revolution," *Washington Post*, December 4, 2020, https://tinyurl.com/2fj6pvu7.

3   Joe Scarborough, "Republicans Were Once the Anti-radicals. They're Now Battering American Democracy," *Washington Post*, December 11, 2020, https://tinyurl.com/52d9h6y9.

4   "Joint Statement."

5   "Voting Laws Roundup: February 2021," Brennan Center for Justice, February 8, 2021, https://www.brennancenter.org/our-work/research-reports/voting-laws-roundup-february-2021.

6   Adam Russell Taylor, "Protecting the Vote in the Name of Faith," *Sojourners*, July 12, 2018, https://sojo.net/articles/protecting-vote-name-faith.

7   "New Voting Restrictions in America," Brennan Center for Justice, October 1, 2019, https://www.brennancenter.org/our-work/research-reports/new-voting-restrictions-america.

8   Interview with Dr. Barbara Williams-Skinner, November 2020.

9   Ronald J. Sider, "For the Common Good," *Sojourners*, April 2007, https://sojo.net/magazine/april-2007/common-good.

10 Adam Russell Taylor, "Democracy Is on the Ballot," *Sojourners*, October 29, 2020, https://sojo.net/articles/democracy-ballot.

11 Wendy R. Weiser, Daniel I. Weiner, and Dominique Erney, "Congress Must Pass the 'For the People Act,'" Brennan Center for Justice, March 18, 2021, https://www.brennancenter.org/our-work/policy-solutions/case-hr1.

12 Selzler, Gonda, and Mohammed, *What Does Spirituality Mean?*, 76.